1992

AMERICA'S CORRECTIONAL CRISIS

Recent Titles in
Contributions in Criminology and Penology

AMERICA'S CORRECTIONAL CRISIS

PRISON POPULATIONS AND PUBLIC POLICY

EDITED BY
STEPHEN D. GOTTFREDSON
AND
SEAN MCCONVILLE

Contributions in Criminology and Penology, Number 17

GREENWOOD PRESS
New York • Westport, Connecticut • London

Library of Congress Cataloging-in-Publication Data

America's correctional crisis.

(Contributions in criminology and penology,
ISSN 0732-4464 ; no. 17)
Bibliography: p.
Includes index.
1. Prisons—United States—Overcrowding.
2. Prison administration—United States.
3. Corrections—Government policy—United States.
I. Gottfredson, Stephen D.   II. McConville, Sean.
III. Series.
HV9469.A78   1987   365'.6   86-27143
ISBN 0-313-25487-7 (lib. bdg. : alk. paper)

Library of Congress Catalog Card Number: 86-27143
ISBN: 0-313-25487-7
ISSN: 0732-4464

First published in 1987

Greenwood Press, Inc.
88 Post Road West, Westport, Connecticut 06881

Printed in the United States of America

The paper used in this book complies with the
Permanent Paper Standard issued by the National
Information Standards Organization (Z39.48-1984).

10 9 8 7 6 5 4 3

Contents

PART I
THE CRISIS

1 Introduction

STEPHEN D. GOTTFREDSON
and
SEAN McCONVILLE

The national criminal justice community is increasingly concerned with what has been called a "crisis in corrections." For many, the crisis is synonymous with overcrowding in prisons and jails.[1] Others insist that this equation is too simple, and stress that the "crisis" involves not just crowding but also confusion and disagreement over the objectives and effectiveness of correctional treatment.[2]

That prison and jail crowding is a major national problem cannot be disputed. Prison populations are now higher than they have ever been and are growing at an extraordinary rate. At present, inmate populations exceed cell capacity in almost all states—in most cases by a very substantial amount.

In addition to being extremely crowded, many prisons and jails are old and in a state of physical decay. They are often inadequately staffed; routine medical care, adequate nutritional requirements, and protection from physical abuse are often lacking. Educational, vocational, and other rehabilitative programs typically are no longer available or have been curtailed sharply.[3]

As of February 1986, 46 states and U.S. territories either were under court order, or were involved in litigation likely to result in court orders, concerning prison conditions.[4] The issue of crowding and other atrocious conditions is central to the overwhelming majority of these suits, and under present interpretation, the U.S. Constitution forbids the kind of treatment prison inmates in almost all states presently receive. Most of these states have been unable to meet the terms of the court orders, and despite periodic drastic action (such as refusals to accept new prison admissions or wholesale releases of inmates), the situation in most jurisdictions is daily getting worse. As a result, we are facing a far-reaching constitutional crisis.

Why is prison crowding a problem? With few exceptions, the people in our prisons have done something deserving of punishment. Why should we be overly concerned with the conditions under which they are imprisoned? In general, there are three types of answer. One is a *humanitarian* argument: it is simply wrong, and an affront to a civilized society, to treat people in this inhumane fashion. Far from simply degrading those so punished, we degrade our society by allowing such conditions to continue.

The second is a *constitutional* argument: the Constitution of the United States, through its Eighth Amendment guarantees, provides that each of us—prison inmates included—has an absolute right to freedom from cruel and unusual punishment. Yet, as already mentioned, the majority of states in this country are in violation of this constitutional guarantee. This alone would suggest that prison conditions and crowding are issues deserving urgent political and administrative attention. Perhaps even more critical is the apparent inability of our state and local governments to provide the remedies required by the courts and by the Constitution, since this fundamentally jeopardizes the Constitution and, by extension, the rights of each of us.

Pragmatic arguments should also persuade us that prison crowding and prison conditions are issues worthy of concern. Our laws generally require that punishments or sanctions not be grossly disproportionate to the crimes to which they are a response. In practice this means that the average inmate spends a relatively short period of time in prison (about two years, on average, across the United States), because most are incarcerated for relatively minor offenses. Of course, some prisoners are incarcerated for very long periods, because their crimes have been more serious. But with these few exceptions, the persons we imprison will shortly be among us again. Common sense alone suggests that it is foolish to incarcerate in conditions likely to worsen prisoners as people and perhaps to increase the probability that they will continue in a life of crime.

A second pragmatic argument addresses the consequences of severe crowding for the administration of our prisons. Empirical studies of the consequences of prison crowding are unfortunately few, but from those that are available, it appears that crowding is related to prison violence and disruptions, and is negatively related to prisoners' health. Certainly prison administrators, at any rate, are quick to point to prison crowding as a major contributory factor in prison riots. A resolution to the prison crowding problem cannot but help to avoid repeating the tragedies of an Attica or a New Mexico.

Essentially, there are only three general strategies that may be taken to resolve prison crowding problems: we can build more prisons; we can reduce intake into the prison system; or we can accelerate releases from the prison system. A fourth possibility, of course, but one that provides no true resolution, is to tolerate the existing and deteriorating situation.

These are not exclusive options, although we appear often to have considered them as such; that is, it is suggested that either we will build more prisons or we will develop alternatives. There is no reason that more than one of these options cannot be considered simultaneously. We do suggest, however, that this brief listing of policy options is in fact exhaustive. There is nothing more that could be done other than to build prisons, reduce intakes, or accelerate releases (or, of course, some combination of these).

We should point out that these apparently simple strategies may in fact be very complex. What sorts of prisons should we build? How many do we need? Where shall we put them? Should we reduce intake through diversion programs? If so, of what sort? Are alternatives to traditional incarceration needed? Again, of what type? How does one go about accelerating releases? What has been tried, and with what sort of success? The unfortunate answer is that most of these strategies have been tried. To date, most have failed.

Attempts to build sufficient prisons to house all those for whom incarceration is felt necessary have routinely failed. In all but a very few instances, states that have engaged in large-scale prison construction projects have found prison capacities exceeded as soon as the new facilities are opened. Further, in this time of fiscal constraint, few jurisdictions may be able to resort to massive prison construction projects as a remedy to the crowding problem. At any time, prison building means that other public spending options must be forgone.

Attempts to reduce prison intakes have rather routinely failed, in the face of perceived public pressure to increase incarceration and to sentence to longer terms. Early parole or emergency and accelerated parole projects also have fallen victim to political and public pressures.

What is responsible for this dismal state of affairs? Indeed, why is the problem worse now than at any other time in our history? These are the central questions to which this volume is devoted.

Part I of this volume defines some of the dimensions of America's correctional crisis and reviews the recent history of judicial involvement in prison administration, the costs of traditional and nontraditional correctional sanctions, and some of the policy constraints under which our public officials operate in attempting to meliorate prison conditions.

The past few decades have seen both the rise and the partial decline of judicial intervention as a method of prison reform. While the 1950s and 1960s have been characterized as decades of the "hands-off" doctrine,[5] the early 1970s were characterized by an increasing willingness on the part of the Supreme Court to become involved in issues concerning the fundamental rights of prison inmates.

Indeed, in the last decade, litigation concerning prisoners' rights so flourished that reviews of such litigation now are quickly dated and tend to be voluminous.[6] As an illustration of the magnitude of the increase in volume of such litigation, consider that petitions brought by prisoners increased from 218 in 1966 to over 11,000 by the end of fiscal year 1979.[7]

Perhaps partly in reaction to the volume of litigation, and perhaps partly in a return to the earlier "hands-off" doctrine, more recent decisions, such as *Bell v. Wolfish*,[8] have tended to demonstrate an increasing reluctance to invalidate rulings, decisions, or practices of correctional institutions or personnel. Singer provides a particularly well-articulated discussion of this issue in general, and of *Bell* in particular.[9] A complete review of prisoners' rights litigation would require (at a minimum) discussion of the First, Fourth, Eighth, and Fourteenth Amendments. However, since our focus is on issues of prison crowding, attention in this volume concentrates on Eighth Amendment issues.

Litigation concerning prison and jail crowding has primarily concerned rights guaranteed by the Eighth Amendment: "Excessive bail shall not be required, nor excessive fines imposed, nor cruel and unusual punishments inflicted." Simple in language and in concept, the amendment provides that each of us—prison inmates included—has the absolute right to freedom from cruel and unusual punishments.[10] It is in the determination of practices and conditions that violate this right that difficulties arise.

It has been suggested that three rather broad and vague tests appear to provide contemporary guidelines for the interpretation of the Eighth Amendment: (1) whether the punishment shocks the general conscience of a civilized society; (2) whether the punishment is unnecessarily cruel; and (3) whether the punishment goes beyond legitimate penal aims.[11] Applying these guidelines, federal and state courts have found specific practices (for example, physical abuse, crowding), the totality of conditions of confinement, and even entire prison systems to be in violation of the Eighth Amendment. Barton L. Ingraham and Charles F. Wellford describe this litigation—its causes and effects—in Chapter 2.

As already noted, few states have been able to build their way out of the correctional crisis. Nonetheless, there remains the need to consider, along with other strategies, the possibility that more prisons may be needed. Indeed, they certainly will be needed unless alternatives, such as those to be suggested later in this volume, can be agreed upon and effectively implemented.

However, the costs associated with prisons and their construction are truly staggering. Estimates of the annual costs of operation per inmate, excluding the costs of the facilities themselves, range from about $10,000 per inmate per year to around $40,000 per inmate per year.[12] The costs of prison construction also are phenomenal, ranging from about $30,000 per bed[13] to about $80,000 per bed or higher.[14] Further, since most prisons are built with borrowed money (that is, through bond issues or other loans), interest rates significantly increase the costs of the facilities. For example, estimates made in 1981 suggested that given then-current interest rates, the eventual price of one prison cell built in that year could well exceed $200,000. These issues of correctional costs are detailed by Todd R. Clear and Patricia M. Harris in Chapter 3.

Earlier we stressed the point that some feel it is simplistic to limit discussion of a correctional crisis to crowding alone. In addition to rising prison populations, the past decade has been marked by a rising tempo of debate over the objectives of our penal system. The relative merits of rehabilitation, deterrence, punishment, and incapacitation are under reconsideration in many quarters. In part, concern over goals and objectives arises from debate over the *effectiveness* of correctional treatment. Although the problem of assessing effectiveness of correctional treatment is difficult indeed, and debates concerning this issue are involved,[15] many have found the available evidence discouraging. Thus, concern over the objectives of incarceration, and success in meeting those objectives, is a second dimension to the crisis in corrections.

A limited number of policy options are available to those charged with the resolution of the crisis in corrections, and these options are subject to a number of interactive constraints. Although rarely recognized as such, issues of moral and legal philosophy provide the most obvious constraint on policy options. Indeed, these constraints are embodied in the Constitution, which has provided the framework within which correctional administrators must operate. Thus, while we hear occasional cries to "line them up and shoot them" or to "let them rot," these simply are inconceivable alternatives to the resolution of the crowding problem.

More frequently recognized as constraints on policy options are issues such as economic resources (as discussed by Clear and Harris in Chapter 3), objective parameters of the criminal justice system, and the political milieu within which correctional systems and their administrators must operate. It is these latter constraints that define the policymaking arena and provide much of the remaining substance of this volume. As described by Stephen D. Gottfredson and Ralph B. Taylor in the final chapter of Part I, political and policy administrators may well find that more options are available to them than they may perceive: based on surveys conducted in the State of Maryland, it appears that correctional policymakers could well profit from more accurate knowledge of the goals and policies that the general public would permit—and indeed, may favor—over those that typically are implemented.

While Part I of this volume focuses largely on the problem, Part II attempts to develop both an understanding of its nature and possible means toward its melioration. In Chapter 5, Joan Mullen summarizes results of a national survey of policy options that have been or are being attempted across the country as correctional administrators struggle with the intractable difficulties facing them, and in Chapter 6 Sean McConville and Eryl Hall Williams summarize the dimensions of, and responses to, the English penal crisis. It has been noted that correctional administrators are in the peculiar business of attempting to run a hotel without benefit of a reservation service[16]—that is, they don't know who's coming to stay, or for how long.[17] Don M. Gottfredson provides in Chapter 7 an example of ways in which discretionary decisions affecting imprisoned populations may be structured, within the context of the release decision, and the effects of sentencing strategies on prison populations are considered in some detail in Chapter 8 by Alfred Blumstein. Alan T. Harland and Philip W. Harris describe the process necessary to ensuring that alternatives to traditional incarceration may be rationally developed and, more important, successfully implemented. A provocative chapter by M. Kay Harris suggests that we may need to reconsider the entire framework from which we now make sanctioning decisions.

Finally, there has recently been renewed interest in possible private sector initiatives in corrections (a development that is part of a wider political interest in privatizing many public sector services and institutions). As a result of rapidly increasing prison populations and more complex service demands, and in the face of limitations on public resources, correctional agencies at all levels are beginning to investigate the potential of involving the private sector in service delivery. In Chapter 11, Sean McConville discusses aspects of the history of privately run prisons and jails and draws some conclusions for current policy decisions.

With almost three-quarters of a million Americans currently incarcerated, given the heat with which penal policy issues are debated, the vast expenditures, the far-reaching decisions that are taken in the uncertainty of crisis or in pursuit of political compromise, we make no apology for addressing at such length what all too often is seen as an arcane field of public policy. The standards we impose upon the hidden worlds of public administration reflect as surely upon our national sensibilities, hopes, and morale as does the quality of administration we bring to more obviously positive public institutions. We hope here to have provided the material for more informed and balanced debate and for the encouragement of productive and acceptable solutions to problems that can be neglected only at some considerable risk to our nation's future.

NOTES

1. See, for example, *Maryland Law Review* 36 (1976): 182–211; New York City Board of Correction, *Crisis in Prisons: New York City Responds* (New York: Board of Correction, 1972); J. Flanagan, "Imminent Crisis in Prison Populations," *American Journal of Correction* 37 (1975): 20–36; and Council of State Governments, *Task Force Committee on Correctional Problems: Seminar on the Crises in Correction* (Atlanta, GA: Council of State Governments, 1976).

2. See, for example, N. Morris and J. Jacobs, *Proposals for Prison Reform* (New York: Public Affairs Committee, 1974); and N. Carlson, "Future of Prisons," *Trial* 12 (1976): 27–34.

3. *Inmate Programming/Inmate Idleness*, Report of the Maryland Criminal Justice Coordinating Council (Baltimore: Maryland Criminal Justice Coordinating Council, January 1986).

4. American Civil Liberties Foundation, *Status Report—The Courts and Prisons* (Mimeo, National Prison Project, February 20, 1986).

5. A. Bronstein, "Prisoners' Rights: A History," in G. P. Alpert, ed., *Legal Rights of Prisoners* (Beverly Hills, CA: Sage, 1980); R. Singer, "The *Wolfish* Case: Has the *Bell* Tolled for Prisoner Litigation in the Federal Courts?" in Alpert, ed., *Legal Rights*.

6. See, generally, Alpert, ed., *Legal Rights*; National Association of Attorneys General, *Implementation of Remedies in Prison Conditions Suits* (Raleigh, NC: Committee on the Office of the Attorney General, 1980); American Bar Association, *Prisoners' Legal Rights: A Bibliography of Cases and Articles* (Washington, DC: Resource Center on Correctional Law and Legal Services, 1974); and American Correctional Association, *Correctional Law: A Bibliography of Selected Books and Articles* (College Park, MD: American Correctional Association, 1977).

7. J. F. Short, Jr., Foreword to Alpert, *Legal Rights*.

8. 441 U.S. 520 (1979).

9. Singer, "The *Wolfish* Case."

10. *Logan v. United States*, 144 U.S. 263 (1892).

11. Bronstein, "Prisoners' Rights."

12. D. McDonald, *The Price of Punishment: Public Spending for Corrections in New York* (Boulder, CO: Westview, 1980), pp. 17, 55.

13. Ibid., pp. 51–52.

14. G. Funke, "Who's Buried in Grant's Tomb?: Economics and Cor-

rections for the Eighties and Beyond" (Mimeo, Institute for Economic and Policy Studies, Inc., Alexandria, VA, April 1982), p. 3.

15. R. Martinson, "What Works?: Questions and Answers about Prison Reform," *Public Interest*, 1974: 22–54; D. Lipton, R. Martinson, and J. Wilks, *The Effectiveness of Correctional Treatment* (New York: Praeger, 1975); National Research Council, *Deterrence and Incapacitation: Estimating the Effects of Sanctions on Crime Rates* (Washington, DC: National Academy of Sciences, 1978); and M. R. Gottfredson, "Treatment Destruction Techniques," *Journal of Research in Crime and Delinquency* 16, no. 1 (1979): 39–54.

16. M. R. Gottfredson and D. M. Gottfredson, *Decision-Making in Criminal Justice* (Lexington, MA: Ballinger, 1980).

17. That correctional administrators alone can do little to resolve the crowding problem is well documented. See S. D. Gottfredson, "Institutional Responses to Prison Crowding," *New York University Review of Law and Social Change* 12, no. 1 (1983–84): 259–73.

2 The Totality of Conditions Test in Eighth-Amendment Litigation

BARTON L. INGRAHAM
and
CHARLES F. WELLFORD

Sixteen years have passed since U.S. District Judge Henley was the first to find the entire prison system of a state (Arkansas) to be in violation of the Eighth Amendment cruel and unusual punishment provision.[1] As of the end of 1984, prison institutions in about two-thirds of the states (33) were under court orders or consent decrees requiring them to improve conditions, and in four additional states legal challenges were still pending.[2] The usual complaint in these lawsuits, although not the only one, is that overcrowding has created intolerable living conditions as well as violence. That overcrowding should be a frequent source of complaint is hardly surprising. Since 1974 inmate populations in state and federal prisons have more than doubled, rising from 229,721 in 1974 to 490,041 by the middle of 1985.[3] These numbers mean that most prisons in the United States are filled far beyond their design capacities, and that inmates are living in very cramped and crowded space. The situation in most of the nation's jails is no better.

Overcrowding is said to contribute to the following conditions in prisons, many of which have been held to be unconstitutional:

1. continual and abnormal violence, including sexual assaults;[4]

2. poor health and the spread of diseases among inmates;[5]

3. the increasing idleness and stagnation of prison life, as recreational, vocational, and educational programs have to be cut back;[6]

4. total loss of privacy and inhuman suffering as more and more inmates
   are forced to share cells designed for the occupancy of fewer people or
   dormitories in which almost every inch of available space is occupied
   by a bunk or mattress.[7]

It has often been held by federal courts that the combination of
these conditions (the "totality of conditions") may constitute cruel
and unusual punishment in violation of the Eighth Amendment.[8]
When pretrial detainees in jails are involved, the totality of conditions in the jails may constitute such an unjustifiable deprivation
of basic amenities that the confinement will be found to be "punishment" without due process of law contrary to the Fifth Amendment or Fourteenth Amendment rights of the detainees.[9]

A variety of different strategies have been employed by prisoners
and their legal counsel to obtain a judicial remedy for the deplorable
conditions caused by overcrowding in prisons and jails. One approach has been to attack each of the offending conditions separately
as a violation of the Eighth Amendment right against cruel and
unusual punishment, and to ask the court to fashion a remedy that
addresses each condition specifically. For example, inadequate or
neglectful medical care is attacked because it leads to unnecessary
suffering;[10] the failure to provide a sufficient number of prison guards
is attacked because the lack of surveillance leads to a high level of
inmate-inmate assaults or rapes;[11] an inadequate classification system is attacked because it places potentially violent inmates in the
same living or working space as inmates with no history of violence,
thus exposing them to victimization;[12] and so on. The other approach, and the one that seems to be favored, is to make a broadside
attack on virtually every aspect of the prison's administration on the
ground that it is irrational and contributes in significant ways to the
generally deplorable and unconstitutional overall condition of the
prison or jail. This approach, where successful, apparently is believed to justify a more holistic judicial remedy, one that addresses
all the needs of reform and will, it is supposed, result in more lasting
improvements. Examples of this latter approach that come readily
to mind are Judge Pettine's reformation of the Rhode Island penitentiary system in *Palmigiano v. Garrahy*, Judge Johnson in *Pugh
v. Locke* (Alabama prison system), and Judge Justice in *Ruiz v.
Estelle* (Texas prison system). [13]

There can be little doubt or serious argument that these and similar far-ranging judicial decrees, emanating principally but not entirely from the federal courts, have brought about much-needed reforms and the partial alleviation of some of the most gross and shocking conditions in this nation's prisons and jails.[14] However, it is still a matter of legitimate dispute whether the legalistic approach—that is, the approach that tries to solve the endemic problems of prison existence, as well as the special problems created by overcrowding, through litigation and the judicial application of minimum constitutional standards—is the best way to handle these problems. We believe that it is also open to argument whether the second legal strategy mentioned above, the broadside attack on the totality of prison conditions (considered cumulatively and not individually), accompanied by a judicial decree that specifies in great detail all the changes that must be made and perhaps also accompanied by the appointment of a special master to oversee compliance and report it to the court, conforms in any way to the law as it has been stated by the U.S. Supreme Court on at least three separate occasions. In this chapter we shall deal with the second question first. Then, in the second part, we shall review the social science research bearing on the relationship between overcrowding and prison violence and inmate health problems. Both violence and inmate health concerns are still major problems in prisons today, and it is generally assumed by the courts that overcrowding contributes to or aggravates both problems. We shall review and comment upon recent research conducted in these areas and the methodological problems encountered in establishing causal connections.

SUPREME COURT DECISIONS IN HUTTO, BELL, AND RHODES

On the basis of Judge Henley's original decisions and decrees in the seminal case of *Holt v. Sarver*,[15] a triad of Supreme Court cases we shall refer to hereafter as *Hutto*,[16] *Bell*,[17] and *Rhodes*,[18] and several lower court opinions we think are consistent with the holdings, dicta, and rationales of those three cases, we have derived the following set of 11 legal propositions that are the law as it stands today with regard to the sufficiency and remediability of prison conditions and administrative practices under Eighth Amendment standards. After stating these 11 propositions, we shall attempt to justify them by discussing the controlling decisions of the U.S. Supreme Court, the triad of cases mentioned above, and particularly Justice Powell's decision in the last of these cases (*Rhodes v. Chapman*). Finally, we shall close this section with a brief discussion of the disagreements that persist in the lower federal courts with respect to the "totality of conditions" test and how it should be applied to correct deplorable prison conditions related to or directly proceeding from overcrowding.

Eleven Propositions

1. Conditions of confinement, whatever they may be (overcrowding, excessive violence, inadequate food, sanitation, or medical care), may be considered in isolation or in combination with other conditions, but some specific conditions must be found to be in violation of Eighth Amendment standards before the court may intervene and decree remedies for those conditions. The mere aggregation of bad conditions that are not themselves unconstitutional does not add up to an unconstitutional jail or prison [*Rhodes v. Chapman*, 452 U.S. 337, 347 (1981); *Madyun v. Thompson*, 657 F.2d 868, 874 n.10 (7th Cir. 1981); *Hoptowit v. Ray*, 682 F.2d 1237, 1247 (9th Cir. 1982); *Ruiz v. Estelle*, 679 F.2d 1115, 1140 n.98 (5th Cir. 1982)].

2. The appropriate standard to be applied under the Eighth Amendment to prison conditions asks whether the condition involves "the wanton and unnecessary infliction of pain" or is "grossly disproportionate to the severity of the crime warranting imprisonment." In considering whether a prison condition or practice is "wanton and unnecessary," it may be asked whether the practice or condition is "totally without penological justification" [*Rhodes v. Chapman*, 452 U.S. at 346; *Gregg v. Georgia*, 428 U.S. 153, 183 (1976); *Estelle v. Gamble*, 429 U.S. 97, 103 (1976)].

In deciding this question, the federal courts must accord great deference to the penological justification offered by prison experts; they cannot ignore them in preference of the testimony of plaintiffs' experts, except where such justifications are totally lacking evidentiary support and are frivolous [*Rhodes v. Chapman*, 452 U.S. at

352]. To do otherwise is to substitute the judgment of the court for the judgment of prison administrators, which the Supreme Court has repeatedly condemned [*Procunier v. Martinez*, 416 U.S. 396, 404-05 (1974); *Bell v. Wolfish*, 441 U.S. 520, 562 (1979); *Rhodes v. Chapman*, 452 U.S. at 351-52].

3. Standards of what is a constitutionally sufficient prison environment are set not by minimum standards promulgated by semiofficial professional organizations, but by the courts interpreting the Constitution [*Rhodes v. Chapman*, 452 U.S. at 348-49 n.13].

4. The Supreme Court and lower federal courts have established certain areas—shelter, sanitation, food, personal safety, adequate clothing, and adequate medical care—in which the serious deprivation of basic human necessities renders the confinement unconstitutional in violation of the Eighth Amendment [*Rhodes v. Chapman*, 452 U.S. at 347; *Stickney v. List*, 519 F. Supp. 617, 619 (D. Nev. 1981); *Grubbs v. Bradley*, 552 F. Supp. 1052, 1122 (M.D. Tenn., 1982)].

5. Although double celling is not per se cruel and unusual punishment (*Rhodes v. Chapman*), overcrowding in prisons and jails in living quarters and isolation cells, especially when combined with other intolerable conditions (filth, rodent and insect infestation, lack of exercise, the constant threat of violence), may constitute a failure to provide the inmate with the basic need of shelter [*Ramos v. Lamm*, 639 F.2d 559, 568 (10th Cir. 1980); *Villaneuva v. George*, 659 F.2d 851, 854 (8th Cir. 1981); *Grubbs v. Bradley*, 552 F. Supp. at 1122].

6. The Eighth Amendment also requires the maintenance of reasonably sanitary conditions in prisons, especially in the housing, food preparation, and service areas. In general, conditions must be sufficiently sanitary that inmates are not exposed to an unreasonable risk of disease [*Ramos v. Lamm*, 639 F.2d at 569-72; *Villaneuva v. George*, supra; *Lightfoot v. Walker*, 486 F. Supp. 504, 524 (1980); *Grubbs v. Bradley*, 552 F. Supp at 1123].

7. Medical and dental services must be offered and be available to prisoners. The failure to offer such services and complete indifference to the health needs of the inmates have been held on several occasions to constitute cruel and unusual punishment [*Estelle v. Gamble*, 429 U.S. at 104; *Ramos v. Lamm*, 639 F.2d at 575; *Todaro v. Ward*, 565 F.2d 48, 52 (2d Cir. 1977); *Laaman v. Helgemoe*, 437

F. Supp. 269, 311-15 (D.N.H. 1977)]. On the other hand, as long as medical care is provided and is adequate, perfect and faultless medical care is not constitutionally required. *Estelle v. Gamble*, 429 U.S. at 106].

8. As for the basic need of personal security from the violence of others, inmates are entitled to be protected from the constant threat of violence and sexual assault [*Jones v. Diamond*, 636 F.2d at 1374; *Ramos v. Lamm*, 639 F.2d at 572; *Woodhous v. Virginia*, 487 F.2d 889, 890 (4th Cir. 1973); *Stickney v. List*, 519 F. Supp. at 620]. On the other hand, no state can guarantee any citizen, let alone a prison inmate, perfect security from personal violence or criminal assault. Thus, the Eighth Amendment is violated not by an isolated or occasional violent episode, but rather by "confinement in a prison where violence and terror reign" [*Woodhous v. Virginia*, 487 F.2d at 890].

9. The Eighth Amendment does not entitle a prisoner to rehabilitation, and thus the failure of prison officials to provide rehabilitative programs is not, by itself, unconstitutional cruel and unusual punishment [*Hutto v. Finney*, 437 U.S. at 686 n.8; *Madyun v. Thompson*, 657 F.2d at 874; *Hoptowit v. Ray*, 682 F.2d at 1254; *Newman v. Alabama*, 559 F.2d 283, 287 (5th Cir. 1977); *Grubbs v. Bradley*, 552 F. Supp. at 1123-24]. However, as we state in the following proposition, insofar as lack of rehabilitative programs contributes to other prison conditions that are unconstitutional (for example, the lack of programs leads to idleness, which leads to violence), they may be subject to change as part of the remedy devised to correct the unconstitutional violation.

10. Prison conditions or practices that are not themselves cruel and unusual may materially contribute to conditions that are. Insofar as they do, their change may be decreed as part of a general judicial remedy [*Hutto v. Finney*, 437 U.S. at 685; *Hoptowit v. Ray*, 682 F.2d at 1264-65 (Tang, J. concurring); *Wright v. Rushen*, 642 F.2d 1129, 1132 (9th Cir. 1981)].

11. Great deference must be accorded the decisions of prison administrators. Absent a clear finding of constitutional violations, the federal courts are without the authority to intervene in prison administration in order to bring it into conformity with what the court considers enlightened correctional management [*Rhodes v. Chapman*, 452 U.S. at 349-50, 351-52; *Jones v. North Carolina*

Prisoners' Labor Unions, Inc., 433 U.S. 119, 126 (1977); *Procunier v. Martinez*, 416 U.S. at 404-05; *Wright v. Rushen*, 642 F.2d at 1134; *Grubbs v. Bradley*, 552 F. Supp. at 1124]. Furthermore, the federal courts "cannot assume that state legislatures and prison officials are insensitive to the requirements of the Constitution" [*Rhodes v. Chapman*, 452 U.S. at 352]. Therefore, federal courts cannot virtually take over the administration of prisons and jails *in the first instance*, without giving prison and jail administrators the first chance of correcting the unconstitutional conditions found to exist within reasonable time limits. If the state, county, or city officials, having been given this chance, indicate a recalcitrance or are excessively slow in complying with the court's initial order, the judicial remedy may be expanded [*Hutto v. Finney*, 437 U.S. at 687].

Three Supreme Court cases are usually cited[19] as bearing on the "totality of conditions" approach to reforming prison conditions through litigation: *Hutto v. Finney*, *Bell v. Wolfish*, and *Rhodes v. Chapman*.[20] Although all of them concerned rather specific prison conditions—*Hutto*, length of confinement in isolation cells; *Bell*, overcrowded jail cells, double bunking, body and cell searches; and *Rhodes*, double bunking of inmates in one cell of 63 square feet— it is clear that in *Hutto* and *Rhodes*, at least, the court was willing to consider the conditions not in isolation but in combinations.[21]

Hutto v. Finney

On this appeal to the U.S. Supreme Court the question to be decided was whether the district court's remedial order forbidding the Arkansas Department of Correction from confining inmates in isolation cells for more than 30 days was required under the Eighth Amendment cruel and unusual punishment clause. The Supreme Court, in an opinion written by Justice Stevens, held that the district court's decision was not that isolation in disciplinary cells for longer than 30 days was under all circumstances unconstitutional, but rather that it might be if the conditions of the cell and confinement were such as to render confinement in isolation intolerable and exceedingly painful.[22] Moreover, the court further held that the interdependence of the prison conditions contributing to the one falling below constitutionally minimal standards permits the district court to fashion a remedy that attempts to deal with the contributing conditions even though they themselves do not fall below the minimum.[23] Thus, the district court's 30-day limit, while not constitutionally required, could be justified on the ground that it served to alleviate the effects of overcrowding and of "deepseated enmities growing out of months of daily friction."[24]

Bell v. Wolfish

Bell was a class action brought by pretrial detainees complaining about several conditions of confinement and administrative practices in the Metropolitan Correctional Center, a new federal jail in New York City. One of the complaints was that the facility was overcrowded, that two inmates were forced to live in cells that had been designed for single occupancy ("double bunking"), and that there were inadequate recreational, educational, and vocational opportunities at the jail as well as insufficient staff.[25] Besides establishing a due process standard for determining the unconstitutionality of conditions in jails in relation to unconvicted pretrial detainees,[26] and holding that previous rulings did not establish a "one-man, one-cell" principle of constitutional law,[27] the majority of the Court in Bell did not concern itself with the totality of conditions at the Metropolitan Correctional Center or with fashioning an appropriate remedy. Instead, the decision is primarily important for the emphasis the court gave to warning the lower courts to treat decisions of prison administrators with more deference and respect:

But under the Constitution, the first question to be answered is not whose plan [for reform] is best, but in what branch of the Government is lodged the authority to initially devise the plan. This does not mean that constitutional rights are not to be scrupulously observed. It does mean, however, that the inquiry of federal courts in prison management must be limited to the issue of whether a particular system violates any prohibition of the Constitution, or in the case of a federal prison a statute. The wide range of judgment calls that meet constitutional and statutory requirements are confined to officials outside the Judicial Branch of Government.[28]

Rhodes v. Chapman

This case raised the single issue of whether the housing of two inmates in a single cell (63 square feet in dimension) at the Southern

Ohio Correctional Facility (SOCF) was cruel and unusual punishment. The prison was a modern one and contained many places for education, meditation, and recreation. The conditions in the cells were crowded but clean, and the plumbing worked. The district court had found that double bunking at SOCF was unconstitutional because, unlike the situation in *Bell*, prison inmates at SOCF were serving long terms of imprisonment and thus would have to suffer the effects of crowding much longer. Other reasons were that the prison housed 38 percent more inmates than its design capacity allowed for; the recommendation of several national and international correctional organizations that each inmate have at least 50-55 square feet of living space; and the fact that most of the inmates spent most of their time in their cells, this being a permanent, not temporary, condition at the prison.[29] The Sixth Circuit Court of Appeals affirmed the decision of the district court, although on slightly different grounds. The Supreme Court reversed.

The majority opinion, written by Mr. Justice Powell, held that none of the five facts raised by the district court was sufficient to render conditions at SOCF unconstitutional under Eighth Amendment standards. The Court took care to define again the meaning of the Eighth Amendment in the prison context, stating that conditions might be harsh, unpleasant, and uncomfortable, but must "not involve the wanton and unnecessary infliction of pain," or "be grossly disproportionate to the severity of the crime warranting imprisonment," nor deprive the inmate "of the minimal civilized measure of life's necessities."[30] Under this standard, the conditions at SOCF were a long way from being cruel and unusual, even if they were punishing.

Not only did the Court in *Rhodes* develop a stricter standard of what kind of prison conditions satisfy the cruel and unusual punishment test, but it also made clear that this test could not be satisfied simply by accumulating (under the "totality of conditions" approach) a number of deficiencies none of which by itself rose to the level of a constitutional violation:

But the Constitution does not mandate comfortable prisons, and prisons of SOCF's type which house persons convicted of serious crimes, cannot be free of discomfort. Thus, these considerations properly are weighed by the legislature and prison administration rather than a court. There being no constitutional violation, the District Court had no authority to consider whether the double celling in the light of these considerations was the best response to the increase in Ohio's statewide prison population.[31]

Thus, to summarize, under the "totality of conditions" test properly applied, prison conditions fall into one of three categories:

1. Prison conditions, practices, or procedures that, in themselves or in combination with others, are cruel and unusual punishment. The court may attempt to remedy these directly by judicial decree or by ordering a change to bring the condition, practice, or procedure into conformity with the Constitution.

2. Prison conditions, practices, or procedures that are not themselves cruel and unusual punishment nor violative of any of the constitutional rights or expectancies of the prisoners ("liberty" interests under the due process clause) but that directly contribute to, cause, or foster the unconstitutional conditions. The court may order changes in these conditions if necessary to bring about the improvement mentioned above in category 1 in the unconstitutional condition(s) found.

3. Prison conditions, practices, or procedures that may be "harsh," "oppressive," and even "contrary to sound penological practices" in the opinion of professional experts or the court but that are not cruel and unusual themselves and do not contribute to others that are. As to these, the federal court simply lacks any constitutional authority to decree a change.

A good illustration of how this test should be applied is presented by the case of *Grubbs v. Bradley.*[32] In this class action under 42 U.S.C. Section 1983 against state officials regarding 12 Tennessee adult penal institutions, it was alleged that a number of different prison conditions and practices violated the inmates' Eighth Amendment rights. One of the conditions or practices challenged was the classification system. The district court held that, in and by itself, the classification system could not be considered an Eighth Amendment violation since it did not inflict needless pain and suffering, nor did it take away any constitutional rights of the inmates.[33] However, deficiencies in the classification system could be considered insofar as they contributed to violence in Tennessee prisons, which *was* found to be an unconstitutional condition.[34] The district court found that "overclassification" of inmates who were of low-violence potential to prisons and wards where dangerous, violence-prone inmates were also confined contributed to increased levels of violence and to the psychological deterioration of nonviolent inmates;[35] and it ordered that overclassification be corrected. However, regarding other complaints made as to the classification system—which would fall into category 3 above—the district court declared itself without the power to intervene and expressed the belief that the correction thereof was better left to the sound discretion of prison officials.[36]

Significantly, the district court in *Grubbs* refrained from entering a long and detailed decree, even though it found seven conditions in the Tennessee prisons it examined to be cruel and unusual punishment. Instead, with one minor exception, it ordered the Tennessee Department of Corrections to submit within 60 days to the special master appointed by the court a plan to remedy certain constitutional violations believed to be in need of immediate correction, and another plan within six months for correcting the remaining constitutional violations. This action we believe is in accord with the often-repeated admonitions of the U.S. Supreme Court to lower federal courts to determine and declare unconstitutionality where they find it, but to rely *in the first instance* on the prison administrator defendants to remove the conditions found to be unconstitutional in their own way.

Prison Conditions and the Lower Federal Courts

All federal courts after *Rhodes* are in agreement that prison conditions should be viewed not in isolation but in the context of other conditions. In that sense, all federal courts apply the "totality of conditions" approach in evaluating prison conditions and administrative practices under the Eighth Amendment when there is a broadside attack.[37] However, there is lingering disagreement among the circuits,[38] and sometimes even within the same district court,[39] over whether viewing prison conditions "alone or in combination" means viewing them in the aggregate or viewing them as contributing to a specific condition that is clearly unconstitutional.[40] In our summary of the law (see propositions 1 and 10) we have adopted the latter view as the correct one, not only because at present it represents the majority view but also because it seems to adhere most closely to the rationale of the majority opinions in *Hutto, Bell,* and *Rhodes.*

Although *Bell* and *Rhodes* made it clear that overcrowding and double bunking were not by themselves unconstitutional under the Eighth Amendment, except perhaps in egregious cases (for example, three men confined to cell space of less than 50 square feet), lower courts have continued to treat overcrowding as if it were the source of all evils, instead of being merely a contributing factor aggravating other sources of violence and deprivation.[41] This has led them to impose population limits on jails and prisons on the assumption that nothing would improve unless something were done to alleviate the pressure of overpopulation.[42] Unfortunately, this most visible and most plausible candidate for the ills of prison existence has led to simplistic thinking on the part of judges intervening in the administration of prisons and jails, causing them to defer other remedies until the crowding problem is "solved"—which may never happen. A more careful examination needs to be made as to how much overcrowding actually contributes to disorder and maladministration in prisons and jails today.

In the following section, we shall concentrate on overcrowding and its correlates and their empirical relationship with prison violence and other clearly objectionable conditions. We hope that this discussion will be useful to lawyers in future prison-condition cases in making the necessary causal linkages we believe need to be made between overcrowding and related conditions that have been held to raise constitutional (Eighth Amendment) issues.

RESEARCH ON THE EFFECTS OF OVERCROWDING

One of the clearest cases of an unconstitutional condition is, as we have seen, the condition of being forced to live in a place where death, serious bodily injury, severe illness, or sexual humiliation are constant threats. It is not difficult to determine in most cases when legitimate order has broken down in a prison, when the guards have effectively lost control over the inmates, and when the stronger inmates are victimizing the weaker for sexual and other favors or using violence to enforce their own brand of vigilante justice. In such an environment, the ordinary prisoner's life is at hazard to a far greater extent than it would be in the free world. Forced confinement in such a world of terrors and risks is not a punishment contemplated by the legislator, and is "grossly disproportionate to the severity of the crime" for which the convict has been imprisoned.[43]

Research on overcrowding has been primarily concerned with the relationship between measures of overcrowding and inmate violence. Violence is the outcome of a very complex interaction of many different kinds of influencing factors, which we shall refer to from now on as "causal variables."[44] These causal variables can be divided into two main classes—personal and situational (or environmental) according to whether they are part of the aggressor's personality and disposition to engage in violent behavior (personal variables) or whether they are part of the situation (environment) in which he finds himself at the time he commits the act of violence (situational variables). Within this scheme, overcrowding is a situational variable.

There is social science research[45] that suggests that personal variables (such as the age of the inmate, his prior criminal history including his history of violence, his Minnesota Multiphasic Personality Inventory [M.M.P.I.] score and classification, and so on) may be more influential (that is, may explain more of the variance in the dependent variable,[46] violence, in statistical tests) than are any situational variables. Therefore, neither overcrowding nor other situational characteristics will ever be able to account for all of the violent acts that occur within prisons. Nevertheless, as we shall show, there is empirical support for the strong inference that overcrowding in particular accounts for a substantial part of the variation in reported violence and other indicators of adverse inmate conditions.

Violence is also the product of an interaction of motivating forces, of opportunities to engage in it, and of the social control applied to restrain it.[47] Overcrowding contributes to violence in prison mainly by providing numerous opportunities for hostilities to break out into open violence. But it also contributes to motivation by creating the stress that leads to the violent resolution of a problem or dispute;[48] and, finally, it may contribute to the breakdown of controls that prison administrators have erected to prevent violence.[49] Overclassification (the practice of placing inmates in higher-security institutions than their background or behavior requires), itself caused largely by overcrowding but, in a circular way, aggravating the overcrowding problem,[50] contributes to violence mainly by providing predisposed aggressors an opportunity to carry out their aggression on victims placed in their midst; but it also contributes in a curious way to motivate aggression.[51] To the extent that overclassification contributes to overcrowding in certain facilities, it is likely to overtax the custodial staff, with the result that controls are lost and aggression is more likely to occur.[52] Finally, idleness, also often caused by overcrowding and with a negative feedback effect on overcrowding, provides the motivation for violence (especially among younger inmates) as well as increasing the number of opportunities for it.[53] As this brief discussion indicates, determining the causal contribution of any environmental or situational factor is an extremely complicated task.[54]

Overcrowding and Inmate Violence

Overcrowding in prisons is a phenomenon that can be defined at the individual or aggregate level either objectively—in square footage of living space per inmate ("spatial density") or in the number of individuals sharing a sleeping unit of whatever size ("social density")—or subjectively in terms of the inmates' perceptions of being crowded. [55] We have already seen that, so far, the U.S. Supreme Court has avoided placing any constitutionally minimal space limits on the size of cells, nor has it yet declared the constitutional maximum for the number of prisoners who may occupy the same living space. This is not to say that there are no such limits. It is difficult to believe that the Supreme Court would contradict a lower federal court's finding of cruel and unusual punishment in confining two inmates in a double-bunked cell measuring less than 50 square feet for more than 10 hours a day, no matter how clean the surrounding areas.[56] On the other hand, prisoners do react in very different ways to crowded conditions, and research indicates that, in general, inmates react less adversely to limited space than they do to space they have to share with others constantly.[57] In other words, there is likely to be more violence in a situation of "social density" crowding than in one of "spatial density" crowding.

While there are numerous studies that clearly establish a relationship between various measures of overcrowding and violence in prisons, much of this research suffers from some obvious methodological problems.[58] Some research has only addressed the relationship between overcrowding measures and violence without considering the effect of personal characteristics of the offender (such as age, prior record, time served) or situational factors other than overcrowding (such as management policies, staff training, classification procedures). While such research demonstrates that overcrowded conditions are associated with levels of violence, it does not establish that overcrowding causes violence.

The measurement of violence and the size and nature of the sample studied have presented problems for research on overcrowding and violence. Violence has usually been measured with incident-data extracted from institutional records. This creates the possibility of significant errors in the estimation of the prevalence and incidence of violence. Violence not observed or reported to staff will not be counted. Also, most studies confound violence between inmates with violent incidents involving inmates and staff. To the extent that record-keeping practices vary across institutions, studies involving more than one prison would face additional sources of invalidity in the measurement of the dependent variable.

Studies of a single institution or a limited range of institutions are characteristic of the research on overcrowding and violence. Using limited samples of institutions (usually selected for their convenience) makes generalization of findings very problematic. This becomes especially troublesome if one wants to control for institutional (situational) characteristics other than overcrowding.

The most comprehensive research on overcrowding and violence was conducted by Gaes and McGuire.[59] This study utilized multiple institutions, longitudinal data, and multiple measures of overcrowding, and the authors introduced into the analysis controls for numerous inmate characteristics (such as age and prior record) and inmate prison activities (such as education and work assignment). Their research found that overcrowding, independent of offender characteristics other than situational factors, was associated with violence. The age factor was found to be especially important in explaining inmate-inmate violence. Nevertheless, they conclude that "crowding, not age, . . . is the best predictor of assault rates," and that the percentage of inmates housed in dormitories is also related to levels of assault.[60] As younger populations are frequently housed in dormitory settings, the impact of age and housing factors must be further considered.

Levels of overcrowding and inmate-inmate violence appear to be closely related. While the best research suggests that this relationship is not eliminated by the introduction of other potential causal variables, the interaction between overcrowding, age, and inmate housing needs further exploration, especially for the understanding of violence between inmates. While we are not yet able to explain why overcrowding is associated with higher levels of violence, nor whether the effect of overcrowding is confounded with age and housing effects, the research has clearly established that overcrowding is an exceptionally strong indicator of levels of violence.

Overcrowding and Inmate Health

Studies of the impact of overcrowding on indicators of the health of inmates face many of the methodological problems noted above. However, the indicators of health (primarily sick calls, illnesses, and blood pressure levels) present fewer problems of measurement than does violence. The research on overcrowding and health clearly demonstrates that various measures of overcrowding are negatively associated with health indicators, especially for inmates housed in dormitory settings.

Adult inmates in overcrowded institutions have been found to have higher rates of tuberculosis,[61] higher rates of request for medical services ("sick calls"),[62] elevated blood pressure,[63] higher rates of psychiatric commitment,[64] increased infection from contagious diseases,[65] and higher rates of suicide and morbidity.[66] Few of these studies have introduced controls for personal or situational characteristics that might account for the relationship between overcrowding and health.

Gaes[67] reports that when controls for criminal history, ethnicity, race, program participation, age, and date of entry into the prison are introduced, there is no significant relationship between space per inmate and clinic utilization. However, other research involving multiple sites, varying housing arrangements, and controls for selected personal characteristics has concluded that "crowding in prisons appears to be related to increased pathology."[68] As in the case of research on violence, these contradictory results reflect the fact that while a significant bi-variate relationship exists between overcrowding and measures of health, the relationship is affected by a host of situational and personal characteristics. When studies use different sites and different measures of apparently similar concepts, variations in results can be expected. While no research has suggested that overcrowding has no significant effect on indicators of inmate health, the level of this effect remains in dispute.

CONCLUSION

Overcrowded prisons have higher rates of inmate-inmate violence and higher levels of various indicators of inmate mental and physical disease. Research to date has not determined the magnitude of the independent causal effect of overcrowding on those measures of prison conditions and effects. It appears that overcrowding, in interaction with age and housing arrangements, accounts for substantial amounts of the explained variation in levels of inmate violence and health.

There are of course other effects of overcrowding that are clearly and substantially determined by the number of inmates in a prison. Increased idleness, inappropriate housing assignments, overclassification, insufficient program resources, decreased staff training, and increased stress on staff result from overcrowding. While research on these consequences of overcrowding is lacking, experience suggests that such outcomes are routinely observable.

NOTES

1. *Holt v. Sarver*, 309 F. Supp. 362 (E.D. Ark., 1969) (*Holt I*); decree first entered in *Holt v. Sarver*, 309 F. Supp. 362 (E.D. Ark., 1970) (*Holt II*); affirmed 442 F. 2d 304 (8th Cir., 1971).

2. *Prisoners in 1984*, Bureau of Justice Statistics Bulletin (Washington, DC: U.S. Department of Justice, April 1985), p. 4.

3. The midyear figure for 1985 was supplied by telephone by the Bureau of Justice Statistics.

4. *Jones v. Diamond*, 636 F. 2d 1364, 1373 (5th Cir., 1981), cert. dismissed sub nom. *Ledbetter v. Jones*, 453 U.S. 950, 102 S. Ct. 27, 69 L. Ed. 2d 1033 (1981); *Ramos v. Lamm*, 639 F. 2d 559, 572 (10th Cir., 1980), cert. den. 450 U.S. 1041, 101 S. Ct. 1759, 68 L. Ed. 2d. 239 (1981); *Gates*

v. Collier, 501 F. 2d 1291, 1308–10 (5th Cir., 1974); *Woodhous v. Virginia*, 487 F. 2d 889, 890 (4th Cir., 1973).

5. Lambert King and George Geis, "Tuberculosis Transmission in a Large Urban Jail," *Journal of the American Medical Association* 237 (1977): 791–92; W. W. Stead, "Undetected Tuberculosis in Prison: Source of Infection for Community at Large," *Journal of the American Medical Association* 240 (1978): 2544–47; Paul B. Paulus et al., *Effects of Crowding in Prisons* (Washington, DC: U.S. Department of Health, Education and Welfare, National Institute of Education, 1977); G. McCain, V. O. Fox, and P. B. Paulus, "The Relationship between Illness Complaints and Degree of Crowding in a Prison Environment," *Environment and Behavior* 8 (1980): 283–90.

6. *Palmigiano v. Garrahy*, 443 F. Supp. 956 (D.R.I. 1977) at pp. 968–70; Peter Suedfeld, "Environmental Effects on Violent Behavior in Prisons," *International Journal of Offender Therapy and Comparative Criminology* 24, no. 2 (1980): 107–16; Lee-Jan Jan, "Overcrowding and Inmate Behavior: Some Preliminary Findings," *Criminal Justice and Behavior* 7 (1980): 293–301, Carl B. Clements, "Crowded Prisons: A Review of the Psychological and Environmental Effects," *Law and Human Behavior* 3 (1979): 217–25, at p. 222.

7. *Pugh v. Locke*, 406 F. Supp. 318 (M.D. Ala., 1976), affirmed sub nom. *Newman v. Alabama*, 559 F. 2d 283 (5th Cir., 1977), cert. den. sub nom. *Alabama v. Pugh*, 438 U.S. 781, 98 S.Ct. 3057, 56 L. Ed. 2d 1114 (1978); Clements, "Crowded Prisons."

8. *Holt v. Sarver*, supra; *Rhodes v. Chapman*, 452 U.S. 337, 363, 101 S. Ct. 2392, 69 L. Ed. 2d 59 (1981) (concurring opinion of Mr. Justice Brennan); *Ruiz v. Estelle*, 679 F. 2d 1115, 1139–40 (5th Cir., 1982); *Villaneuva v. George*, 659 F. 2d 851, 854 (8th Cir., 1981); *Johnson v. Levine*, 588 F. 2d 1378 (4th Cir., 1978); *Nelson v. Collins*, 659 F. 2d 420 (4th Cir., 1981); *Smith v. Fairman*, 690 F. 2d 122, 125 (7th Cir., 1982).

9. *Bell v. Wolfish*, 441 U.S. 520, 99 S. Ct. 1861, 60 L. Ed. 2d 447 (1979).

10. *Estelle v. Gamble*, 429 U.S. 97, 97 S. Ct. 285, 50 L. Ed. 2d 251 (1976); *Ruiz v. Estelle*, 503 F. Supp. 1265, 1307–46 (S.D. Tex., 1980), affirmed in part, reversed in part, 679 F. 2d 1115 (5th Cir., 1982); *Madyun v. Thompson*, 657 F. 2d 868, 872 (7th Cir., 1981), affirming in part, reversing in part 484 F. Supp. 6l9 (C.D. Ill., 1980).

11. *Ruiz v. Estelle*, 503 F. Supp. at pp. 1288–94; *Madyun v. Thompson*, 657 F. 2d at pp. 874, 875; *Hoptowit v. Ray*, 682 F. 2d 1237 (9th Cir., 1982) at pp. 1249–50; *Ramos v. Lamm*, 639 F. 2d 559, 573 (10th Cir., 1980). Often, it turns out that the complaint is not so much the lack of guards, but their refusal to intervene even when they know a fight or sexual assault is in progress.

12. *Hoptowit v. Ray,* 682 F. 2d at p. 1255; *Grubbs v. Bradley,* 552 F. Supp. 1052 (M.D. Tenn., 1982) at pp. 1060–65; *Palmigiano v. Garrahy,* 443 F. Supp. at pp. 981–82.

13. See notes 6, 7, and 10 for district court citations.

14. See James B. Jacobs, "The Prisoners' Rights Movement and Its Impacts, 1960–80," in Norval Morris and Michael Tonry, eds., *Crime and Justice,* vol. 2 (Chicago: University of Chicago Press, 1980), pp. 429–66.

15. See note 1.

16. *Hutto v. Finney,* 437 U.S. 678, 98 S. Ct. 2565, 57 L. Ed. 2d 522 (1978).

17. See note 9.

18. *Rhodes v. Chapman,* 452 U.S. 337, 101 S. Ct. 2392, 69 L. Ed. 2d 59 (1981).

19. See Comment, "Challenging Cruel and Unusual Conditions of Prison Confinement: Refining the Totality of Conditions Approach," *Howard Law Journal* 26 (1983): 227; Rod Smolla, "Prison Overcrowding and the Courts: A Roadmap for the 1980's," *University of Illinois Law Review* 1984 (1984): 389; Claudia Angelos and James B. Jacobs, "Prison Overcrowding and the Law," *The Annals* of the American Academy of Political and Social Science 478 (March 1985): 100.

20. See notes 16, 9, and 18.

21. "The length of time each inmate spends in isolation was simply one consideration among many. We find no error in the court's conclusion that, *taken as a whole,* conditions in isolation cells continued to violate the prohibition against cruel and unusual punishment." *Hutto v. Finney,* 437 U.S. at 687 (emphasis added). "In *Hutto v. Finney* the conditions of confinement in two Arkansas prisons constituted cruel and unusual punishment because they resulted in unquestioned and serious deprivations of basic human needs. Conditions other than those in *Gamble* and *Hutto, alone or in combination,* may deprive inmates of the minimal civilized measure of life's necessities." *Rhodes v. Chapman,* 452 U.S. at 347. (See also concurring opinion of Justices Brennan, Stevens, and Blackmun, 452 U.S. at 362–63.)

22. 437 U.S. at 685–87.

23. 437 U.S. at p. 687.

24. 437 U.S. at 688.

25. 441 U.S. at pp. 5, 541–43.

26. It was well established before *Bell,* and the Court was quick to affirm, that the Eighth Amendment cruel and unusual punishment provision does not apply to pretrial detainees, whose confinement is not intended as criminal punishment. Detainees had to rely on the due process clauses of the Fifth and Fourteenth Amendments. The Court held that under these clauses pretrial detainees had the right not to be "punished" until convicted, and that either the jail conditions and deprivations they suffered had to be

intended by their jailors as punishment or, if not intended as such, they had to amount to "punishment." To amount to punishment, the harsh jail condition or administrative practice would have to lack any rational purpose in terms of a legitimate governmental objective, or it would have to be excessive in relation to the reasons given for it. 441 U.S. at 538–39.

27. 441 U.S. at 542.
28. 441 U.S. at 562.
29. 452 U.S. at 343–44.
30. 452 U.S. at 347.
31. 452 U.S. at 349–50.
32. 552 F. Supp. 1052 (M.D. Tenn. 1982).
33. 552 F. Supp. at 1060.
34. 552 F. Supp. at 1061.
35. 552 F. Supp. at 1063.
36. 552 F. Supp. at 1064.
37. For a theoretical discussion of the differences between a "broadside" (totality of conditions) attack and a "focused" (discrete adjudication) attack, see Comment, "Complex Enforcement: Unconstitutional Prison Conditions," *Harvard Law Review* 94 (1981): 626.
38. See *Hoptowit v. Ray*, 682 F.2d 1237, 1256 (9th Cir. 1982); *Smith v. Fairman*, 690 F.2d 122, 125 (7th Cir. 1982); *Walker v. Mintzes*, 771 F.2d 920, 925–26 (6th Cir. 1985); *Ruiz v. Estelle*, 679 F.2d 1115, 1140 n.98 (5th Cir. 1982); *Union County Jail Inmates v. Di Buono*, 713 F.2d 984, 999 (3d Cir. 1983); *Doe v. District of Columbia*, 701 F.2d 948, 957 (D.C. Cir. 1983); *Jones v. Diamond*, 636 F.2d 1364, 1368 (5th Cir. 1981), cert. dismissed sub nom.; *Ledbetter v. Jones*, 453 U.S. 95, 102 S. Ct. 27, 69 L. Ed. 2d. 1033 (1981); *French v. Owens*, 538 F. Supp. 910, 912 (S.D. Ind. 1982); *Heitman v. Gabriel*, 524 F. Supp. 622, 625 (W.D. Mo. 1981).
39. Compare, for example, the opinion of Morton, J., in *Grubbs v. Bradley*, 552 F. Supp. 1052, 1121–22 (M.D. Tenn. 1982), with the opinion of Nix, J., in *Groseclose v. Dutton*, 609 F. Supp. 1432, 1445 (M.D. Tenn. 1985).
40. For a contrast between the "aggregation" and "spillover" approaches, see Smolla, "Prison Overcrowding and Courts," pp. 409–13. The "aggregation" approach looks to the effect on the inmate of an aggregation of noxious conditions, none of which may be constitutionally deficient by itself, whereas the "spillover" approach abjures resting on "vague conclusions" that the total prison environment is unconstitutionally oppressive. (Cf. *Hoptowit v. Ray*, 682 F.2d at 1256.) The latter approach insists that the focus remain on specific conditions that are unconstitutional. Other conditions that contribute to the specific unconstitutional conditions may then also be dealt with in the judicial remedy seeking to correct the unconstitutional

condition. What cannot be done under the latter approach is justifying a top-to-bottom reform of the prison or jail merely on the basis of a judge's conclusion that the environment in the prison is harsh and oppressive.

41. See Comment, "Challenging Cruel and Unusual Conditions"; *Lareau v. Manson*, 507 F. Supp. 1177, 1194 (D. Conn. 1980); *Inmates of Alleghany County Jail v. Wecht*, 565 F. Supp. 1278, 1297 (W.D. Pa. 1983); *French v. Owens*, 538 F. Supp. 910, 927 (S.D. Ind. 1982); *Benjamin v. Malcolm*, 595 F. Supp. 1357, 1365 (S.D.N.Y. 1983); *McMurry v. Phelps*, 533 F. Supp. 742 (W.D. La. 1982); *Union County Jail Inmates v. Scanlon*, 537 F. Supp. 993 (D.N.J. 1982).

42. Angelos and Jacobs, "Prison Overcrowding and the Law," p. 109.

43. See citations in note 5.

44. The term usually employed in social science is "independent variable"; but, for clarity's sake, we shall hereafter refer to independent variables as "causal variables," not because they have proved to be causes of events or phenomena, but because they are candidates for testing to see whether or not they are causally related to the variables.

45. See J. D. Edinger and S. M. Auerbach, "Development and Validation of a Multidimensional Multivariate Model for Accounting for Infractions in a Correctional Setting," *Journal of Personality and Social Psychology* 36 (1978): 1479–89, at pp. 1486–87; D. Ellis, H. G. Grasmick, and B. Gilman, "Violence in Prisons: A Sociological Analysis," *American Journal of Sociology* 80 (July 1974): 16–43, at p. 23. See also T. J. Flanagan, "Correlates of Institutional Misconduct among State Prisoners," *Criminology* 21 (February 1983): 29–39.

46. The "dependent variable" is the phenomenon or event whose variation is thought to be affected by variation in the "independent (causal) variable." Hereafter, for clarity's sake, we shall refer to this variable as the "outcome variable." Thus, variations in the amount of violence in a prison are assumed, subject to proof or disproof, to be the outcome or result of variations in the causal variables.

47. Albert K. Cohen, "Prison Violence: A Sociological Perspective," in A. K. Cohen, G. F. Cole, and R. G. Bailey, eds., *Prison Violence* (Lexington, MA: Lexington Books, 1976), pp. 3–22.

48. A. F. Kinzel, "Body-Buffer Zones in Violent Prisoners," *American Journal of Psychiatry* 127 (July 1970): 59–64; S. F. Curran, R. J. Blatchley, and T. E. Hanlon, "The Relationship between Body Buffer Zone and Violence as Assessed by Subjective and Objective Techniques," *Criminal Justice and Behavior* 5 (March 1978): 53–62; Clements, "Crowded Prisons"; P. Paulus, G. McCain, and V. Cox, "Prison Standards: Some Pertinent Data on Crowding," *Federal Probation* 45 (December 1981): 48–54.

49. *Pugh v. Locke*, 406 F. Supp. at 325; *Ruiz v. Estelle*, 503 F. Supp. at 1281–82.

50. Carl B. Clements ("The Relationship of Offender Classification to the Problem of Prison Overcrowding," *Crime and Delinquency* 28 [January 1982]: 72–81) argues that overclassification aggravates the overcrowding problem by increasing the disciplinary infractions, causing loss of good time and delayed parole release, and, in general, slowing down the progress of all inmates through the system.

51. Many investigators have noted the seeming necessity for certain prisoners to establish and maintain a position of dominance with respect to weaker prisoners while in prison. This may lead to sexual as well as other forms of violence. See Cohen, "Prison Violence"; Daniel Lockwood, "Sexual Aggression among Male Prisoners" (Ph.D. diss., State University of New York, Albany, 1977); A. Ibrahim, "Deviant Sexual Behavior in Men's Prisons," *Crime and Delinquency* 20 (January 1974): 38–44; R. Wilson, "Homosexual Rape: Legacy of Overcrowding," *Corrections Magazine* 3 (1977): 10–11. Misclassification of young, passive inmates to wards or cell blocks occupied by aggressive inmates who have a need of establishing a reputation for machismo and dominance only acts as a stimulus to violent assault.

52. See citations in note 49.

53. Ibrahim, "Deviant Sexual Behavior," pp. 41–42; Barry Feld, "A Comparative Analysis of Organizational Structure and Inmate Subcultures in Institutions for Juvenile Offenders," *Crime and Delinquency* 27 (July 1981): 336–63, at pp. 358–59; Barry Feld, *Neutralizing Inmate Violence: Juvenile Offenders in Institutions* (Cambridge, MA: Ballinger, 1977), pp. 199–200; Suedfeld, "Environmental Effects on Violent Behavior in Prisons," pp. 112–13.

54. In social science research the following are often cited as the criteria that must be met before a causal relationship can be established: (1) demonstrating an appropriate time-order relationship between the variables (that is, the cause occurs before the effect); (2) demonstrating the existence of concomitant variation between the variables; and (3) demonstrating that the relationship between the variables is not due to some other variable or set of variables. In traditional science, establishing causal relationships involves experimentation. In a basic experiment the subjects to be studied are randomly assigned to experimental and control conditions. The random assignment is to assure that differences existing prior to the experiment are equalized in each group. The control group is not exposed to the cause. Subsequent differences between the experimental and control groups can be attributed to the assumed cause.

While the experimental model is useful in some social and legal research settings, it is highly questionable for most criminal justice research. When experimentation is not possible, surveys, observation, analysis of administration data, and so forth must be used to assess causal relations. The study of the effects of prison overcrowding represents an area of research not available to experimentation. Most of the research discussed in this section involves nonexperimental or quasi-experimental approaches to establishing causal relations.

55. For various attempts to measure crowding in prison objectively, see J. Mullen and B. Smith, *American Prisons and Jails*, vol. 3, *Conditions and Costs of Confinement* (Santa Barbara, CA: Abt Associates, 1980); P. Paulus et al., "Some Effects of Crowding in a Prison Environment," *Journal of Applied Social Psychology* 5 (1975): 86–91; P. L. Nacci, H. E. Teitelbaum, and J. Prather, "Population Density and Inmate Misconduct Rates in the Federal Prison System," *Federal Probation* 41 (June 1977): 26–31. As to subjective measures of overcrowding, see D. Stokols, "A Social Psychological Model of Human Crowding Phenomenon," *Journal of the American Institute of Planners* 38 (1972): 87–115; D. Stokols, "On the Distinction between Density and Crowding: Some Implications for Future Research," *Psychological Review* 79 (1972): 275–77; G. McCain, V. C. Cox, and P. B. Paulus, *The Effect of Prison Crowding on Inmate Behavior* (Washington, DC: U.S. Department of Justice, National Institute of Justice, 1980), p. 13; G. Gaes, "The Effects of Overcrowding in Prison," in Michael Tonry and Norval Morris, eds., *Crime and Justice*, vol. 6 (Chicago: University of Chicago Press, 1985), pp. 95–146.

56. *Battle v. Andersons*, 564 F.2d 388, 395 (10th Cir. 1977) (35-40-square-foot cells); *Detainees v. Malcolm*, 520 F.2d 392, 395 (2d Cir. 1975) (40–square-foot cells).

57. P. Paulus et al., "Some Effects of Crowding," pp. 26–27; D. A. D'Atri, "Psychophysiological Responses to Crowding," *Environment and Behavior* 7 (1975): 237–52.

58. For a thorough review of these studies, see Gaes, "Effects of Overcrowding in Prison."

59. G. Gaes and W. McGuire, "Prison Violence: The Contribution of Crowding versus Other Determinants of Prison Assault Rate," *Journal of Research in Crime and Delinquency* 22 (1984): 41–65.

60. Gaes, "Effects of Overcrowding in Prison," p. 134.

61. Stead, "Undetected Tuberculosis in Prison."

62. Paulus, McCain, and Cox, "Prison Standards."

63. D. A. D'Atri and A. Ostfeld, "Crowding: Its Effects on the Elevation of Blood Pressure," *Preventive Medicine* 4 (1975): 237–50.

64. Paulus, McCain, and Cox, "Prison Standards."

65. B. Walker and T. Gorden, "Health and High Density Confinement in Jails and Prisons," *Federal Probation* 44 (1980): 53–58.

66. V. C. Cox, P. Paulus, and G. McCain, "Prison Crowding Research: The Relevance for Prison Housing Standards," *American Psychologist* 11 (1984): 52–66.

67. Gaes, "Effects of Overcrowding in Prison."

68. McCain, Cox, and Paulus, *Effect of Prison Crowding.*

3 The Costs of Incarceration

TODD R. CLEAR
and
PATRICIA M. HARRIS

Proposals to expand the use of imprisonment are typically founded in nonfiscal concerns, including frustration over increases in crime, a desire to lock up greater numbers of criminals, and an expectation of improved crime control through incapacitation policies. Too often, fiscal and other costs of incarceration are given insufficient consideration in these proposals. When the economic dimension is at last addressed, costs are frequently represented by a general summary figure, such as a per-bed or daily per-inmate cost. The issue of whether proposed changes in incarceration policy are affordable is normally skirted in favor of some all too familiar but fiscally irrelevant dogma: if crime is on the increase (or alternatively, if our need to punish has increased), and if current capacity cannot accommodate larger numbers of convicted criminals, then additional prison space must be created.

Of course, this is both a simplistic and an incomplete way to define the problem of prison policy, as several authors have recently pointed out.[1] The assumption that crime is increasing—or that our need to punish is increasing—is at best questionable.[2] The omission of cost considerations from the penal policy debate is glaring, in light of the generally conservative fiscal attitude adopted by most

This chapter was prepared under grant no. SD-81-11 from the National Institute of Corrections of the U.S. Department of Justice. Points of view or opinions stated in this document are those of the authors and do not necessarily represent the official position or policies of the U.S. Department of Justice.

state governments. There is a need for a broader perspective which would give more weight to fiscal and programmatic concerns. This chapter provides a cost analysis of incarceration, with specific attention given to the costs associated with an expansion in the use of imprisonment. Costs are considered from three points of view: (1) fiscal, or real dollar costs of goods and services; (2) managerial, or costs affected by specific contemporary practices of administrators of corrections institutions; and (3) policy, or the costs of incarceration in comparison to other punishment options.

THE COSTS OF IMPRISONMENT: A FISCAL PERSPECTIVE

In personal finance we normally consider bottom-line costs. In the purchase of a new car, for example, we know that the price of a basic model can differ considerably from the final price. First, we must consider that "extras," such as a radio, air conditioning, and the like—considered virtual necessities by most buyers—will naturally inflate the price of an automobile. To this adjusted price must be further added the cost of tax, destination charges, dealer preparation, license and registration, and insurance. Combining all of these expenses, it is not unlikely that a car that lists for $10,000 will cost us $14,000-$15,000. And if financing is necessary, the eventual cost to the buyer can double the base price of the car. A decision to buy a new car, therefore, should prudently be linked to an assessment of the vehicle's full cost, as well as to an assessment of our buying power with respect to that price. Moreover, such an assessment would typically take into account the relative costs of alternative, less expensive models, as well as other potential uses for our money.

Analogous logic ought to apply to the assessment of the costs of prison policy. That is, "add-ons" and financing, as well as basic costs, should be considered together. Only then would we be able to determine whether we can afford the bottom-line costs. Yet, with respect to incarceration policymaking, the bottom line is hard to find, because only a few attempts have ever been made to establish it. Usually, we are provided with the mere "sticker price"—that is, estimates of per-inmate operating costs. However, a small but careful body of research leads us to believe that the bottom-line dollar amount is more often than not significantly greater than these sticker prices suggest:

1. A study by McDonald of the costs of incarceration in New York prisons revealed that corrections budgets accounted for only 77 percent of the total prison operating costs.[3]

2. An examination by Coopers and Lybrand of the costs of jailing in New York City estimated that the Department of Corrections budget had understated the total cost of jailing by 22 percent.[4]

3. An assessment by Funke and Wayson of the economic impact of the proposed state takeover of one county correctional facility in Massachusetts showed that the correctional center's budget had underrepresented full operating costs by 28 percent.[5]

4. The reexamination by the Institute for Economic and Policy Studies (IEPS) of the reported construction costs of one Connecticut facility found that publicly reported figures accounted for only two-thirds of the actual costs of construction.[6]

Why are the reported figures so inaccurate? Reasons differ depending upon whether we are looking at operating or construction costs.

Operating Costs

The operating costs of a facility are typically calculated by dividing an institution's reported annual budget by its number of inmate days (usually estimated as the average daily population multiplied by 365). Limiting the numerator of this cost figure to the annual budget can be very problematic, since government financial reporting practices, unlike those of the private sector, distribute costs along organizational, as opposed to programmatic, lines. Since a vast number of criminal justice agencies—including correctional facilities—are dependent upon the services of other public agencies, such as those that offer social services, to meet program needs, it is easy to see how a particular operating budget can underrepresent the total true costs of the agency in question. In particular, these budgets ordinarily will be deficient in the following ways.

As a rule, the operating budgets of correctional institutions will not report the costs of pensions, vacations, sick leave, and other fringe benefits, which can account for at least 20 percent of operating expenses. Since the operation of any correctional facility is labor-intensive (largely because of security needs), employee benefit plans will always represent a substantial cost. In New York State, Mc-Donald found that pensions and fringe benefits alone composed 21 percent of the total true costs of operation. In the same audit, it was revealed that through a part-time contractual agreement with one physician, the state eventually paid approximately twice as much as it would have had the full-time services of one doctor been employed by the Department of Corrections.[7]

Organizational budgets also fail to reflect the contribution of contractual services to total program costs where it may not make good sense for an institution to maintain its own staff. Justifications for contractual services include the lack of a need for full-time personnel; the need for diverse but irregular services; and the difficulty associated with attracting highly qualified personnel to work in a prison setting. Although the use of contractual services in these cases may be in fact a fiscally sound policy, this is not to say that it is inexpensive. An audit of corrections costs completed for the Indiana State Legislature in 1981 found that $13,118,802 had been charged to the state over and above the corrections budget, for medical services provided for inmates outside their institutions.[8] McDonald's analysis of New York State found that $1.5 million of the total costs of incarceration in New York State was actually borne by the Department of Mental Hygiene, for psychological and psychiatric services to prison inmates in fiscal year 1978, and that $75,000 had been spent by the State Division of Substance Abuse Services for drug therapy treatment of inmates during that same period.[9] Neither of these costs had been reflected in the Department of Corrections budget.

Corrections budgets often omit the cost of operating an institution's physical plant. In New York City, for example, payments for plant maintenance and utilities are drawn from a citywide general services budget.[10] Funke and Wayson discovered that although the corrections budget maintained categories for phone, heat, and utilities, the amounts budgeted had in fact underrepresented their actual use.[11]

Corrections budgets do not reflect the contribution of grant monies, which can be responsible for the support of various programs within an institution. These monies constitute one of the hidden costs of incarceration, since the receiving jurisdiction may be required to pick up the costs of the funded programs upon each grant's expiration. In McDonald's study, grant monies accounted for as much as 1.7 percent of the total costs of incarceration in New York State.[12]

Finally, corrections budgets do not reflect lost taxes, welfare payments to family members, and other expenses that may arise whenever a person is imprisoned and thus removed from family and place of employment. One examination of these hidden costs concluded that such expenses could as much as equal the total amount of the corrections budget of the jurisdiction under study.[13]

Construction Costs

Construction costs are usually given as per-bed expenditures. These costs tend to be underreported, not because of any set of idiosyncrasies related to public financial disclosure methods, but for a variety of other reasons.

Costs of essential goods are often simply omitted from the calculation of total construction expense. Critical omissions discovered by the Institute for Economic and Policy Studies in its reexamination of the publicly reported estimates of a proposed Connecticut facility included architectural fees (8 percent of total construction costs); the cost of construction supervision (2.3 percent); agency fees (3.5 percent); change-order contingencies (5 percent); equipment costs (10 percent); insurance and bid fees (1 percent); and finance charges (10-15 percent). When the cost of omitted goods and services was figured in, the total per-bed estimates rose a full 50 percent from $50,000 per cell to $75,000 per cell.[14]

Construction costs may deliberately be underestimated in order to increase the chances of a project's approval. McDonald cites the case of one prison proposal in which the costs of the facility's furnishings had been excluded from the publicly reported estimate. It was found that the cost of furnishings accounted for 10 percent of the total cost of construction.[15]

Construction costs may also be underestimated because of the delay that often accompanies prison construction, given that the selection of a site is such a volatile issue. In a nationwide survey of prison and jail construction, Abt Associates discovered that site selection can often take as long as five years.[16] In the interim, construction costs can rise roughly at the annual rate of inflation. Applying these figures to the adjusted cost of the proposed Connecticut facility, IEPS demonstrated how a $75,000 per-cell estimate could inflate into an actual cost of $118,000.[17]

Finally, the most considerable of construction expenses—the amortized debt—is virtually ignored by most policymakers. In the private sector, construction and other capital costs are built into the operating budget over a number of years until the capital stock has fully depreciated. In public financial disclosure, however, corrections debts are aggregated with all other forms of public debt, and thus amortization costs fail to be reflected in construction estimates. This is a significant omission: first, because most correctional facilities are constructed with the support of some form of financing; and second, because financing can as much as quadruple original cost estimates. Such was the effect of amortization upon the cost of one proposed New York facility, using an interest rate as low as 9 percent.[18] In most cases, information regarding the operating value of existing capital stock will be difficult to obtain, so that even those operating cost proposals that have taken hidden costs into consideration will continue to underestimate substantially the real costs of running prisons and jails.

Real Costs

Just as was true in the case of the purchase of a new car, the "purchase" of the incarceration sanction involves payments that will be substantially higher than what the buyer—the policymaker and the taxpayer—may first be led to believe. In contrast to the former case, however, in which the enforcement of laws regarding truth in lending painstakingly ensure the buyer's understanding of all committed monies, there is no similar mechanism to ensure the policymaker's or taxpayer's recognition of funds expended for the support of correctional facilities. Responsible policymaking requires that these various hidden costs be revealed before decisions are taken that involve major financial commitments for a generation or more.

PRISON COSTS: A MANAGEMENT PERSPECTIVE

Because imprisonment is expensive, the question arises whether there are strategies that administrators of correctional institutions can pursue in order to reduce or otherwise stabilize costs. Current political demands for an increased use of imprisonment lends particular urgency to this question. Usually, solutions to the problems of rising prison populations are narrowly focused: the increases are accepted as given, and efforts are undertaken to house the extra number of prisoners by means of a more efficient employment of current capacity, or through its expansion. Each of these strategies has a negative fiscal impact.

The More Efficient Use of Existing Facilities

If a given facility houses an increasing number of inmates, it would seem prima facie true that the cost per inmate will be reduced. However, while the total department of corrections' budget may remain unaffected by changes in inmate populations (since much of an institution's budget is devoted to personnel costs, and since a relatively small proportion of total funding is spent on inmate-specific needs, such as food and clothing),[19] a prison that operates over capacity can force real costs upward in a number of unsuspected ways.

To begin with, crowding exacerbates unfavorable conditions of prison life that the Supreme Court has held are relevant to the issue of the constitutionality of confinement. In *Rhodes v. Chapman*,[20] the most influential of Supreme Court decisions regarding this issue, the Court approved the practice of double celling in the Southern Ohio Correctional Facility chiefly because inmates tended to be locked in their cells only during that portion of the day devoted to sleeping, and because the increase in population within that facility had not negatively affected any other aspect of institutional life. Similar reasoning was used in *Bell v. Wolfish*,[21] which also involved double celling and its related effects in a new facility. Both decisions merely reinforce earlier Court rulings in such cases as *Holt v. Sarver*[22] and *Laaman v. Helgemoe*,[23] in which was developed what is now known as the "totality of conditions" doctrine. (See "The Totality of Conditions Test in Eighth Amendment Litigation," Chapter 2 in this volume.) This doctrine bases the state's obligation to intervene on behalf of inmates on an assessment of the sum of the institution's conditions, and on their effects upon the imprisoned. For example, in *Pugh v. Locke*,[24] the Court found that overcrowding compounded other defects in the Alabama penal system. In *Costello v. Wainwright*,[25] testimony supported a relationship between crowding, inadequate health care, and violence.

Thus *Bell* and *Rhodes* provide respite from the fiscal pressures of incarceration for only a limited number of corrections administrators who are fortunate enough to have been placed in charge of relatively new facilities. Yet little more than a third of all state and federal facilities were constructed after 1970, and most maximum-security facilities were constructed prior to 1925.[26] Since the degree to which crowding is legally permissible is inextricably linked to the quality of other prison conditions, the corrections administrator who wishes to employ existing capacity to house growing populations must maintain prison conditions at an acceptable level. Several criteria have evolved in recent years to help determine the acceptability of a prison's conditions. Most influential of these are the standards developed by the American Correctional Association,[27] compliance with which is necessary for accreditation by the Commission on Accreditation for Corrections. Although accreditation is seldom required of institutions, it is considered prestigious because it sometimes paves the way for increased funding. But more important, it has been recognized by the courts as one indicator of the acceptability of an institution's conditions.[28]

However, compliance with standards is likely to entail substantial costs. While compliance with many of the more mundane standards requires little expenditure, the standards relating to matters most likely to be raised in inmate suits can be very expensive, especially if they involve capital expenditures. Since there is usually more than one way to achieve compliance with a standard, it is difficult to estimate with precision the costs of compliance. Some indication is provided by the Institute of Economic and Policy Studies, which conducted a series of analyses in a number of states on this issue.[29]

These analyses found compliance costs in Iowa institutions to be $28.6 million; in Colorado institutions, between $14.5 million and $17.8 million; in Maine, $18.1 million; in New Jersey, between $17.5 million and $19.5 million; and in Connecticut, $2.0 million—

a low figure only because the Department of Corrections in that state had already established a funding plan for the accreditation effort. All of these costs are in 1981 dollars, represent first-year compliance costs only, and do not include expenditures necessary for maintaining compliance in later years. To translate these figures into 1986 dollars would require increases of about 25 percent. Significantly, most of the costs were incurred for compliance with only a few standards, usually involving capital expenditures. In Iowa, for example, more than 90 percent of the costs of compliance was required to meet just three standards: cell enlargement, the construction of recreation facilities, and the expansion of inmate work programs.

Given the sentiment of the Court in *Bell* and *Rhodes*, it would seem that an institution's capacity could be expanded constitutionally by dispersing inmates to other areas of the prison during non-sleeping hours. Yet this solution has a fiscal Catch-22: as reliance on cells for physical security needs is decreased, the dependence on personnel for meeting security needs is increased. There is some indication that inmate-staff ratios are highest in maximum-security settings and lowest in minimum-security settings. In New York State, for example, the inmate-security staff ratios are 3.5:1 for maximum-level institutions, 2.5:1 for medium-level institutions, and 2.1:1 for minimum-level institutions,[30] probably because increased freedom of inmate movement requires enhanced staffing. Since wages and salaries account for over half of the costs of operating prisons in New York (excluding capitalization of debt), any plan to reduce capital costs by increasing personnel costs may backfire. In one innovative prison, inmates were provided with modules, or wings, containing single rooms, kitchens, and recreation areas, but administrators failed to realize until too late that additional security personnel were needed to transport inmates from one self-contained module to another.[31]

The tradeoff between the more expensive physical features of maximum-security settings and the high cost of increases in custodial staff for less secure facilities may balance in favor of the latter, since there is indication that the former sometimes incur additional, unexpected expenses. In *Ramos v. Lamm*,[32] a suit brought by the inmates of the Colorado State Penitentiary, testimony suggested that the architecture of the cell houses contributed to inmate violence. In another case, inmates in the maximum-security division of a Virginia prison were awarded $600,000 in damages in their successful fight to obtain more security personnel.[33] The construction of reduced security systems does not guarantee that those systems will ultimately survive as money savers: inmates at the federal Metropolitan Correctional Center in New York, one innovative detention facility using normative living arrangements, brought suit against that institution, charging that the innovative design constituted an unfair detention practice that unreasonably restricted inmates' movement.[34]

Since prisons are inherently expensive to operate, policymakers may seek ways to make them pay for themselves, by attempting to develop productive industry within the walls. Prisons have traditionally operated state industries and employed inmates in the maintenance of the facility itself. That this labor pool should be reorganized to prepare goods and services for public purchase, in order to generate a profit that will cover institutional cost, is an appealing notion. Attractive as the idea might seem, there is reason to believe that prison industries founded on this ideal might suffer substantial economic losses.

To avoid competition with the private sector, prison industries have been prohibited from selling their products on the open market. Consequently, prison industries have produced a limited number of goods, for use only by other state offices, and it is this fact that has been blamed for the generally unprofitable character of the traditional prison industry. In recent years, these prohibitions have been lifted on an experimental basis. A form of prison industry known as the Free Venture Model[35] has been authorized and developed in seven states. This model, which adopted some aspects of private industry, including hiring and firing, a profit motive, and productivity standards, was generally regarded as a vehicle that could steer prison industries to financial health. An evaluation of the new model found, however, that contrary to its promise, only a minority of the new shops were able to make a profit.[36] Successful shops were primarily those that called for few inmate skills; unsuccessful shops were those that made little use of market forecasts and analyses and revenue projections. Furthermore, an audit of Indiana prison industries, which originally suggested that the industries there were profitable, found upon closer scrutiny that the cost accounting system, particularly regarding labor and materials, was notably inaccurate.[37] Moreover, overhead costs had not been incorporated into the industry's budget. Perhaps the biggest financial impediment confronting prison industry is the need for a supervisory force that must serve simultaneously as security personnel. The salaries of a larger number of personnel will inevitably cancel out a significant portion of the cost savings that could be realized through the use of a relatively low-paid labor force. Exacerbating this problem is the prevalence of featherbedding, or overstaffing of inmates in prison industries, which arises because there is usually a dearth of engaging and productive work in prison.

The Expansion of Prison Capacity

If the more efficient use of current capacity is an unlikely achievement, one may be led to postulate that increasing prison populations can be managed via expansion of capacity. Expansion options include the construction of new facilities, the conversion of other buildings into prisons, and the expansion of existing institutions.

We have already outlined the costs involved in the construction of new facilities. In light of these steep costs, which some may perceive as prohibitive, the question for policymakers is whether there are other options for expanding prison capacity that entail less expense.

The limited body of research that has addressed this issue suggests, however, that alternatives to new prison construction are not always inexpensive. For example, when McDonald reviewed the New York State plan to take over the city-owned Rikers Island correctional complex, he discovered total per-cell costs of $65,000, exclusive of financing.[38] Conversion costs, which included perimeter security, special custody areas, vehicles and program equipment, recreational facilities, and security hardware and necessary renovation, would have been substantially higher had site selection and purchase been an issue.

An alternative to conversion is the enlargement of existing prisons. This may not be an appropriate solution to a crowding problem, however, if only because experts and authoritative agencies recommend maximum capacities of 500 or fewer inmates.[39] Nonetheless, some expansion programs have been cost-estimated, and the per-cell figures range from $7,800 (1978 dollars) to $30,000 (1978 dollars).[40] It is not clear whether the normally hidden costs we described earlier have been incorporated into these figures.

INCARCERATION COSTS: A POLICY PERSPECTIVE

The discussion so far has demonstrated two points: (1) that imprisonment is a far more costly punishment than many policymakers realize; and (2) that there is little that corrections administrators can do on their own to minimize costs of increasing inmate populations. This is similar to a situation in which a person desires to purchase a new car because of anticipated increases in driving at a time when it is felt that an older car cannot handle a heavier demand for its use: new cars are painfully expensive, cheap cars have too many shortcomings, older cars require too much repair. Ultimately, the buyer must face the question of whether he can afford to drive as much as he had planned, and whether the benefits of driving support the expense it will entail.

The same question faces those who propose increased public expenditures for corrections. The benefits of imprisonment—deterrence, incapacitation, and rehabilitation—are more often than not presented as certain. It is concomitantly felt that more prisons lead to more of each of these benefits, or to more crime control. This seems reasonable, but a closer inspection of policy research suggests that the relationship is not as it is often stated. Since this evidence is reviewed in detail elsewhere (see "A Brief for Deescalating Criminal Sanctions," Chapter 10 in this volume), for the sake of brevity we shall summarize only its main points.

Research methodology is too poor to allow confident conclusions about rehabilitation,[41] and the less questionable research on this issue provides no indication that treatment can be more effectively administered in a prison setting than elsewhere.[42] Research on deterrence has produced similar uncertainty. Given the possibility of simultaneous, alternative explanations for the phenomenon under study,[43] it is unlikely that researchers can ever demonstrate an incontrovertible deterrent effect. What little firm evidence exists on this topic indicates that the system is most effective when it promotes swift and certain punishments.[44] But celerity and certainty are rarely characteristic of the criminal justice process.

Regarding incapacitation, two generalizations can be made. First, the number of crimes that can be prevented through the practice of collective incapacitation is likely to be very low and will be obtained only by very large increases in prison populations.[45] Second, attempts to use incapacitation selectively will be met with high rates of error, as our present state of knowledge regarding correlates of career criminal behavior is not yet very discriminating.[46]

Of course, just as an individual could simply desire a new car, as opposed to needing one, there are some who believe that we should punish through incarceration not in anticipation of potential crime control benefits but merely because criminals deserve to be punished. Hence, prisons may be seen as a necessity of justice. But it may not be possible, or necessary, to fulfill the requirements of a system of just deserts through imprisonment.

First, the extreme costs and substantial delays that are associated with new construction mean that there cannot be timely increases of capacity sufficient to meet increased demands for punishment. Moreover, since there is some indication that increases in inmate populations may stem partially from temporary growth in the number of young adults in this country,[47] additions to capacity that are initiated in the present may prove to be unnecessary at a later time.

Second, one may question the need for the maximum level of security under which many inmates are currently incarcerated. There is evidence which suggests that overclassification is responsible for the placement of inmates requiring only minimum- or medium-security status in maximum-security settings. Following *Pugh v. Locke*, a major reclassification effort revealed the suitability of minimum or community levels of supervision for over half of the inmates in Alabama's penal system.[48] Similarly, another study found that arbitrary classification procedures had led to the placement of nearly all inmates at the New Mexico State Penitentiary in medium-security custody.[49] The concept of desert is not inconsistent with the less arbitrary, more careful use of custody classification, and the latter—inasmuch as it can lead to the avoidance of expensive new construction and the encouragement of less expensive minimum-security settings such as the work camp—may provide a more fiscally sound way to use incarceration to meet desert needs.

Third, there are opportunity costs associated with the extensive use of incarceration. Vast public expenditures channeled toward the expansion of a jurisdiction's prison capacity can no longer be spent for other necessary services such as public transportation, schools, and health care.

Despite these factors, legislatures still fund prison capacity expansion, just as people buy new cars. The analogy is a good one, for both economic decisions are costly, involve hidden expenses, produce continuing long-term revenue losses, and are normally based upon emotional as well as practical concerns. But here the analogy collapses—since for most people, the automobile is a necessity. New cars offer safer transportation than older models, as well as providing a more efficient use of fuel. Prisons, on the other hand, provide little real benefit to justify their very high cost, and they sap resources that could be used to address other social needs. Moreover, it is possible to meet punishment needs through a variety of other mechanisms, ranging from shortened terms of imprisonment to an expanded use of community supervision. For the price we have paid for traditional uses of imprisonment, it is possible to purchase a greater number of alternative "punishment experiences."[50]

For this reason, we believe that policymakers need to reevaluate the emphasis given to imprisonment as the punishment of choice. We think that a new perspective is needed that recognizes both the increased demand for and high cost of imprisonment. It is a perspective that acknowledges that neither of these critical issues can be addressed effectively within a traditional, reactive framework.

We suggest the adoption of proactive strategies involving a wide range of criminal justice system administrators and policymakers. A proactive strategy is demand-focused and recognizes the relatively invariable character of prison capacity in comparison to other punishments. It is a strategy focused on the regulation of a relatively fixed amount of punishment resources.

Proactive regulation of offenders can occur at any of three points, which we shall call the entry, location, and exit stages. Although regulation need not be restricted to only one point, for the sake of clarity we will review each individually.

Regulation at the entry stage affects the number of offenders sent to correctional institutions. It is the most powerful kind of regulation, for two reasons: this stage presents the greatest number of opportunities for regulation, and the participation of a wide variety of policymakers can be enlisted to increase entry control. Entry regulation strategies occur both before conviction (for example, diversion) and after (for example, increased use of community supervision). Legislators, prosecutors, and judges play a critical role in entry regulation policies. Of course, gaining the cooperation of these decision makers in regulating input is often difficult.

Location is a second, albeit also problematic, mode of regulation. Regulation by location involves the use of a wide range of types of prison. This is currently difficult to achieve since we have unfortunately limited the majority of our incarceration options to maximum- and medium-custody settings. It is a significant form of regulation because as other forms of location, such as minimum-security camps, become more available, it will be possible to provide residential, custodial settings for many offenders without incurring the capital costs that are associated with traditional forms of incarceration.

Regulation at the exit stage occurs when offenders are moved more rapidly through prisons. Of the three stages, exit regulation is now the most threatened, given that parole, certainly among the most effective of exit stage mechanisms, has been eliminated in some states and restricted in others. Other useful exit stage mechanisms include executive clemency, furlough, work release, and emergency crowding measures. All of these options can play a significant role now, because the crowding problem is immediate and, obviously, currently incarcerated populations cannot be housed adequately using existing capacity.

In the public policy arena, it is standard practice to place limits on the expenditure of public dollars for services to citizens. Under recent political leadership, this practice has become something of a measuring stick for any policy's feasibility. Yet in the area of corrections, the theme of fiscal conservatism has been much less strong than in areas of direct social service such as welfare and education. Demands for expanding correctional expenditures often go relatively unchallenged in public debate.

This is ironic, since proposals for correctional expenditures often seriously underestimate the true or eventual costs of those initiatives, while vastly overestimating their benefits. There are a large number of responsible means for managing offenders without incurring the sometimes drastic costs of correctional expansion. The

time has come to establish reasonable limits on the level of public
expenditures on punishing offenders.

NOTES

1. See, for example, Michael Sherman and Gordon Hawkins, *Impris-
onment in America: Choosing the Future* (Chicago: University of Chicago
Press, 1981); Alfred Blumstein, Jacqueline Cohen, and William Gooding,
"The Influence of Capacity on Prison Population," *Crime and Delinquency*
29 (1983): 1-51; Todd R. Clear, Patricia M. Harris, and Albert L. Record,
"Managing the Cost of Corrections," *Prison Journal* 62 (1982): 1-63; and
M. Kay Harris, *Reducing Prison Crowding: An Overview of Options* (Draft
of a report submitted to the National Institute of Corrections, July 1981,
in partial fulfillment of NIC grant CQ-9).

2. Federal Bureau of Investigation, *Uniform Crime Reports, 1984*
(Washington, DC: U.S. Department of Justice, 1985).

3. Douglas McDonald, *The Price of Punishment: Public Spending for
Corrections in New York* (Boulder, CO: Westview, 1980).

4. Coopers and Lybrand, *The Cost of Incarceration in New York City*
(Hackensack, NJ: National Council on Crime and Delinquency, 1978).

5. Gail S. Funke and Billy L. Wayson, *Comparative Costs of State and
Local Facilities* (Washington, DC: Correctional Economics Center, 1975).

6. Gregory P. Falkin, Gail S. Funke, and Billy L. Wayson, *Revising
Connecticut's Sentencing Laws: An Impact Assessment* (Alexandria, VA:
Institute for Economic and Policy Studies, 1981).

7. McDonald, *Price of Punishment*, pp. 15-16.

8. Indiana Legislative Services Agency, Office of Fiscal and Management Analysis, *Sunset Performance Audit of Corrections and the Judiciary*,
February 1982, p. 100.

9. McDonald, *Price of Punishment*, pp. 36-38.

10. Coopers and Lybrand, *Cost of Incarceration*.

11. Funke and Wayson, *Comparative Costs*, pp. 15-16.

12. McDonald, *Price of Punishment*, p. 16.

13. Val Clear, Scott Clear, and Todd Clear, *Eight Million Dollars* (Anderson, IN: Anderson College Press, 1977).

14. Falkin, Funke, and Wayson, *Revising Connecticut's Sentencing
Laws*, pp. A34-37.

15. McDonald, *Price of Punishment*, p. 52.

16. Kenneth Carlson et al., *American Prisons and Jails*, vol. 2, *Population
Trends and Projections* (Washington, DC: National Institute of Justice,
1980), p. 2.

17. Falkin, Funke, and Wayson, *Revising Connecticut's Sentencing Laws*, pp. A34-37.

18. McDonald, *Price of Punishment*, p. 54.

19. McDonald found that during fiscal year 1978, as little as $666 was spent per inmate for food. Ibid., p. 29.

20. *Rhodes v. Chapman*, 101 S. Ct. 2392 (1981).

21. *Bell v. Wolfish*, 441 U.S. 520 (1979).

22. *Holt v. Sarver*, 309 F. Supp. 363 (E.D. Ark. 1970).

23. *Laaman v. Helgemoe*, 437 F. Supp. 269 (N.H. 1977).

24. *Pugh v. Locke*, 406 F. Supp. 381 (MD Ala. 1976).

25. *Costello v. Wainwright*, 397 F. Supp. 20 (MD Fla. 1975).

26. Joan Mullen and Bradford Smith (principal authors), *American Prisons and Jails*, vol. 3, *Conditions and Costs of Confinement* (Washington, D.C.: National Institute of Justice, 1980), pp. 25-26.

27. See *Standards for Adult Correctional Institutions*, 2d ed., (College Park, MD: American Correctional Association, 1981), and Supplement.

28. For example, when inmates at one Virginia prison brought suit to obtain more correctional officers at that facility, the Court raised the number of security staff from 122 to 152, the number called for by correctional standards. See *Doe v. District of Columbia*, USDC DC (1980).

29. Robert C. Grieser, ed., *Correctional Policy and Standards: Implementation Costs of Correctional Standards* (Washington, DC: Law Enforcement Assistance Administration, 1980).

30. McDonald, *Price of Punishment*, p. 22

31. John Blackmore, "Prison Architecture: Are Advanced Practices Really Dead?" *Corrections Magazine* 4 (1978): 42-53.

32. *Ramos v. Lamm*, 638 F. 2d 559, 573 (CA10 1980).

33. *Doe v. District of Columbia*, USDC DC (1980).

34. *Wolfish v. Levi*, 573 F. 2d 118 (2d Cir. 1978).

35. For a discussion see Econ, Inc., *Study of the Economic and Rehabilitative Aspects of Prison Industry*, vol. 5, *Analysis of Prison Industries and Recommendations for Change* (Washington, DC: U.S. Government Printing Office, 1978).

36. Gail S. Funke, Billy L. Wayson, and Neal Miller, *Assets and Liabilities of Correctional Industries* (Lexington, MA: Lexington Books, 1982).

37. Indiana Legislative Services Agency, *Sunset Performance Audit*, pp. 78-79.

38. McDonald, *Price of Punishment*, p. 51.

39. Standards regarding maximum occupancy have been promoted by the Department of Justice (a limit of 500 inmates per decentralized unit); the American Correctional Association (a limit of 400 inmates per decentralized unit); and the National Advisory Commission on Criminal Justice

Standards and Goals (a limit of 300 inmates per component or institution). See U.S. Department of Justice, Office of Public Affairs, *Federal Standards for Prisons and Jails* (Washington, DC: U.S. Government Printing Office, 1980), p. 16; American Correctional Association, *Standards*, p. 341; and National Advisory Commission on Criminal Justice Standards and Goals, *Corrections* (Washington, DC: U.S. Government Printing Office, 1973), p. 309.

40. Mullen and Smith, *American Prisons and Jails*, vol. 3, p. 125.

41. For a discussion, see Lee Sechrest, *The Rehabilitation of Criminal Offenders: Problems and Prospects* (Washington, DC: National Academy of Sciences, 1979).

42. We are referring to research reported in Robert R. Ross and Paul Gendreau, eds., *Effective Correctional Treatment* (Toronto: Butterworth, 1980).

43. For a discussion, see Daniel Nagin, "General Deterrence: A Review of the Empirical Evidence," in Alfred Blumstein, Jacqueline Cohen, and Daniel Nagin, eds., *Deterrence and Incapacitation: Estimating the Effects of Criminal Sanctions on Crime Rates* (Washington, DC: National Academy of Sciences, 1975).

44. See the discussion in Andrew von Hirsch, *Doing Justice: The Choice of Punishments* (New York: Hill and Wang, 1976), pp. 41-44.

45. See, for example, Stephen Van Dine, Simon Dinitz, and John Conrad, "The Incapacitation of the Dangerous Offender: A Statistical Experiment," *Journal of Research in Crime and Delinquency* 14 (1977): 22-34; and Joan Petersilia and Peter W. Greenwood, "Mandatory Prison Sentences: Their Projected Effects on Crime and Prison Populations," *Journal of Criminal Law and Criminology* 69 (Winter 1978): 604-15.

46. For an overview of this and other issues related to prediction, see Andrew von Hirsch and Don M. Gottfredson, "Selective Incapacitation: Some Queries about Research Design and Equity," *New York University Review of Law and Social Change* 12 (1983–1984): 11-51.

47. See Alfred Blumstein and Jacqueline Cohen, "A Theory of the Stability of Punishment," *Journal of Criminal Law and Criminology* 64 (Summer 1973): 198-207; Alfred Blumstein, Jacqueline Cohen, and Daniel Nagin, "The Dynamics of a Homeostatic Punishment Process," *Journal of Criminal Law and Criminology* 67 (Fall 1977): 317-34; and Alfred Blumstein and Soumyo Moitra, "An Analysis of the Time Series of the Imprisonment Rate of the States of the United States: A Further Test of the Stability of Punishment Hypothesis," *Journal of Criminal Law and Criminology* 70 (Fall 1979): 376-90.

48. Carl B. Clements, "The Relationship of Offender Classification to the Problems of Prison Overcrowding," *Crime and Delinquency* 28 (1982): 72-81.

49. Carl B. Clements, "Crowded Prisons: A Review of Psychological and Environmental Effects," *Law and Human Behavior* 3 (1979): 217-25.

50. For a discussion of the concept of "punishment experiences" and an overview of the relative costs of different sanctions, see Gail S. Funke, "Who's Buried in Grant's Tomb? Economics and Corrections for the Eighties and Beyond" (Unpublished paper, Institute for Economic and Policy Studies, Inc., Alexandria, VA, April 1982).

4 Attitudes of Correctional Policymakers and the Public

STEPHEN D. GOTTFREDSON
and
RALPH B. TAYLOR

Representative democracy requires at least a fairly high level of accurate information about constituency attitudes and opinion. Without that . . . [policymaking] institutions may provide the stamp of legitimacy and perform other functions, but they do not provide a decision-making system that reflects the views and values of the citizenry.[1]

A basic assumption of representative democracy is that public policy should be responsive to the public will. This principle applies to both the legislative and the administrative branches of government—including those branches concerned with criminal justice and corrections. Indeed, Luttbeg argues that "linkage between the public and its leaders is the mechanism that allows public leaders to act in accordance with the wants, needs, and demands of their public."[2] These wants, needs, and demands may be made manifest in a variety of ways, including the ballot box, letters to representatives, interviews given to the press, and answers given in public opinion polls.

Political scientists studying linkages between public opinion and policy formulation have offered a number of suggestions concerning the nature of the assumed ties between representatives and their constituencies. For example, Miller and Stokes have observed that

Authors' note: Frank J. Kearney contributed to the work presented in this chapter. Some portions were presented at the Annual Meeting of the American Psychological Association (1982), and some are adapted from S. D. Gottfredson and R. B. Taylor, *The Correctional Crisis* (Washington, DC: National Institute of Justice, 1983).

correlations between constituency opinion and congressional representatives' estimates of that opinion vary across issues. In that study, good correspondence was found with respect to civil rights issues, but the representatives were found to be inaccurate in assessing constituency opinion of foreign affairs and social welfare issues.[3] Hedlund and Friesma have compared Iowa legislators' perceptions of public opinion with voting results in referenda on these same issues, finding that the legislators were more accurate in assessing constituency opinion on major issues than on lesser ones.[4]

Riley and Rose have summarized various characterizations of the general public's attitudes toward corrections and correctional issues as (1) ambivalent, (2) vague, (3) unconcerned, (4) apathetic and uninformed, (5) uncertain and lacking consensus, (6) disinterested, (7) punitive, (8) ignorant, and, infrequently, (9) optimistic.[5] However (and as noted by Riley and Rose), the sources of these sentiments typically provide little, if any, data supportive of their rather gloomy characterizations.[6]

Given the relative paucity of information available concerning the general public's actual attitudes toward corrections, it is surprising that correctional policymakers so readily claim knowledge of what these views are.

In 1973, Berk and Rossi conducted a study of correctional policymakers in three states (Florida, Illinois, and Washington). Of principal concern was the understanding of policymakers' attitudes toward correctional goals and proposals for change. The sample of policymakers was defined to be "persons who were potentially instrumental in initiating, approving, and carrying out programs within state corrections systems." It was also reasonably assumed that these would be "persons occupying positions of power and influence."[7] While Berk and Rossi noted important variations in opinions of and receptivity to different change strategies among the members of different groups within the sample, more striking were the differences they observed between the opinions and attitudes of the policymakers and their assessments of the public view on these issues. In general, it appeared that the correctional policymakers held personal views that could be characterized as liberal, reform-oriented, and rehabilitative. In stark contrast, they saw the general public as punitive and generally concerned only with its own protection and safety.

In a study conducted in the State of Maryland, we have observed this same pattern of findings.[8] Our sample of correctional policymakers appeared to hold relatively liberal views of the proper goals for correctional systems: they stressed rehabilitation, they opposed the abolition of parole, and they typically did not favor simple retributive punishment. Also clear was that they perceived the positions of the general public to be very different from their own views—at least their own views as expressed to us when they were guaranteed absolute confidentiality and anonymity of individual expressions of opinion.[9]

This chapter examines the accuracy of policymakers' views of public opinion. Berk and Rossi,[10] although clearly concerned with this issue, were unable to examine it with their data. However, in 1975, Riley and Rose[11] conducted a large-sample survey of residents of Washington State, one of the states whose policymakers (n = 83) were surveyed by Berk and Rossi in 1973. In the main their findings do indeed suggest (1) correspondence between the views of the policymakers and those of the general public, but (2) important misperceptions of the public view on the part of the policymakers. As we shall see, our findings confirm those of Riley and Rose.

OVERVIEW OF SAMPLES

The Correctional Policymakers

In the summer of 1980, an interview schedule containing both structured and open-ended items was administered to 80 members of a group we defined as Maryland's correctional policymakers. In keeping with Berk and Rossi's[12] suggestion that such a group should consist not only of those who initiate and approve programs within state corrections systems, but also those charged with carrying out those programs, our sample included both those who make policy decisions (elected officials, judges, corrections administrators) and those who implement these decisions (institution supervisors, sheriffs and chiefs of police, prosecutors). The sample was chosen to reflect the major components of the criminal justice system and included correctional administrators, planners, and other officials (both elected and appointed) representing the state (n = 16); correctional administrators, planners and other officials representing local jurisdictions (n = 13); local-level elected officials (mayors, county executives, state legislators) (n = 14); supervision officials (wardens, superintendents) (n = 15); law enforcement officials (sheriffs, chiefs of police) (n = 11); and representatives of the legal system (judges, prosecuting and defense officials) (n = 11). Interviews were completed with 91 percent of the 88 persons contacted.

It should be noted that those interviewed as part of this policy-making sample were not selected to be representative of the groups listed. Rather, this is a carefully selected and biased sample, generated from historical/archival sources and discussions with persons intimately concerned with corrections. Thus, it consists of persons who can be presumed to be extremely knowledgeable and concerned about correctional issues.[13] Thus, the following discussion of attitudes and perceptions should not be generalized to the larger groups (for example, judges or law enforcement officials) from which our policymaker sample was drawn. We did conduct a comprehensive survey of these broader groups, and discussion of these findings is given elsewhere.[14] The present discussion pertains specifically and only to correctional policymakers as defined here.

The interview schedule was designed to be administered in person, and contained both open and structured questions concerning (1) the problems and assets of Maryland's correctional system; (2) perceptions of a "crisis" in corrections and the reasons underlying it; (3) short- and long-term solutions to prison crowding problems in both state and local jurisdictions; (4) attitudes toward proposed policy changes; (5) assessments of the attitudes of others concerning proposed policy changes; and (6) goals and philosophies for corrections.

The General Public

In December of 1980, we conducted a public attitude survey in 13 of Maryland's 24 counties. The counties were selected to sample the constituencies of the policymakers interviewed earlier. A random digit dialing telephone sampling approach was used, and the sample was stratified by sex and restricted to residents, age 18 or older, of those 13 jurisdictions. Just over 600 interviews were obtained, and the response rate was 64 percent. The same basic information on attitudes toward correctional goals and proposed policy changes was collected, but using a simpler format.

Subsequent analyses showed that the sampling strategy was successful, and that the proper proportion of interviews was achieved across jurisdictions. Unsampled jurisdictions, all of which are predominantly rural, account for 12.7 percent of the entire state population.[15] While rural jurisdictions are very well represented in our sample, this slight underrepresentation relative to the entire state population should be considered in the interpretation of statewide findings.[16] Finally, it should be noted that our intent was to sample the constituencies of the policymakers interviewed; and this was achieved.

ASSESSMENTS OF GOALS

In our face-to-face interviews with policymakers, we were able to obtain rankings of the priorities they assigned (or felt were assigned) to each of four possible correctional goals: incapacitation, punishment, deterrence, and rehabilitation. These were defined as in the Berk and Rossi study:[17]

1. Incapacitation: protecting the public by removing offenders from the community where they might commit additional crimes.
2. Rehabilitation: rehabilitating offenders so that they might pursue non-criminal lives.
3. Punishment: administering punishment to offenders as retribution for the crime they have committed.
4. Deterrence: deterring crime by showing potential offenders the serious consequences of committing a criminal offense.

Given the relative complexity of a ranking task, we used a simpler, two-stage rating approach for administration to the general public over the telephone.[18] Thus, while we can obtain mean ranks for the priorities assigned by the policymakers and mean ratings for the priorities assigned by the general public, the two metrics are not commensurate. Accordingly, we have transformed each to rank-order measures for the analyses that follow, and the policymakers' opinions are here represented by rank-ordered mean ratings. The reader should bear in mind the characteristics of ordinal data when considering our discussion: successive intervals are assumed to be successive in order only—no interpretation of the magnitude of differences between numbers is possible or appropriate. Indeed, in some cases the differences between values in the original metric were small—although in all cases (but for instances in which ranks are presented as tied) they exceeded at least one standard error in magnitude.[19]

Figure 1 illustrates our findings with respect to the accuracy of our policymakers' perceptions of the value the general public assigns the goals of corrections. A striking lack of correspondence is apparent from simple inspection; and indeed, the rank-ordered correlation between the two assessments is large and negative ($\rho = -.84$).[20] While the policymakers feel that the public prefers (in this case, by a wide margin) the goal of incapacitation, this goal is in fact the second lowest priority in the public view. While policymakers likewise feel that the general public strongly supports the goal of retributive punishment (also, in this case, by a wide margin in the original metric), this goal is actually assigned the lowest priority by our sample of the public. It is therefore not surprising that while the policymakers feel that the goal of rehabilitation would be lowest in the public esteem (and by a very wide margin indeed), this goal is in fact tied with that of deterrence for the public's highest priority. Quite clearly, then, there is considerable misperception of the public viewpoint on the part of the correctional policymakers.

What of the correspondence between the policymakers' own views and those of their constituents? Figure 2 summarizes these findings. Considerably more agreement is manifest; while moderate, the correlation between the two sets of viewpoints is at least positive ($\rho = .28$). Policymakers and the general public agree that simple retributive punishment is the least desirable goal for a correctional system, and both assign high priority to the goal of rehabilitation or treatment. Such disagreement as exists is over the goals of incapacitation and deterrence.

If we find concordance over goals, what of assessments of the functioning of the correctional system relative to the public's desired goals? Figure 3 suggests that the public should be disappointed: the relation between the policymakers' assessments of present correctional system priorities and the priorities desired by the general public is negative ($\rho = -.27$). Indeed, respondents in our survey of

Figure 1
Relation between Public Opinion of Four Correctional Goals and
Policymaker Perceptions of Public Opinion

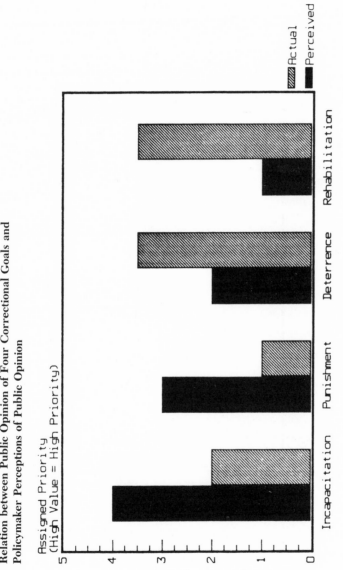

Figure 2
Relation between Public and Policymaker Opinions of Four Correctional Goals

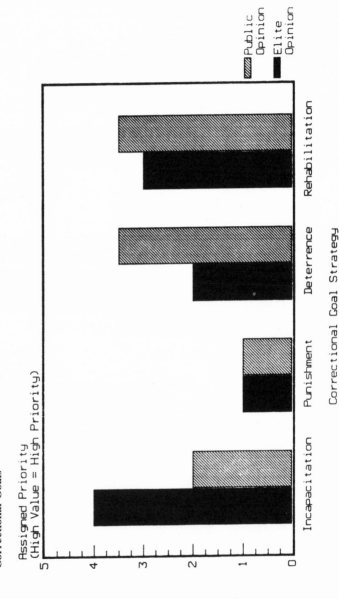

Figure 3
Relation between Policymaker Assessments of the Present Correctional System's Priorities and the Public Opinion of What These Priorities Should Be

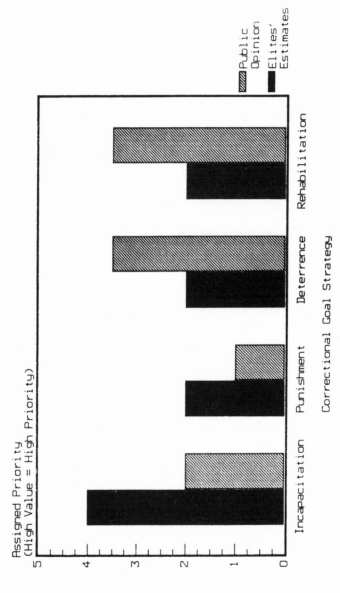

the general public reported overwhelmingly that the Maryland corrections system was doing a very poor job at meeting any of its
proper goals. When asked about Maryland's attempts to implement
these four goals, less than half of the sample responding felt—irrespective of the specific goal—that Maryland was doing a good job
at implementation. Further, and again not surprisingly, a very large
proportion of the respondents (ranging from 79 percent for the goal
of incapacitation to 70 percent for the goal of rehabilitation) reported
that realistically more could be done to meet these correctional
goals.

The picture presented thus far suggests not only that Maryland's
policymakers are poor judges of the public's wants, but that the
system they are charged with operating is not responsive to the
priorities as assigned by the public. Further, since their own views
are similar to those of the public, the system is also seen as not
meeting the goals of the policymakers themselves. This evidence
would seem to suggest that with respect to correctional system goals,
at any rate, those whom we charge with public responsibility are
failing to meet that charge.

But are they? Figure 4 illustrates the relation between the policymakers' perception of the public will and their perception of how
our present correctional system functions. The relation is high and
positive ($\rho = .78$), suggesting that correctional policy may indeed be
practiced in accordance with the public will, as the policymakers
perceive that will. While there is little differentiation perceived
among most system functions, the overall pattern, given the priority
assigned to the goal of incapacitation, is consonant with the perceived public will. This, of course, is the critical point: the extent
to which our policymakers misperceive or misunderstand the views
of the public may determine the extent to which public policy is
nonresponsive to the public will.

ASSESSMENTS OF CHANGE STRATEGIES

In our interviews both with correctional policymakers and with
the general public, we asked for assessments of several proposals
for correctional change that were then prevalent in the correctional
policy debate in Maryland. These proposals for reform had figured
prominently in public, administrative, and legislative debates over

Figure 4
Relation between Policymaker Estimates of the Priorities Under Which the Present Corrections System Operates and Their Estimates of the Priorities Which the General Public Would Assign Four Correctional Goals.

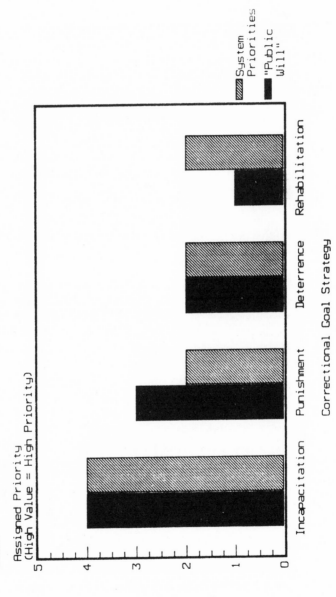

correctional policy for several years. The four proposed change strategies that we studied were (1) a proposal to abolish parole; (2) a proposal to incarcerate a larger proportion of the inmate population at the local (as opposed to the state) level; (3) a proposal to establish Community Adult Rehabilitation Centers (CARCs) on a widespread basis; and (4) a proposal not to build any large new state prison facilities.

In addition to asking policymakers and the general public for their own positions on each of these issues, we asked our policymakers to give their assessments of public support for (or opposition to) each one. Figure 5 graphically displays our findings.

On all issues but one (the establishment of CARCs), the policymakers' positions and the positions of the general public are the same. The only statistically significant difference is with respect to the widespread establishment of CARCs; more policymakers support this proposed change than do members of the general public— 93 percent versus 73 percent ($\chi^2_1 = 16.60$; p < .01).

Although policymakers and the general public agree on three out of four possible reform strategies, the policymakers' perceptions of the public view are at variance with the reality on three out of four: only with respect to the building of at least one new state institution do policymakers' perceptions and the actual public view correspond. Substantial and statistically significant differences in perception occur with respect to the abolition of parole ($\chi^2_1 = 38.98$; p < .01), the movement of inmates to local as opposed to state facilities ($\chi^2_1 = 25.32$; p < .01), and the widespread establishment of CARCs ($\chi^2_1 = 32.01$; p < .01).

SUMMARY AND CONCLUSIONS

It has often been assumed that the general public is not only uninterested in correctional issues, but ignorant of these issues as well. We know from our survey that this is not the case—at least in Maryland. We found that the vast majority of our sample are very interested in corrections and correctional issues. They are quite aware of the major problems facing the state corrections system, and they follow these issues rather regularly in the media. Finally, they hold strong opinions concerning the proper goals of a correctional system. Contrary to general belief, we found the general

Figure 5
Policymaker Attitudes, Public Opinion, and Policymaker Perception of
Public Opinion on Key Correctional Issues

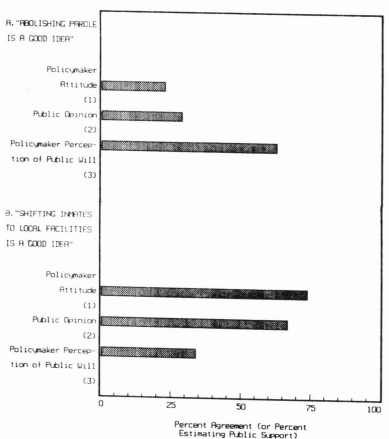

Figure 5—*continued*

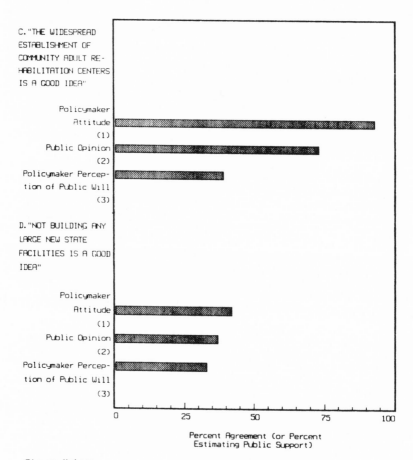

C. "THE WIDESPREAD ESTABLISHMENT OF COMMUNITY ADULT RE-HABILITATION CENTERS IS A GOOD IDEA"

Policymaker Attitude (1)
Public Opinion (2)
Policymaker Perception of Public Will (3)

D. "NOT BUILDING ANY LARGE NEW STATE FACILITIES IS A GOOD IDEA"

Policymaker Attitude (1)
Public Opinion (2)
Policymaker Perception of Public Will (3)

Percent Agreement (or Percent Estimating Public Support)

Figure Notes:

A: $X^2_{(1)}(1,2) = 1.067$; n.s.

$X^2_{(1)}(2,3) = 38.974$; p < .01

B: $X^2_{(1)}(1,2) = 1.354$; n.s.

$X^2_{(1)}(2,3) = 25.317$; p < .01

C: $X^2_{(1)}(1,2) = 16.602$; p < .01

$X^2_{(1)}(2,3) = 32.013$; p < .01

D: $X^2_{(1)}(1,2) = 0.562$; n.s.

$X^2_{(1)}(2,3) = 0.199$; n.s.

public not to be especially punitive—rather, they stress more utilitarian goals, such as rehabilitation, deterrence, and incapacitation. These attitudes are reflected in the public's views of the various proposals for correctional reform. The reform strategies that receive most support stress rehabilitation and increasing localization of correctional programs and facilities. The majority of the general public in Maryland feel that more institutions are needed, but unfortunately it cannot be determined from our data whether this stems from a simple concern over a lack of space, or from knowledge of the conditions in Maryland's present facilities (or both).

Almost without exception, these attitudes are echoed by our sample of policymakers. In no important respect do the attitudes of the policymaker sample differ from the attitudes of the public. In fact, where they do differ, the views of the policymakers would appear more liberal and more reform-oriented.

We also discovered that our policymakers feel that they know the public mood—and that the public's attitude concerning correctional issues is at substantial variance with their own. This chapter has systematically assessed the accuracy of that perception. What we have observed is almost complete congruence between the public and the policymakers with respect to most key corrections issues, but severe misconceptions among policymakers of the public will with respect to these same issues.

Concerning correctional system goals, we find a striking lack of correspondence between the policymaker group's assessment of public opinion and the reality of that opinion: the correlation (rank-order) between the two is large and negative ($\rho = -.84$). While the policymakers report that the general public would strongly support the goal of retributive punishment and would offer only very weak support to the goal of rehabilitation, this is not the case. However, we find relatively good agreement between the policymakers' own goals for corrections and those of the general public ($\rho = .28$). Both groups assign high priorities to the goal of rehabilitation or treatment and agree that simple retributive punishment is the least desirable goal for a correctional system. Thus, both the public and those who are charged with setting and implementing correctional policy appear to support utilitarian, as opposed to retributive, goals.

From the policymaker sample, we gathered assessments of the priorities that the Maryland corrections system apparently assigns

these goals. When we correlate actual system functioning—as perceived by the policymakers—with the priorities as assigned by the
public, we again find a negative relation ($\rho = -.27$). That the public
is aware of this lack of correspondence is clear: the general public
overwhelmingly responds that Maryland's corrections system is
doing a very poor job at meeting any of its proper goals. Fewer than
half of the respondents feel—irrespective of the specific goal—that
Maryland is doing a good job at implementation. Further, a very
large proportion of the sample report that realistically more could
be done to meet these intended correctional purposes.

We observed virtually this same pattern in the assessment of
various proposals for correctional reform. Virtually no important
differences exist between the policymakers' assessment of various
change strategies and the public assessment of these same strategies.
Yet with the exception of the building issue, the policymakers consistently misperceive the public sentiment. While the attitudes of
both the public and the policymakers can be characterized as rather
liberal, nonpunitive, and reform-oriented, the policymakers attribute almost the reverse to the public.

Several studies concerned with different policy arenas have observed this same phenomenon,[21] and the only other study concerned
specifically with correctional policy confirms our findings.[22] We
therefore feel it extremely unlikely that our results are spurious or
in error.

To what should we attribute these findings? Hedlund and Friesma
have argued that policymakers are better at assessing constituency
opinion on major issues than on minor ones.[23] It could readily be
argued that the building controversy is the most important, or most
visible, of the issues we addressed. If so, our findings support Hedlund and Freisma's argument, since the policymakers' assessments
of public opinion on this issue are quite accurate. Harris has argued
that while the public supports the concept of community-based
corrections in theory, the public also feels that opposition from
neighbors would be so great as to render nil the practical chances
that such a program would succeed.[24] If so, our policymakers may
be justified in their lack of faith in public support for this proposal.

Alternatively, one could take the position that the policymaking
and implementing groups we studied are failing to meet the responsibilities with which they are charged. A basic assumption of

representative democracy is that public policy should be responsive to the public will; and one can argue that this principle applies to both administrative and legislative branches of government. The picture we have seen clearly suggests not only that our policymakers are poor judges of the public's wants, but that the system they are charged with operating is not responsive to the priorities as assigned by the public. To this point, then, the evidence would seem to suggest that with respect to correctional system goals and their implementation, those whom we charge with public responsibility are failing to meet that charge.

We prefer a less cynical interpretation, and in fact feel that the data better fit a model of "pluralistic ignorance"—a term commonly used to describe situations in which persons underestimate the extent to which others share their beliefs and sentiments.[25] We also (see Figure 4) examined the relation between policymakers' perception of the public will and their perception of the functioning of our present correctional system. The relation was high and positive ($\rho = .78$). It appears that correctional policy may indeed be made and implemented in accordance with the public will, as the policymakers perceive that will. This, of course, is the critical issue: the extent to which policymakers misperceive or misunderstand the views of the public may determine the extent to which public policy will be nonresponsive to the public will. If existing mechanisms used by policymakers to assess public opinion are inadequate, it is important that policymakers recognize this limitation. As Riley and Rose suggest, "If the model of a representative democracy is indeed operative, then providing decision makers with empirical data obtained by using scientific survey techniques [could and] should lead to greater responsiveness to public opinion."[26]

NOTES

1. R. D. Hedlund and H. P. Friesma, "Representative Perceptions of Constituency Opinion," *Journal of Politics* 34 (1972): 730–52, at 736.
2. N. R. Luttbeg, "Political Linkage in a Large Society," in *Public Opinion and Public Policy: Models of Political Linkages* (Homewood, IL: Dorsey, 1968).
3. W. E. Miller and D. E. Stokes, "Constituency Influence in Congress," *American Political Science Review* 57 (1963): 46–56.

4. Hedlund and Friesma, "Representative Perceptions."

5. P. J. Riley and McN. Rose, "Public Opinion vs. Elite Opinion on Correctional Reform," *Journal of Criminal Justice* 8 (1980): 345–56.

6. Cf. National Advisory Commission on Criminal Justice Standards and Goals, *Corrections* (Washington, DC: U.S. Government Printing Office, 1973); E. Doleschal, "Public Opinion and Correctional Reform," *Crime and Delinquency Literature* 2 (1970): 456–76; E. H. Johnson, *Crime, Correction, and Society* (Homewood, IL: Dorsey, 1974); C. E. Reasons, "Correcting Corrections," in C. E. Reasons, ed., *The Criminologist: Crime and the Criminal* (Pacific Palisades, CA: Goodyear, 1974); Chamber of Commerce of the United States, *Marshaling Citizen Power to Modernize Corrections* (Washington, DC: Chamber of Commerce of the United States, 1972); D. L. Smith and C. Lipsey, "Public Opinion and Penal Policy," *Criminology* 14 (1976): 113–24; D. Stang, "Problems of the Corrections System," in Reasons, ed., *The Criminologist*; J. M. Taves and A. L. Mauss, "Corrections and Punishment," in A. L. Mauss, ed., *Social Problems in Social Movements* (Philadelphia, PA: Lippincott, 1975); R. Henshel and R. A. Silverman, eds., *Perception in Criminology* (New York: Columbia University Press, 1975); and D. Skolar, "Future Trends in Juvenile and Adult Community-Based Corrections," in G. Perlstein and T. Phelps, eds., *Alternatives to Prison* (Pacific Palisades, CA: Goodyear, 1975).

7. R. A. Berk and P. H. Rossi, *Prison Reform and State Elites* (Cambridge, MA: Ballinger, 1977), p. 3.

8. S. D. Gottfredson and R. B. Taylor, *The Correctional Crisis* (Washington, DC: National Institute of Justice, 1983); S. D. Gottfredson and R. B. Taylor, "Public Policy and Prison Populations: Measuring Opinions about Reform," *Judicature* 68, nos. 4–5 (1984): 190–201.

9. On this point it is interesting to note that the "private" and "public" expressions of sentiment of several members of our sample of policymakers also were often at variance.

10. Berk and Rossi, *Prison Reform.*

11. Riley and Rose, "Public Opinion vs. Elite Opinion."

12. Berk and Rossi, *Prison Reform.*

13. Because of budgetary restrictions, we of course did not interview all such persons. In this sense, then, this can be considered a sample of the larger policymaking group. We do believe that our sample is biased toward the "heavily involved" portion of this larger group.

14. See Gottfredson and Taylor, *Correctional Crisis.*

15. Based on 1980 census counts; see A. Goodman and R. Talalay, *Census Note 1* (Baltimore, MD: Center for Metropolitan Planning and Research, Johns Hopkins University, 1981).

16. However, a rural-urban-suburban locational analysis yielded little in the way of important differences.

17. Berk and Rossi, *Prison Reform.*

18. The approach is described in detail in S. D. Gottfredson and R. B. Taylor, *Corrections in Court: Prison Populations and Public Policy*, Final Report to the National Institute of Justice (Silver Spring, MD: NCJRS, 1982).

19. All analyses are based on slightly different numbers of cases, since not all respondents answered every question we asked.

20. With only four ranks, one must obtain a value of ρ equal to 1.00 to achieve traditional levels of statistical significance. It should be pointed out, however, that the data discussed here represent mean ranks, and are based on very large numbers of cases. Accordingly, the ranks discussed may be considered to be quite stable. Where differences between mean ranks did not exceed at least one standard error in magnitude, ranks are represented as tied. Our use of ρ is intended simply as an aid to interpretation.

21. For example, Miller and Stokes, "Constituency Influence"; Hedlund and Friesma, "Representative Perceptions."

22. Riley and Rose, "Public Opinion vs. Elite Opinion."

23. Hedlund and Friesma, "Representative Perceptions."

24. L. Harris, "Changing Public Attitudes toward Crime and Corrections," *Federal Probation* 32 (1968): 9–16.

25. See R. K. Merton, *Social Theory and Social Structure* (New York: Free Press, 1968); H. J. O'Gorman, "Pluralistic Ignorance and White Estimates of White Support for Racial Segregation," *Public Opinion Quarterly* 39 (1975): 313–30; and H. J. O'Gorman, and S. L. Garry, "Pluralistic Ignorance: A Replication and Extension," *Public Opinion Quarterly* 40 (1976): 449–58.

26. Riley and Rose, "Public Opinion vs. Elite Opinion," p. 347.

PART II
POLICY OPTIONS

5 State Responses to Prison Crowding: The Politics of Change

JOAN MULLEN

Based on a review of 1979 data, a national study of American prisons and jails concluded that the population boom of the 1970s could be attributed to a rise in the number of new admissions to prison rather than increases in time served.[1] More recently, analysts have suggested that crowding in the 1980s is the product of tougher parole policies and longer sentences. "Perhaps what we have here," suggests Franklin Zimring, "is the two punch of a one-two combination."[2]

In an effort to reduce the massive crowding in state prisons, a variety of strategies have been devised to regulate the flow of new admissions to prison or to control the length of time served. At the outset, it is probably fair to conclude that many of these actions have served only to ameliorate short-term crowding problems, while others that have promised more enduring relief have failed to take hold on any serious scale. Despite staggering costs and dubious results, prison construction remains the preferred state response to crowding.

Considering the political environment of corrections, it is hardly surprising to find nonconstruction remedies dominated by quick fixes and faltering steps toward lasting reform. While lip service is given to the notion that prison space is a scarce resource that needs to be wisely allocated, the nation's lawmakers clearly believe that the public is fed up with crime and wants nothing more than to "lock the bastards up."[3] Since the fiscal climate is equally conserv-

ative, it is hard to find resources for prison construction, let alone
the funds to develop more deliberate solutions to prison crowding.

When crisis occurs (generally in the form of a riot or court order),
state governors turn to their appointed correctional administrators,
who are powerless to resolve the dilemma that occurs when rising
prison populations are not matched by increases in the funds allocated to corrections. So the governor buys time by setting up a blue-
ribbon commission to study the problem or by replacing the corrections commissioner. Then, with administrators mindful of the
need to do something now, a handful of remedial measures are
quickly installed to quiet the crisis. The trouble is, of course, that
crisis remedies often do well in addressing the effects of a problem,
but typically do little to attack its underlying causes. A new round
of effects may not be felt for one or two elections into the future,
but sooner or later the problem will outlive its solutions.

"The absence of coherent corrections policy" has become a popular phrase to describe the problem that lies beneath the surface of
crowded institutions. In effect, the nation's prisons have been or-
phaned by a distribution of authority that wreaks havoc with traditional notions of rational public policymaking. In theory, the
primary responsibility for prison policy development lies with the
legislature. By prescribing penalties, the legislature decides who
will go to prison and for how long. By authorizing funds for construction, staffing, and maintenance, the legislature also dictates the
conditions of confinement.

In practice, by virtue of extremely broad statutory limits on the
use of imprisonment, decisions about who goes to prison are in most
states effectively delegated to the judiciary, whose members operate
independently, following policies that may not be uniformly defined
or consistently implemented. For all practical purposes, judges are
left at large, "wandering in the deserts of uncharted discretion," too
often indulging their own values.[4] A New York Supreme Court judge
achieved brief notoriety when he publicly tossed a coin to determine
a robber's sentence. Having captured the attention of the press, the
judge pointed out that this sentence was different only in publicity;
the sentences of other judges were just as random, and possibly less
fair.

Although judges are also given nominal authority over length of
stay, here their decisions are largely symbolic. The executive branch

effectively controls time served through its various releasing powers, most notably parole. Like the judicial gatekeepers at the front door of corrections, parole boards open and shut the back door "without orderly and uniform criteria of judgment, often moved by political pressures or the winds of public opinion."[5]

Now and again, the legislature reasserts its authority with a mandatory sentencing law intended to thwart the discretionary prerogatives of judges or parole commissions. These, however, merely sharpen this picture of decentralized authority by strengthening the charging decisions of local prosecutors. As Zimring reminds us, "no serious program to create a rule of law in determining punishment can ignore the pivotal role of the American prosecutor."[6]

Out of this labyrinth of decisions made across levels and branches of government comes a state prison population. Remarkably, much of the public and many of its elected leaders seem to believe that the prisoners arrived as a result of conscious policy, in response only to events (crimes) that are not within anyone's control. The fact that there is neither a coherent policy nor, as a result, any predictable relationship between rates of crime and trends in the use of prison is a detail that escapes public notice.

In addition to delegating its control over the use of imprisonment, the role of the legislature in setting standards for the conditions of confinement has been pro forma at best. This responsibility has been delegated to the executive branch, despite the fact that many of the decisions that affect prison conditions are beyond its control. In the absence of any legislative direction on what constitutes an appropriate prison living space, definitions of the capacity of state institutions are vague and elastic. Capacity has become a yardstick of convenience that may refer to the number of inmates a facility was originally designed to hold, the number that corrections officials believe the space can accommodate, or even the number who are actually living in the space. In the end, not only can just about anyone go to prison, but just about any conditions of confinement are permissible—until, of course, the federal courts decide that enough is enough and step into the void left by legislative default.

There is no doubt that lawmakers have too long abdicated their basic responsibility for deciding what is an appropriate standard of prison living and for apportioning punishments accordingly. It is not necessarily wise to ask that legislators assert direct control, for reallocating all power to the legislature "means gambling on our ability to make major changes in the way elected officials think, talk and act about crime."[7] It is reasonable to ask that state legislatures pay far more attention to the process and results of their delegation of authority.

STRATEGIES FOR CONTROLLING PRISON ADMISSIONS

The beginnings of state imprisonment policy are clearly revealed in a number of state efforts to influence or accommodate prison admission decisions. Discussed below are three general approaches. Included are attempts to limit prison commitments in the course of developing more uniform sentencing policies; efforts to ensure that if those limits are exceeded, they are also funded; and various attempts to shift the population burden to other types of sanctions, other levels of government, or even the private sector. While each strategy has differed in process and results, all lead to a common conclusion: effective population control may be out of our reach until the decentralized discretionary nature of sentence decision making is adequately addressed and the resulting state policies are clearly linked to the resources available to the corrections function.

Revising Sentencing Law and Practice

By now, the evolution of America's penal laws has become a familiar story that needs little reiteration. Originally based on a theory of retribution, the nation's criminal laws were patterned after those in England, which prescribed fixed sentences for specific offenses. In the late nineteenth century, reformers disavowed the punishment purpose of criminal sentencing and turned more to rehabilitation. The new approach called for indeterminate sentences, under which the time a prisoner served was only broadly specified by the sentencing judge ("five years to life") and most of the term-setting power was given to parole authorities. Over the next 80-odd years, the system adapted to contemporary needs partly because this indeterminate model gave its users considerable latitude in selecting appropriate penalties.

Since the 1960s, efforts to return to more determinate sentencing models have multiplied in response to persistent criticism of the inconsistent results of a sentencing process that has given so much discretion to its decision makers. Beginning with complaints that the uncertainties and disparities were unfair, the line of argument has become more conservative, and many have alleged that the failure to mete out certain and consistent punishment is a threat to public safety. To these broader arguments has now been added the recognition that while discretionary sentencing decisions certainly produce a prison population, they hardly form a coherent corrections policy. As a result, states have no direct control over prison populations nor any rational basis for making decisions about construction or any of its alternatives.

Unfortunately, the recent history of sentencing reform provides little guidance on how best to structure sentencing discretion. Legislative efforts to introduce more determinacy in sentencing—through various forms of penal code revision—have often done little more than transfer the discretion from one part of the system to another. In this result, the system has been likened to a waterbed, where the distribution of water may shift but the total is always conserved. Equally troubling is the prospect of leaving sanctioning decisions open to the political maneuvering of the legislative process:

It implies no disrespect for our legislative leaders, but only a recognition of plain reality, to observe that sentencing, prisons, and correctional practices generally do not attract sustained and steadily coherent attention among lawmakers, state or federal.[8]

The delicate scheme of priorities in any well-conceived sentencing proposal can be torpedoed by amendment with ease and political appeal.[9]

The inflexibility of statutory remedies is another source of complaint. While legislatively determined sanctions are frequently driven by transient political motives, the laws so created have remarkable endurance and cannot readily adapt to subtle changes in public standards or criminal activities. The mechanisms for setting sanctions, having once been activated, are now static, and further legislative action is required to adjust sentences if conditions change.

If law reform, by itself, is not the answer, neither is an exclusively administrative approach. Several jurisdictions have tested voluntary sentencing guidelines that provide judges with decision rules for setting sanctions—rules established and policed solely by administrative means. A number of evaluations have now been completed. The most recent is as firm as its predecessors in concluding that voluntary compliance is not guaranteed to change anything.[10]

To date, the most reasonable compromise has emerged in the form of statutory guideline systems that divide policy-setting authority between the legislature—responsible for providing broad policy direction—and an independent sentencing commission authorized to set specific sentencing standards. In such a scheme, the legislature retains its supervisory authority, but deliberations on specific sentencing policies are removed from the caprice of competitive politics and placed in the more studious hands of a staff-assisted, permanent commission composed of public and judicial representatives as well as the leaders of key criminal justice agencies. Judicial compliance with the sentencing structure thus formed is encouraged by the legislative imprimatur of the commission as well as the provision for appellate court review of any sentencing decisions that deviate from recommended ranges. Continuous monitoring by commission staff is also essential to detect and counteract repeated judicial departures from the guideline ranges or shifts in legislative priorities or prosecutorial practices.

By itself, determinate sentencing—in this or any other form—provides no assurance of prison population control. Guidelines or other determinate schemes are merely structures for expressing the sentencing values of their architects. Indeed, in many states greater determinacy and increased severity have gone hand in hand—a development that has promised to put further strain on overburdened state facilities. More definite sentence decision making is essential for placing clearly defined bounds on the use of imprisonment. In order to control prison crowding, those bounds must be shaped at the outset by carefully balancing normative judgments about who ought to be in prison with practical estimates of how much prison space is available or affordable.

Ironically, while there is ample evidence that the amount of available prison space has entered into individual judges' sentencing calculus, there has been little interest in avoiding the inevitable disparities by elevating that practice to the level of system policy. Merely to mention the concept evokes the idea of a "just" sentence compromised because the state system was filled to capacity at the time of conviction. Of course, this idea (or any approximate reality) is unacceptable. Sanctioning choices geared to accommodate resource constraints are not decisions made at the point that an individual offender is facing sentencing; the choices are made long before that moment, when the state confronts the need to develop uniform sentencing policy and decides that a particular class of offender should not remain in the community. Instead, perhaps those offenders should be imprisoned for twice as long as current practice if the state is willing to reduce the resources allocated to lesser offenders in order to achieve that result. The state is simply deciding—as a matter of policy—what resources are available and how they should be applied. Punishments are still fashioned to fit the crime (or whatever sentencing rationale is chosen), and not simply the available space. Space merely serves as the limiting criterion—a little something to restrict what might easily become endless ideological debates over the presumed merits of particular sanctions.

Minnesota provides the leading example of a state that has tailored its guidelines to fit within its existing prison capacity. The Minnesota legislature originally directed the Sentencing Guidelines Commission to "take into substantial consideration prior sentencing and release practices and correctional resources, including but not limited to the capacities of local and state correctional facilities." For several reasons, the commission considered it both legitimate and essential to implement this broad mandate by imposing a firm population constraint on the guidelines structure:

First, the state has an obligation to avoid subjecting confined citizens to inhumane conditions, and such conditions are more likely to develop in overcrowded correctional institutions.

Second, the Sentencing Guidelines Commission is not a legislative body, and cannot appropriate funds required to provide additional prison bed spaces. Failure to consider prison populations in formulating the sentencing guidelines would result in restricting legislative options in correctional appropriation decisions.

Third, if the Commission ignored the population impacts of their decisions (producing Guidelines under which populations exceeded capacity), and if the legislature did not appropriate funds for additional prison beds . . . overcrowded prisons would present a much more inviting target for constitutional challenge. [11]

On a more pragmatic level, the formation of guidelines that exceeded the state's prison capacity was considered a self-defeating exercise. To the extent that capacity issues were not explicitly accommodated, population pressures might prompt the early release of offenders, and the guidelines themselves would have no consistent influence over time served.[12]

Finally, common sense called for a reality constraint to moderate the temptation to prescribe prison merely to satisfy political objectives. As the commission reported, "phrasing the problem in terms of the rational use of existing space served as a catalyst in resolving the divergent interests represented on the Commission. For example, where prosecution and defense might be strongly committed to different positions, both parties had an external reason—impact on population—to reach an accommodation."[13]

Notably, while effective population management was a clear goal of Minnesota's new sentencing structure, the guidelines were intended primarily to address issues of equity and fairness by achieving greater sentence uniformity and proportionality. Ironically, on these latter measures, the system has produced somewhat ambiguous results. After a successful first year, prosecutors adapted their charging and bargaining practices, judicial departures from prescribed sentences increased, and neither the commission nor the legislature chose to reassert state policy by making compensatory adjustments in the guidelines system. In contrast, both the commission and the legislature were strongly committed to the goal of population management and worked together to ensure that overall population levels remained within the bounds of the state's existing prison capacity.[14]

While many other states have undertaken the development of sentencing guidelines, few have rushed to emulate Minnesota by incorporating resource constraints into their deliberations on sentencing policy. In many fields of public service, the concept of linking public policy to the public purse is elemental. If states lowered the compulsory school age to require public education starting at three years of age, unless there were surplus school capacity those states would clearly face the prospect of matching their commitment to longer primary education with additional funds to house and teach the new student populations. In fact, the policy would probably be abandoned if the states could not afford the consequences, since children and their teachers would bear the burden.

In corrections, where the most immediate beneficiaries of a link between policy and resources are the staff and inmates of institutions that operate far from public view, there is no constituency for rational allocation schemes. Since lawmakers themselves are hardly eager to bring home the responsibility for prison policy development, it has been easier, it seems, to hide behind perceptions of public indifference or hostility than to consider efforts to educate and involve the citizenry in corrections reform.

Preparing Impact Statements

Although most states have been reluctant to advertise a direct relation between sentencing and prison resources, several have been willing at least to consider the impact of new sentencing laws on prison populations by developing prison impact statements. Under this scheme, new bills or administrative guidelines are accompanied by calculations that estimate the resources required to accommodate the changes proposed. The mathematical exercises are quite similar to those undertaken by a sentencing authority that uses the available space to define the bounds of sentencing policy. The key difference is in the application of the results. In Minnesota, where space served as a limiting criterion, policies were debated and their impact on population tested until guidelines were found that satisfied the punishment priorities of the commission without exceeding the state's prison capacity. In states that prepare impact analyses to accompany proposed revisions in sentencing policy, the statements merely serve as an announcement of the consequences. The objective is not to avoid the estimated impact by making tradeoffs elsewhere in sentencing, but to accommodate the results by informing the legislature of the need for expansion and its probable costs.

By recognizing the possibility that additions to prison capacity may be necessary, this method of linking policy and resources has far broader political appeal than proposals to constrain policy to match existing capacity. The appeal is not without substance. However tempting it may be to argue that existing prison capacity in most states is sufficient, the argument is foolhardy. "How much is

enough?" remains a question of values that will be answered in
different ways by different states. As long as the state is willing to
pay the price of its sanctioning policies, expansion can be considered
a rational choice.

But will the state pay the price? Does the preparation of an impact
statement announcing the need for expansion imply that the legislature will authorize the funds? Because the funding decision remains stranded on the battleground of competitive politics, there
is no guarantee that the legislature will accept the responsibility for
matching policy and resources. Describing a battle with successful
results, Blumstein reports on the progress of a mandatory-minimum
sentencing bill submitted to the legislature by the governor of
Pennsylvania:

> A prison impact analysis indicated that the prison capacity needed to house
> the extra prisoners would be excessive. Using the impact analysis in
> negotiation with the previous bill's sponsors, he got them to join him in
> endorsing a legislative package that combined a call for five-year mandatory
> minimum sentences for a narrowly limited group of offenses with a request
> for a legislative authorization of [a] $134 million bond issue to provide 2,880
> additional prison spaces to accommodate the anticipated increase in prison
> population; and the governor let it be known that approval of the sentencing
> legislation without the bond issue would lead to a veto. Both components
> were passed with virtually no opposition.[15]

Considering the politics of this encounter, it is not hard to imagine
a situation where the legislature might disregard the resource implications of a change in policy, or where a bond issue authorized
by the legislature would fail to obtain voter approval. Under these
circumstances, the impact statement has served to place the resource question on the record, but it has not produced greater
legislative accountability for the conditions of confinement. Only if
the legislature is forced to abandon or modify unfunded commitments to get tough will the impact statement have more than symbolic value.

Developing Alternative Sanctions

Turning to a more widely discussed method of controlling prison
admissions, by now it is clear that expanding the use of alternative

sanctions is a strategy that has fallen between the cracks of our decentralized system of corrections decision making. In the decade of the 1960s, corrections reformers enthusiastically endorsed the community corrections ideal, and hundreds of disparate programs were established as "community-based alternatives to incarceration." Over the decade of the 1970s, a major difference between rhetoric and reality became apparent as evidence mounted that many alternatives might simply be diverting "alternative" offenders and not those who might otherwise be imprisoned. The "widened net of social control" became a popular label for this unintended consequence of the diversion movement.

The discovery that alternatives often reached non-prison-bound offenders should not have been particularly surprising. Convicted offenders do not come before the judge with clear labels calling for a particular disposition. The upper 10 percent and lower 10 percent may be clearly recognizable (though no two judges might agree), but the intermediate 80 percent represent largely discretionary choices. If an alternative were introduced somewhere at the lower end of this range, it would be expected to draw clients from the dispositions both above and below it in severity. In the face of public demands to get tougher across the board, the alternative could be used almost exclusively to toughen the punishments of lesser offenders.

Achieving more true diversion from prison to alternative sanctions requires not only changing the ways that sanctioning decisions are made but also reconsidering the labels and contents of the sanctions themselves. If one believes that not only do words express what people think but "language can influence *how* people think," the labeling problem is significant.[16] As long as nonprison sanctions are advertised as "alternatives," attention is drawn to the opposing possibility and "the real thing" may inevitably win greater popular support. Given the public's perception that an offender either goes to prison or gets nothing for his trouble, a system composed of prison and its alternatives is a system in which everyone belongs inside the walls but we have scrambled to make something out of nothing in order to deal with the pressures of prison crowding. A more sensible picture of corrections policy contains a legitimate continuum of sanctions in which prison is the last resort in an array of penalties of increasing severity. Recasting alternatives as "intermediate" sanctions, known to apply to cases of middling severity (and not to prison-bound offenders), might go a long way toward reinforcing this model in perception and practice.

In fact, many states have begun to address the task of developing intermediate sanctions by increasing the weight of traditional probation supervision in higher-risk cases. The new "intensive supervised probation" programs emphasize restitution and work requirements, mandated curfews, periodic blood and urine testing, intensive surveillance, and related measures for offender supervision and control. Other intermediate sanctions include so-called split sentences that involve probation with confinement in residential community corrections programs or brief periods of "shock" imprisonment.

Yet even the most determined effort to develop satisfying intermediate punishments may fail to reduce prison crowding unless fundamental changes are also made in the framework for sentence decision making. Just as prison populations are the imperfect result of thousands of inconsistent decisions, intermediate sanctions may be overused or neglected by prosecutorial or judicial prerogative. It is the entire range of sanctions, not simply sentences to prison, that can benefit from clear decision guidance and a centralized monitoring apparatus.

A significant shortcoming of the sentencing guideline efforts implemented in the early 1980s (including those in Minnesota) has been their exclusive focus on regulating only the imprisonment decision and not also the decisions to place offenders under community supervision. Only in Delaware has an effort emerged to ensure the consistent assignment of offenders to various levels of noncustodial supervision. The approach proposed in Delaware is a sequential sentencing model with 10 levels of accountability that reflect increasing degrees of offender supervision. Assignment of offenders to various levels is regulated by a sentencing guidelines structure that considers both the nature of the offense and the offender's background.[17]

As other jurisdictions begin to experiment with similar sentencing schemes, it is reasonable to hope that decisions about the use of intermediate sanctions will also be tied to funding decisions. Just as a state's use of prison must be linked to its capacity to build and operate institutions, there must be a similar connection between the funds allocated to nonprison sanctions and the decisions to place offenders under community supervision. In the absence of that link, it may be impossible to maintain any reasonable caseload standards, supervision will deteriorate, and the next generation of corrections observers will be left to talk about crowding and the loss of credibility in the new community corrections programs.

Consider the dilemma of probation—now the most widely used nonprison sanction. Probation capacity is not defined by bricks and mortar; nor have overloaded probation caseloads been the subject of judicial challenge. But the same loss of correctional control has resulted from the failure to establish sentencing standards that recognize capacity limitations. While prison crowding dominates the news, there are about three times as many offenders being supervised in the community.[18] Since probation has become a vast dumping ground for all kinds of petty criminals and lesser felons—and the caseload of a single probation officer may number in the hundreds—it is hardly surprising that judges worry about the quality of supervision and researchers confirm their worst fears by suggesting that placing felons on probation constitutes a serious threat to public safety.[19]

Richard Lynch of the American Bar Association has described the dilemma of a sentencing judge confronted with an offender who has never been imprisoned, now convicted of some "halfway violent street crime":

And what are your options?...You could send him to prison for a few months or a year and you know he will only come out worse and be back on the street. You could put him on probation, but you know that the overburdened probation officers aren't going to be able to give him any serious attention. [So] you sentence him to a few months in prison, because you feel like you have to do *something*. Then you go into the bathroom and you throw up.[20]

The new intermediate sanctions are unlikely to solve this dilemma unless capacity limitations are carefully installed and rigorously enforced. If more intensive supervision is to be provided to some offenders, then something has to give—either funds must increase to meet the demand for more stringent supervision, or fewer controls must be placed on lesser offenders. In some cases, fewer controls will mean no supervision at all and greater use of unconditional discharge, warnings, fines, and restitution orders unattached to probation. While the concept of reducing the weight of any penalties may not be politically palatable, "it is foolish to pretend that we can deliver on a promise to get tougher, more helpful, and more controlling across the board."[21] By avoiding the prospect of reducing the sanctions applied to lesser offenders, we may only succeed in diluting our ability to exert meaningful control over more serious cases.

Shifting the Burden to Other Levels of Government

Efforts to relieve crowded state facilities have often taken the form of mechanisms to redistribute the population burden to other levels of government. At the simplest extreme, many states have resorted to purchasing space in local jails; some have turned to neighboring state facilities or federal institutions. (Amusing examples can even be found of preemptive actions by the judiciary to divert troublesome cases to other jurisdictions. On the heels of a Florida case in which a convicted prostitute was given the option of going to prison or leaving for California, an Iowa judge provided the offender in an obscenity case with a one-way, nonrefundable bus ticket to the same state.)[22]

In a more serious vein, by delaying the transfer of offenders to state facilities following sentencing, or by revising policies that determine whether offenders can even be sentenced to state facilities, an increasing share of the population burden has been diverted to the local level. In the process, however, many locally confined state prisoners have confronted the irony of confinement in conditions far worse than those declared unconstitutional at the state level.

The intergovernmental dimensions of the corrections function magnify the irony. Local authorities—who make the decisions to send offenders to state prisons or to use local sentencing options—are given strong incentives to place offenders in state custody where they both are removed from the community and become a state rather than local financial burden. When those local decisions begin to clog state facilities, a variety of shell games are played to shift the burden back to the local level, which typically remains ill-equipped to handle offenders under local jurisdiction, let alone to absorb state prisoner overflows.

Recognizing the need to expand local corrections capabilities, more and more states have been pressed to support the development of a broader array of local sentencing options. The use of state funds to support local corrections programs achieved prominence with the California Probation Subsidy, instituted in 1966. From 1967 to 1978, California counties were given over $200 million to expand local supervision programs. Funding allocations were directly tied to the number of prison-bound offenders retained in the community. The state established a specific quota for each participating county and provided $4,000 for every eligible offender who was not sent to prison. In 1973, Minnesota's Community Corrections Act established a similar financial incentive for reduced prison commitments, and in the late 1970s, Oregon, Kansas, and Indiana followed suit with community corrections legislation that included chargeback provisions if particular classes of felons were sent to state prison.

Most programs hoped not only to reduce or stabilize prison commitments but also to enhance local sentencing options by developing intermediate sanctions to occupy the open territory between traditional probation and prison. The conflict between these goals soon became apparent—at least in the research literature. While the diversion goal asked for less control over some prison-bound offenders, the goal of enhancing sanctions implied the exertion of more control over some probationers. Not surprisingly, the results have been mixed. A number of evaluations found that enhanced local supervision had succeeded in increasing the severity of sanctions for lesser offenders. But the available data have generally failed to support any strong claims of impact on prison population. Since many judges may have been indifferent to the payback provisions or unaware of their details, it is likely that the financial incentives have been too remote to influence judicial sentencing behavior. Rather, judges had to be induced to sentence differently based on the availability of stronger local programs. Some judges may have found the inducements sufficient; others may have been less persuaded.[23] Once again, we see the perils of expanding sanctions without installing uniform guidelines for their use.

Several other states have established statewide community corrections subsidies but have declined to attach specific incentives for reduced commitments. Local resistance to chargeback provisions, state concerns about the difficulty of controlling their funding ob-

ligations, and the administrative complexities of devising an appropriate formula and tracking placements have frequently discouraged
the incentive subsidy concept. While these states may fare no worse
than those with chargeback provisions, in the absence of guidelines
to regulate whether and how local programs will be used, they are
unlikely to do any better in the business of prison population control.

Shifting the Burden to the Private Sector

Contracting with the private sector to provide confinement services is an emerging response to crowding that has received ample
media attention and, in a few states, serious legislative consideration. Without engaging in the debate about the propriety or prac-
ticality of delegating a function of social control to private
entrepreneurs, a few observations can be made. (A more detailed
view of the history and future prospects of private prisons is provided
in Chapter 11, "Aid from Industry? Private Corrections and Prison
Crowding.")

The largest user of privately operated facilities has been the federal Immigration and Naturalization Service (INS), which is responsible for the detention of aliens pending deportation. Since
immigration law violators are not a criminal population, INS facilities
are simply designed to provide decent holding space for aliens whose
average length of stay is about 10 days. Faced with cumbersome,
time-consuming federal building procedures, limits on the number
of authorized federal staff positions, and a diminished ability to buy
space in crowded local jails, the INS has found contracting to be an
expedient way to meet rising demands for detention space.

Although the publicity that has surrounded INS contracting practices has led many to infer a national trend toward "prisons for
profit," state corrections agencies have proceeded with caution. In
early 1986, facility contracting at the state level was still reserved
largely for community-based facilities that closely resembled the
private halfway house or prerelease model that has been a standard
feature of state corrections practice for many years. Only in Kentucky had the state contracted for a facility to provide primary custody rather than secondary prerelease services. Even here,
however, the facility is a minimum-security installation that operates
on the grounds of an abandoned Catholic college under the super-

vision of the community corrections division. (Although interest in private jail facilities has been slightly less restrained, only a handful of local jails had been turned over to the private sector by early 1986.)[24]

If the private sector were used more aggressively, could states resolve their prison crowding problems? In theory, private vendors can operate equivalent facilities at lower cost because of staffing efficiencies that may be realized in the absence of civil service regulation, lower private sector pension and benefits costs, and greater market incentives to increase productivity. Yet even if these efficiencies are proved in practice, it is foolish to suggest that the private sector could eliminate crowding given the same levels of population and the same funding allocations. In many jurisdictions, the corrections function is so underfunded in relation to the number of offenders confined that greater efficiency is unlikely to yield the needed improvements.

Recall, however, that the private sector would never tolerate the imbalance between prisoners and funds that exists in many jurisdictions. Consistent with sensible business practice, private sector contractors would insist on a clear link between the number of offenders confined and the funds provided for their confinement. Under these terms, it is reasonable to expect that crowding would disappear, but it may be equally plausible to suggest that if public sector managers could negotiate the same deal with their legislatures, they might do as well.

Under a typical confinement service contract, vendors are responsible for locating an acceptable site, leasing or constructing an appropriate building, and providing all the staff and services necessary to operate the facility. Much as in the business of running a full-service hotel, room rates are based on capital investments, operating costs, and expected occupancy, and the government is charged by the day for each unwilling guest.

Now, consider the case of a 200-bed facility that is fully occupied for one year. At $25 per inmate per day (a typical cost for a minimum-security private facility), the annual cost of $1.825 million might compare favorably with the costs of building and operating the same facility in the public sector (depending on how one treats such things as the state's loss of equity in the physical plant and the costs of its contractor supervision). But what happens when the facility is consistently expected to handle 300 inmates? The answer is both simple and reasonable: the contractor is more than happy to build another 100-bed facility to house the overflow, and to charge the governemnt accordingly—in this case, an additional $912,500 per year. There is a certain irony in the introduction of such rational behavior into the corrections setting. After years of scholarly and professional entreaties to link imprisonment policies with corrections funding decisions, it may be the new corrections entrepreneurs who bring home the simple point that more prisoners require more resources.

STRATEGIES FOR REGULATING TIME SERVED

For the simple reason that most states have centralized control over time served (through parole and other discretionary release mechanisms), it has been far easier to regulate prison populations by adjusting release than by adjusting intake decisions. Since a court-imposed sentence frequently leaves corrections authorities with discretionary leeway that is greater than average time served, parole boards could double (or halve) the inmate population if they were inclined to do so. Small changes in time served can result in large changes in incarcerated populations. In a state with a two-year average term of imprisonment, each week added to or substracted from the sentence will change the inmate population by 1 percent.

The extent to which those weeks really matter is open to considerable interpretation. States vary widely in the severity of sanctions imposed. The limited data that are available often suggest that the most important factor in determining time served for many offenses may be the side of the state border on which the offense was committed. Thus, for instance, in 1982, serious property criminals were confined an average of about 10 months in Delaware, but stayed over twice as long (22 months) in Maryland's prisons. In Oregon, robbers served an average of 25 months, while the same offense in Washington was worth about 39 months.[25]

What can we infer from this diversity of sanctioning levels from state to state? First, if there is an objective basis for setting sanctioning levels, most states are not following it. The famed four horsemen of Deterrence, Rehabilitation, Incapacitation, and Retribution ride in and out of fashion, but sentencing practices have built up under them all, and prisons—in both architecture and action—often predate any of them.

Second, even supposing we could agree on a rationale for sentencing, this would yield only relative, not absolute, levels of sentencing. The members of a sentencing commission might agree that $10 shoplifters should get less severe sentences than corrupt judges, but they would have no guidance on whether the respective sentences should be 1 and 10 weeks, or 1 and 10 years. Even the most utilitarian incapacitation formula fails to provide much guidance. We know that some offenders commit offenses at a much higher rate than others. One option is to lock these people up for very long terms. On the other hand, we also know that arrest rates decrease annually as offenders age past their early twenties. This suggests that by the time we know enough about the high-rate offenders to classify them, they have aged past the peak offending years.

Aside from the unaffordable prospect of waiting for the criminal population to get older, there seems to be little that prisons can do to influence the offense rate of their releases. Other things being as nearly equal as statistical analysis can make them, people who serve long prison terms generally are rearrested about as often as their cohorts who get out early. These comparisons are inevitably confounded by the preference of parole boards to release low-risk offenders first, but the net result is to leave no conclusive empirical basis for selecting sentence lengths on the basis of predicted postrelease behavior. Like the initial in/out decision, some offenders may be clearly assigned to one extreme or the other, but the majority will be on the margin, and the margin is always arbitrary.

Historically, the criteria for setting time served have relied on a parole board's estimation of the readiness of inmates to reenter the community. The nature of the offense, the inmate's history of substance abuse, disciplinary record, performance in prison treatment programs, and postrelease plans have all contributed to the release decision. Because the weights attached to these factors have typically reflected the personal predispositions of parole authorities or prevailing political moods, attention has focused on correcting the resulting uncertainty and disparity by fixing terms more precisely at the point of sentencing.

So what then happens to parole? A number of states have abolished parole release on the theory that the function has no utility if judges are to impose more definite, real-time sentences. Yet a number of cautions are in order. Unless sentencing decisions are carefully guided, the elimination of parole release may considerably enhance judicial discretion, further decentralizing the imprisonment decision and diminishing the state's ability to exert direct control over prison populations. In at least four states that have abolished parole, judges have been left with relatively broad powers. While real-time sentences are now imposed by judges in those states, their range of choice is sufficiently broad that the result may be more rather than less disparity in time served.

Even if judicial decisions are carefully guided, the total abolition of parole removes an important safety net. While the current disaffection with rehabilitation may be persuasive in the majority of cases, there may always be exceptions in which the costs of continued incarceration are far higher than the risks of early release. Particularly with respect to sentences of long duration or those that fall outside of guideline ranges, Zimring has argued that some sentence review mechanism ought to be retained.[26]

In a number of jurisdictions, efforts to forestall the abolition of parole release decision making have taken the form of parole guidelines that provide a structure for setting a definite parole release date shortly after imprisonment on the basis of a matrix of offense and offender characteristics. In fact, the origins of the sentencing guideline concept can be found in the early efforts of the Federal Parole Commission to use a guideline system to rationalize parole release decisions. By the early 1980s, 3 states had installed statutory guideline systems and at least 14 other states operated parole guideline systems by administrative policy.

No state has explicitly used the amount of available space as a criterion in establishing guidelines for parole release. Nonetheless, adjustment of release policy through accelerated parole has been widely—albeit quietly—used throughout the history of American corrections as a device for regulating prison population. "In a system that seems addicted to barking louder than it really wants [or is able] to bite,"[27] a parole system allows judges to appear draconian for the media, knowing "that everything will be set quietly to rights down the road."[28] In addition to resolving wildly discrepant terms of confinement, numerous examples can be found of parole boards responding to administrative pressure to lower prison population by liberalizing the criteria for parole release. For the most part, however, because facility capacity is seldom explicitly defined and the use of accelerated parole release has been informal and erratic, the results have been equally haphazard.

Even if one could install a more uniform regulatory system at this juncture, it is not at all clear that the parole release decision should be the place to resolve basic questions of sentencing policy or to reconcile disparities between those policies and the available resources. While back-door adjustments may be more convenient and less visible (at least at the outset), "expediting release of prisoners while doing nothing to stem the flow of admissions is like bailing water from a boat without repairing the gaping hole in its bottom."[29]

Described below are two broad courses of action that states have pursued to regulate time served by adjusting the parole process. In the first category are basic efforts to expedite parole release by speeding the flow of inmates through state facilities. The second category includes more forceful mechanisms to reduce time served. While these latter mechanisms illustrate the utility of a "bailing" device, they also demonstrate the dangers of using a mechanism of last resort as a primary means of population control.

Speeding Inmate Flows

Strategies in this category range from basic efforts to grease the administrative wheels of the parole process to more ambitious attempts to facilitate release by improved classification and prerelease programming:

1. Several states have advanced parole hearing schedules in order to permit the early identification and timely release of parole-eligible inmates. Allowing more time to develop approved living and work arrangements means that fewer paroles have been delayed beyond the inmates' eligible release dates. A number of states have also increased the frequency of parole hearings or lengthened the number of days in each hearing period in order to clear backlogs of parole-eligible inmates.

2. Many states have shown considerable forbearance in their parole revocation policies. A greater tendency to overlook violations, or efforts to change the conditions of parole or to increase parolee

supervision, has commonly substituted for reincarceration on technical violations.

3. Reclassification of inmates according to the degree of risk they present to the community, and in turn the degree of control that must be exercised during their incarceration, is an activity that has occasionally offered significant opportunities for speeding the flow of inmates through the system. To the extent that a system is overperforming its control function and classifying inmates at a higher-than-needed level of security, resources are wasted and the state's ability to move inmates to prerelease or parole status is unnecessarily limited. A number of states have been prompted (by court demand, legislative request, or administrative initiative) to develop rational standards for inmate classification, many observing a point system issued by the National Institute of Corrections.

4. An important result of an effectively managed classification process is the identification of candidates for release to so-called phased reentry programs. Virtually all states have some form of halfway house, work release, prerelease, or furlough program intended to provide a period of transition between secure confinement and release to the community. To the extent that these community facilities and programs are underutilized, they present a logical opportunity to shift some portion of the population burden to another corrections component.

For the most part, all of these strategies are sensible inmate management tools—independent of crowding; many offer at least modest opportunities for relieving the pressures on major institutions. While some states have looked toward the expansion of community reentry programs as an important means of population control, it should be emphasized that any alternative—not just those at the front end of the system—may be used for supplementing instead of replacing traditional means of offender treatment. Precisely because it is generally acknowledged that few inmates should go cold turkey from institutions to community, expanding the availability of transition programs may increase the demand for this form of correctional supervision. In some cases, the additional supervision may be a wise investment. The danger is that without clear guidelines for the use of prerelease controls, discretion will have its way, and the result may be an inadvertent expansion in overall terms of confinement.

Accelerating Release

In the absence of incarceration policies framed to avoid the overcommitment of prison resources, many states have temporarily reconciled gaps between prison use and prison capacity by resorting to brute force. Relying on the various releasing powers of the executive branch, these states have checked gross discrepancies between the number of prisoners and the available space by offering quiet sentence discounts or by declaring a state of emergency and quickly pushing excess prisoners out the back door.

1. Good time. Two types of good-time programs are available in the majority of states: automatic good time, which is dispensed as credits against time served (credits that are lost in the event of misconduct); and merit time, which rewards inmates for meritorious conduct or participation in work or education programs. A common strategy for supplementing or (where parole has been abolished) replacing the sentence discounting functions of the parole board, the application of good time is authorized by statute and granted almost wholly at the discretion of corrections officials. In response to crowding, behavior standards for granting good-time credit have been lowered, proposals to abolish automatic good time have been held in abeyance, and schemes to grant merit time have flourished.

2. Emergency release provisions. By 1986, at least a third of the states had developed laws or administrative policies authorizing early release under emergency conditions. Under these policies, parole eligibility dates are rolled back 90 to 180 days for selected nonviolent offenders. Emergency release procedures are typically triggered when a facility has suffered a continuous excess of prisoners over an explicitly defined capacity level, or when state executives are convinced that facility populations have reached "unsafe levels."

3. Sentence commutations. In states where emergency release has yet to be formalized, corrections authorities have called on the clemency powers of their governors. In at least five states, the chief executive has responded by expanding traditional holiday and birthday commutation practices or accepting the pleas of corrections officials to release inmates on special commutations or reprieves.

While states have shown little interest in more considered methods of recognizing resource constraints on the use of prison, this list of expedient, ex post facto adjustments has been widely adopted.

During 1983 alone, an estimated 21,420 inmates from 15 states received early releases.[30] To be sure, no state has warmly embraced the undisguised intent of an emergency release procedure. Most have simply accepted the need for a crisis remedy, hoping that it can be quickly administered and soon forgotten.

If prison crowding were merely a transitory crisis, it would be simple enough to swallow a crisis remedy and return to business as usual, confident that the problem had been solved—however distasteful the means. But the crisis, in this case, is hardly a one-shot problem. If we review the history of imprisonment in America, a picture emerges of a system never out of crisis. In 1931, the Wickersham Commission reported serious crowding in federal and state institutions, citing examples of the deplorable conditions that existed in many states. Thus continued a story that began in 1801, when Philadelphia's Walnut Street Jail—widely considered a sire of the American penitentiary—became so overcrowded that its inspector resigned in disgust. Throughout the twentieth century, with the exception of two significant interruptions, prison populations have continued to rise, accelerating rapidly since the early 1970s and producing crowding crises with persistent regularity.

Unless the problems that have produced this legacy of crowding are addressed coherently, a crisis remedy is bound to lose its potency. Designed to cope with emergencies but used instead to fill the void left by the absence of more deliberate policy, emergency release procedures may have a number of unfortunate consequences. Unless the procedure is applied with rigorous consistency, the reductions in time served will perpetuate disparities in the treatment of similarly situated offenders. Yet if the procedure is applied consistently, it is sure to become more visible and less acceptable over time. Sooner or later, the emergency release strategy may become useless even to ameliorate crisis. Either public opposition will preclude its legitimate use, or the pool of inmates considered eligible for release may be exhausted and the crisis remedy will need its own emergency repairs.

STRATEGIES FOR CHANGING THE POLITICS OF CHANGE

While the absence of coherent policy is the primary curse on corrections, a closely related second is the lack of any popular constituency for corrections reform. The political grandstanding and symbolic rhetoric that have so often characterized legislative responses to crime and punishment are seldom challenged in public debate. The American public is not dumb, but it is preoccupied and, as John Conrad reminds us, corrections strikes no chord of personal interest:

The constituency for the correctional establishment is narrow, specialized, and seldom influential....Except when public attention is riveted by a spectacular failure of the system, we are out of sight and out of mind. No initiative we can take will change this state of affairs. It is an unremedial condition which must be confronted realistically and constructively.[31]

Doubting that a strong and durable constituency for fundamental change in corrections can ever be built, Conrad suggests we look instead for the incremental improvements that can be won by cultivating special-purpose constituencies, however temporary and fragile they may be. Conrad also acknowledges that the negotiation of those constituencies will rely on the leadership of strong correctional innovators—a rare breed of men and women of restless intellect and forward vision.

Though the prospect of waiting for a kind of leadership likely to emerge in only a handful of people every generation may be discouraging to the impatient reformer, it is nonetheless realistic. Over and over again, a successful program is dissected using the most sophisticated tools available to social science researchers who must ultimately confess that it is the quality of the program's leadership that seems to make a difference.

More discouraging to the prospects of achieving even incremental progress on the issue of prison crowding is the inability to step outside the political arena and identify who is responsible and might reasonably be expected to lead the charge for prison population control. Decisions about prison construction and the development of alternatives, standards of confinement, and sentencing and release policies are closely linked in their impact on prison population. But in most states, these decisions are made by separate groups that are often poorly informed about the intentions of other policymakers or the implications of their decisions. As a result, decisions are made collectively but incoherently. Now and again, one of John Conrad's innovators emerges with a remedy for one part of the problem, but the reform is soon coopted by forces at work elsewhere in the system. Sometimes the ability of one part of the system to nullify the decisions made in another is useful in prohibiting ill-advised measures to function as intended. Even so, one might accept the risk of something going badly wrong if the reward were a chance to change the direction of corrections policy.

Recognizing the need for a coordinated, systemwide assault on the crowding problem, in the early 1980s the Edna McConnell Clark Foundation and the National Institute of Corrections mounted an effort in four states to develop a political constituency for prison population control. In each state, policy groups were formed, composed of key leaders from all three branches of government at the state and local levels. These groups differed from the more typical blue-ribbon task force or study commission in that the products of the groups' deliberations "were to be actions, not merely reports."[32] Supported by a full-time staff and guided by a central project leader, the groups were encouraged to understand all the decisions that affect corrections policy; to examine the results of those decisions; to establish standards of prison living by defining the capacity of state institutions; to reach consensus on a set of options to relieve crowding; and to take the responsibility for implementing the measures proposed.

The educational benefits of the project have been significant. As the South Carolina group, for instance, began to explore the composition of the state's prison population (information that is surprisingly inaccessible to the public and its political leaders), it learned that 400 inmates were under custodial supervision for writing bad checks and failing to make child support payments. Confronted with these and related facts, even the most conservative members of the panel became advocates of more rational allocation.[33]

Over the two years that the policy groups received funding support, time permitted the installation of only short-term solutions to crowding. Only history will reveal whether the constituencies formed in those years will persist in working toward more durable methods of prison population control. In the most rewarding result, these groups and their facsimiles in other states would eventually create or become permanent state commissions on penal policy. The new commissions would resemble the policy groups in their focus on population control, but their reach would extend to all aspects of the corrections apparatus—not merely prisons. They would also resemble today's sentencing and parole guidelines commissions charged with regulating who goes to prison and how long he stays. But here too the mandate would be broadened to consider which offenders would be assigned to what types of noncustodial supervision. All of these decisions would be guided, in part, by a realistic assessment of the state's capacity for correctional supervision—an assessment that would add questions of economics to the moral, ethical, and scientific debate.

Once the new commission had promulgated guidelines for all sentence decision making, commission staff would persistently monitor compliance and review any new legislative proposals pertaining to the criminal justice system. Since any proposal that changes the status quo at any point in the system potentially affects correctional populations, the commission's review and recommendations would assist the legislature in deciding whether the probable results justify the impact on the system and whether the impact can be tolerated or accommodated. A strong standard for departures from the commission's recommendations would be established to moderate the temptation to implement overzealous, underfunded legislative proposals.

What possible incentives can be fashioned to prompt the legislature to cede power to a commission that would enforce more rational decision making? After all, for all its flaws, the current system has the appeal of allowing the legislature to fashion penalties that win votes, even if they fail to make rational use of corrections resources. Why would any politician endorse a system that might hamper this freedom to posture about law and order without regard for the system's ability to deliver on those promises?

Apart from the possibility that legislators might welcome the opportunity to delegate an increasingly unmanageable problem, the creation of any external pressure for change is likely to rely on the cultivation of a more informed public. This is not to suggest that efforts be mounted to build a constituency for upgrading prison conditions. While an element of the public may find the conditions in many prisons morally offensive, it is probably fair to say that most citizens are able to look the other way and are willing, if pressed, to tolerate just about any nonlethal degree of crowding.

But does the public know what is being purchased with its corrections dollar? If legislators in South Carolina were surprised to
learn that bad-check and nonsupport cases were routinely incarcerated, is there any reason to believe that the public is more enlightened? Those who have not been intimately involved in the
debate on prison population size are invariably shocked at how much
we do not know—not only about the effects of sanctions, but even
about their use. Proponents of reducing the use of prison sanctions
suggest that many facilities are clogged with nonviolent offenders
who might be perfectly acceptable candidates for less restrictive
sanctions. Opponents of reduced reliance on prison suggest that a
variety of pressures (court orders to reduce population, fiscal re-
straints, and difficulties locating publicly acceptable sites for new
facilities) have pushed state prison populations toward increasing
concentrations of violent offenders.

All of this, however, is conjecture. Where data are available, the
level of detail is often too broad to provide an individual state with
a convincing demonstration of whether any of its policies can be
changed. Facts about length of time served as a function of various
case characteristics are equally spotty. Anecdotal evidence and isolated studies in single jurisdictions frequently suggest that crowding
has had a homogenizing effect, resulting in roughly equivalent terms
of confinement for disparate classes of violent and nonviolent offenders. While deteriorating conditions of confinement might not
cause undue public anxiety, the notion that a crowded system might
be able to apply force where needed would surely jolt both conservative and liberal sensibilities.

As it now stands, the only information that is freely available to
the public is contained in media reports of particularly heinous
crimes or gross failures in the system's treatment of particular cases.
While the resulting public outcry undoubtedly shapes policymakers'
perceptions of the public mood, it is not at all clear that public
reactions to specific incidents can be generalized to the broader
issues of sentencing and corrections policy. Since Chapter 4, "Attitudes of Correctional Policymakers and the Public," has discussed
the complex nature of public opinion on criminal justice issues, it
will suffice to say here that the available data are virtually impossible
to translate into clear preferences on incarceration policy.

Given the primary role that perceived opinion appears to play in the development of corrections policy, it is not unreasonable to suggest that we improve the accuracy of our knowledge of public opinion and, conversely, that more deliberate efforts be made to improve public knowledge of sentencing and corrections issues. Correctional officials have long been aware of the role of public sentiment in promoting or restraining the development of specific programs. Successful administrators have typically responded with extensive efforts to educate and involve the public in their endeavors. Public meetings, presentations by key officials, television and radio announcements, endorsement by community leaders, and the cultivation of media relations through meetings with editorial staff, contacts with reporters, and consistent use of press conferences have frequently helped to build constituencies for particular reforms. Extending this function, Conrad suggests that the responsibility of correctional leadership for interpreting broader policy issues to the public is so critical that executives who cannot make the case for reason and economy "should be removed, regardless of their other qualifications."[34]

To dispel the ignorance that has allowed the public and its elected leaders to operate largely on faith requires a monumental effort to reveal the process by which prisons are filled and the results of that process. Bismarck's famous principle—that the public should not know too much about what goes into making sausages or laws—cannot be applied when public opinion is itself a justification for the laws. While public tolerance of prison crowding may know no bounds, none of us looks favorably on chaos, or even inefficiency, in the organizations we support. If the public thought of criminal sanctioning as a practice with no articulable goal, no rational procedure, and no authoritative leader, it might be less tolerant of perpetual crisis appropriations and more supportive of formal structures charged with bringing rationality to our chaotic corrections enterprises.

NOTES

1. Kenneth Carlson, *American Prisons and Jails*, vol. 2, *Population Trends and Projections* (Washington, DC: U.S. Department of Justice, National Institute of Justice, October 1980).

2. Stephen Gettinger, "The Prison Population Boom: Still No End in Sight," *Corrections Magazine* 9, no. 3 (June 1983): 10.

3. James B. Jacobs, *The Politics of Prison Construction* (New York: New York University School of Law, March 1983).

4. Marvin Frankel, *Criminal Sentences, Law without Order* (New York: Hill and Wang, 1972), p. 7.

5. Ibid., p. 94.

6. Franklin Zimring, "A Consumer's Guide to Sentencing Reform," in Franklin Zimring and Richard Frase, *The Criminal Justice System* (Boston: Little, Brown, 1980), p. 937.

7. Ibid., p. 938.

8. Frankel, *Criminal Sentences.*

9. Zimring, "A Consumer's Guide," p. 938.

10. Deborah Carrow and Judith Feins, *Guidelines without Force: An Evaluation of the Multijurisdictional Sentencing Guidelines Field Test* (Washington, DC: U.S. Department of Justice, National Institute of Justice, July 1985).

11. Minnesota Sentencing Guidelines Commission, *Preliminary Report on the Development and Impact of the Minnesota Sentencing Guidelines* (Washington, DC: National Institute of Corrections, July 1982), p. 14.

12. Andrew von Hirsch, "Constructing Guidelines for Sentencing: The Critical Choices for the Minnesota Sentencing Guidelines Commission," *Hamline Law Review* 5, no. 2 (June 1982): 177.

13. Minnesota Sentencing Guidelines Commission, *Preliminary Report,* p. 14.

14. Kay A. Knapp, "What Sentencing Reform in Minnesota Has and Has Not Accomplished," *Judicature* 68, nos. 4–5 (October-November 1984): 181.

15. James Q. Wilson, ed., *Crime and Public Policy* (San Francisco: ICS Press, 1983).

16. Michael Sherman and Gordon Hawkins, *Imprisonment in America* (Chicago: University of Chicago Press, 1981), p. 4.

17. Thomas Quinn, "Focus for the Future: Accountability in Sentencing," *Federal Probation* 48, no. 2 (March 1984): 10–18.

18. *Probation and Parole Statistics* (Washington, DC: U.S. Department of Justice, Bureau of Justice Statistics, February 1986).

19. Joan Petersilia et al., *Granting Felons Probation* (Washington, DC: U.S. Department of Justice, National Institute of Justice, January 1985).

20. Eric Black, "Criminal Elements," *Ambassador*, March 1983, p. 66.

21. M. Kay Harris, "Reducing Prison Crowding and Nonprison Penalties," *The Annals* of the American Academy of Political and Social Science 478 (March 1985).

22. *Criminal Justice Newsletter* (National Council on Crime and Delinquency) 14, no. 7 (March 18, 1983).

23. Deborah Carrow et al., "An Evaluation of State Subsidies of Locally Administered Community Corrections Programs" (Unpublished draft, National Institute of Corrections, 1985).

24. Privately operated jails include two facilities in Bay County, Florida, a small regional facility in Minneapolis, a 300-bed facility in Hamilton County, Tennessee, and a regional facility located in Allegheny County, Pennsylvania.

25. Herbert Koppel, *Bureau of Justice Statistics Special Report: Time Served in Prison* (Washington, DC: U.S. Department of Justice, June 1984).

26. Zimring and Frase, *Criminal Justice System,* p. 1004.

27. Marvin Frankel, "Remarks as Presenter," in ibid., p. 1001.

28. Zimring, "A Consumer's Guide," p. 934.

29. Harris, "Reducing Prison Crowding," p. 158.

30. *Prisoners in 1983,* Bureau of Justice Statistics Bulletin (Washington, DC: U.S. Department of Justice, 1984).

31. John P. Conrad, "Corrections and Its Constituencies," *The Prison Journal* (Pennsylvania Prison Society) 64, no. 2 (1984): 47.

32. Gerald Kaufman, "The National Prison Overcrowding Project: Policy Analysis and Politics, A New Approach," *The Annals* of the American Academy of Political and Social Science 478 (March 1985): 165.

33. Edna McConnell Clark Foundation, *Time to Build?* (New York: Edna McConnell Clark Foundation, 1984), p. 12.

34. John P. Conrad, "Charting a Course for Imprisonment Policy," *The Annals* of the American Academy of Political and Social Science 478 (March 1985): 127.

6 The English Response to the Penal Crisis

SEAN McCONVILLE
and
ERYL HALL WILLIAMS

Prison crowding has been the chief symptom of the protracted criminal justice crisis that has gripped England and the United States since the mid-1970s. English government and parliamentary thinking, as well as other informed comment, has increasingly seen solutions arising from and extending to spheres beyond the system of prison administration and policymaking. This chapter will outline the nature and extent of the main English prison problems and will consider a number of possible solutions.

THE ENGLISH PENAL CRISIS

The average daily prison population in England has grown by some 11 percent over the past decade.[1] In 1975 the then home secretary Mr. Roy Jenkins expressed fears that if the national prison population were to exceed 42,000, a major crisis would ensue. The numbers have rarely fallen below that level since then, and they now well exceed it. In April 1986 the prison population rose to 46,600, the highest ever recorded, and has been increasing ever since.[2] The certified normal accommodation (CNA) of the system is 39,400, but even the gap of over 7,000 between capacity and actual population does not fully reveal the extent of the overcrowding. In

Authors' note: Portions of this paper are based on work performed under contract for the National Institute of Corrections in 1982. The views expressed are those of the authors only.

the first place, because of the specialized nature of many prisons in England, institutions cannot be regarded as being simply interchangeable. Adult sentenced prisoners cannot be kept in establishments for young persons or in remand (pretrial) accommodation; high- and low-security prisoners cannot properly be mixed, while those serving long sentences are eventually sent to training prisons rather than local prisons (a rough equivalent to jails in the United States). Overcrowding is therefore very unevenly distributed.

Partly because of policy (a desire to provide more decent and stable regimes for the long-term population) and partly because of demand, the greatest overcrowding occurs in the big urban prisons. For example, the population of Manchester prison (CNA 1,024) reached 1,756 at one time in 1985. With an average population of 1,384 in that year, many prisoners were held two and three to a cell. The Prison Department in its most recent published report pointed out that nationally there were 17,236 prisoners sharing cells.[3] Overall, about one-third of the English prison population is held two or three to a cell (which in the vast majority of cases was built over 100 years ago for one person).

The second reason why the number in excess of the CNA does not fully represent the extent of overcrowding is that the CNA is based on an acceptance, in many prisons, of standards that are already low and include an amount of "permissible" crowding. Moreover, although the CNA is 39,400, practical usable capacity is lower. Representatives of the prison governors' (wardens') association, in evidence to a House of Commons select committee, pointed out that to estimate true capacity some 5 percent of capacity must be deducted from the CNA figures, to allow for cells taken out of use for refurbishment, the repair of damage, and the like.[4] With prisoners sleeping in corridors, classrooms, and recreation areas, and with the establishment of special camps and the use of police station cells as stopgaps, the administration of the English prison service is conducted on a knife-edge: there is no room for mistakes, and a disturbance involving damage has consequences far beyond the walls of the prison in which it occurs. As the director-general observed in his 1981 report, "the sudden loss of an establishment or part of an establishment could have disastrous consequences for the management of the prison population."[5]

Coping with excessive numbers is a major component of the problem, but it is not the only one. The English penal estate has been neglected by successive governments for decades and is now grossly inadequate for its task. Out of 120 prisons in England, 42 (which hold the majority of prisoners) were built before 1900, and so slow was the pace of construction, and the recourse to ex-army camps, converted country estates, and the like, that only about a quarter of all English prison accommodation was built for twentieth-century purposes. The heavy wear and tear to which overcrowding subjects this old and largely dilapidated stock adds greatly to the problems of the prison administrators. An official from the section of the Prison Department responsible for buildings (including forward planning) told a House of Commons inquiry that "the whole estate is, to put not too exaggerated a view on it, collapsing around our ears and it needs a massive injection of capital if we are to have prisons standing at the end of this decade."[6]

The consequences of overcrowding for the lives of staff, inmates, and their relatives need not here be dwelt on to any great extent. It is worth pointing out that staff having to work in sordid, dangerous, and unhealthy conditions are likely to be resentful of management, quite demoralized, and, from time to time, uncooperative to the point of industrial action. Such staff relations make it very difficult to initiate changes, or to involve officers in a development of their roles and responsibilities.

The Scottish Prison Officers' Association used a significant expression in its evidence to the House of Commons Expenditure Committee: "The inmates' living conditions amount to the staff's working conditions."[7] Staff are fearful of the dangers arising from the supervising of inmates in crowded conditions. Although grateful for the extra income arising from overtime payments, they are conscious of the physical strains associated with excessive hours of work, and the pressures upon family life brought about by long absences, greatly restricted recreation, and the tendency to "bring the job home." Many staff are also worried about the possibility, in congested and inadequately regulated conditions, of catching contagious diseases and of exposing their families to such risks.[8] These strains and worries have undoubtedly contributed to the exceptionally bitter industrial relations that have beset the English prison service in recent years. There has been a national confrontation between the Prison Officers' Association and the government, brought to an end only by a major committee of inquiry, emergency-powers legislation, and the use of army personnel and facilities. At the time of this writing (May 1986) another hostile encounter looms.

Unlike American and most Western European prison systems, English prison cells (though larger than those in the United States) are generally not equipped with lavatories or washbasins. Inmates in local prisons, a substantial portion of whom are remand prisoners or are serving short sentences, are frequently held for 23 out of 24 hours locked in their cells where, even with multiple occupancy, they eat and carry out their bodily functions. The unsanitary nature and degrading effects of these conditions need not be labored. And, of course, overcrowding affects not only the cells, but all the support facilities of the prison: kitchen, laundries, bathing, and visiting facilities. The daily emptying of chamber pots ("slopping out") has to be done in cyclical order to avoid overwhelming sewage systems installed 100 years ago for half the present population. Visits from families and friends have to be curtailed because of lack of space. Even the routine bathing of prisoners becomes a major exercise in administration when, as in some prisons, only 10 to 20 showers or baths are available for maybe 1,000 prisoners.

All of this leads to strains that are self-evident. English prisoners do not have the equivalent of Fifth, Eighth, or Fourteenth Amendment protections, the provisions of which are quite clearly violated by some of these conditions. Not only are inmates thereby denied an important safeguard, but those civil servants involved both centrally and locally in prison administration are constrained by the results of normal interdepartmental competition for resources, without the goad that court orders can often usefully supply. One other observation may be pertinent here: the word "crisis," which suggests an imminent outcome or resolution, may be quite inappropriate to apply to developments in prison administration. Given a political willingness to tolerate progressive deterioration in conditions already poor, double and triple celling can allow the prisons to absorb greater numbers than hitherto has been thought possible.

In summary, the English prison system is beset with difficulties: an inflated and growing inmate population, decaying plant, and an apparent inability to regulate the demands that are made upon it. This last point has repeatedly been stressed by prison administrators and commentators, who note that the prisons are virtually unique among criminal justice institutions in that they *must* accept all persons who are presented to them with a valid warrant; from policing and prosecution through to probation and psychiatric care, all other criminal justice bodies are able to a considerable degree to match work to resources. This is a consideration to which we shall return; for the moment it is sufficient to observe that, quite uncertain from month to month of the demands that may be made upon them, English prison administrators are unable to forecast or plan realistically. Their most rational activity and chief hope is to agitate for the greatest amount of funds that the government will allocate to them. Agreeing that "planning" in any real sense of the word is virtually impossible, the director of regimes and services of the Prison Department told the Home Affairs Committee, "Because the chasm between what we have and what we need is so large and because there is an enormous refurbishing programme required, we cannot go wrong in providing our present programmes. What we are providing would be badly needed on any analysis."[9] This drop-in-the-bucket type of planning would be only too regrettably familiar to penal administrators in many parts of the United States as well.

RESPONSES

Providing Greater Resources?

At first sight, it would seem that the most obvious solution would be to provide more resources. In fact, expenditure on prisons (capital and current) has grown enormously during the past decade, from 172 million (sterling) ($296 million) in 1971 to 580 million (sterling) ($812 million) in the year ending 1985. Virtually all Western governments are now operating under considerable financial constraints, and to add to the already large burdens of operating a prison system, the additional costs of expanding capacity and rectifying existing shortcomings is a major political problem. Thus, although governments have repeatedly acknowledged the grave nature of the physical and social problems confronting the English prisons, it has equally often been said that money cannot, in present circumstances, be found to end overcrowding, to carry out necessary refurbishment to minimum standards, and to install integral sanitation.

Eleven years ago the home secretary estimated that (based on a population of only 42,000) about $1.75 billion would be required to implement this modest tripartite program. Inflation and the increase in prison population have already increased this cost substantially, and allowing for contract "slippage," continuing inflation over the years the work is to be carried out, an increasing trend in prison numbers, and the constant deterioration in prison plant, figures of $4 billion to $5 billion are now reasonable estimates. It must be emphasized that such vast expenditure would provide only a basic standard of decency in English prisons; no frills or special facilities of any kind are included within it. A sum of this size is unobtainable now or in the foreseeable future. Even with an expanding economy and swelling revenues, it would be a doubtful proposition politically, but given tightly restricted or shrinking welfare and education budgets, it is probable that no political party could successfully seek a mandate for such vast capital expenditure. The only approach that seems prudent in present circumstances is to increase expenditure modestly to meet the worst features of dilapidation, and to provide accommodation at least sufficient to maintain the system at its present capacity with, possibly, a slight expansion. Alongside this, however, a major effort must be made to bring demands upon the criminal justice system into line with the available resources.

In keeping with this strategy, the present government has shown itself willing to embark on a program of modest expansion, refurbishment, and replacement. An experiment whereby every third cell is converted into sanitary facilities for the two adjoining cells has been started in several of the Victorian prisons, while in some of the postwar prisons electrical unlocking has been introduced, to allow nighttime access to lavatories. The problem with both these approaches, apart from cost, is that the work takes a long time to complete, causes complications in the daily routine of establishments while work is in progress, and will take out of use at least 10 percent of accommodation in the already crowded Victorian prisons.[10]

Some accommodation has already passed beyond the point where it would be economical to attempt refurbishment, and that, together with the expansion in population, requires that there be some program of new building. Nevertheless, the Prison Department has given priority to redevelopment and refurbishment. Although the general plan is to provide 11,700 new or refurbished places by the end of the decade, there is much uncertainty as to the impact this will have on overcrowding, since the rate of decay or mishap to existing stock is uncertain, as are the trend in crime rates and the reactions of Parliament and the courts. Neither can it be said to what extent successive governments will continue the program of capital funding (and in the past there has been much fluctuation).[11] Yet another imponderable is the changing nature of the prison population, which, when combined with the long period between prison planning and completion, may make finished accommodation unsuitable for current needs.[12] To meet these difficulties, the Prison Department now plans for adaptable new establishments:

we try to invest in institutions which will be of a sufficiently high flexibility to cope with the pressure in the system, and which will be all purpose in the sense that if necessary at a later stage and before they are commissioned they can be used for other purposes.[13]:

Making Better Use of Resources

Siting of new prisons. Besides seeking to plan for adaptable types of new prisons, a major concern of Prison Department planners is to build in locations in which running costs, and the expenses of other criminal justice agencies, will be as low as possible. City-center land is extremely expensive, of course, and since (so far) no skyscraper prisons have been built in Britain, the current land requirement for a new prison is 20 acres.[14] The only urban areas where building on such a scale could be contemplated would be redevelopment sites such as derelict dockland, and even there expenses are high, as are opportunity costs. The result of this familiar problem is that although one-third of all reported crime in the United Kingdom occurs in the London metropolitan police district, there is a chronic shortage of prison accommodation there; many defendants have to be produced for the courts from prisons outside the area; and sentenced prisoners (other than those serving short sentences) must usually expect to spend some or all of their sentence at some distance from their family, friends, probation officers, and prospective employers. For the public purse, there are all the considerable expenses of ferrying prisoners around, as well as the additional staffing costs and social problems of maintaining prisons in out-of-the-way, relatively isolated locations. The recent report by the Home Affairs Committee emphasized the need for coordination in planning new courts and the prisons that will serve them, as well as the general desirability of providing more urban locations.[15]

Escorts. A related consideration is the extent to which prisoner escorts may be coordinated in order to reduce expense as far as possible. In England, court productions (apart from the initial production to the committing magistrate's court) are dealt with by the prisons. This necessarily means that a substantial proportion of the staff of some prisons is engaged in escort and court duty. As a number of prisons may produce to the same courts, there is also duplication in staffing. A study carried out by specialist staff in the London prisons showed that substantial savings could be made by setting up a planning unit that would arrange escorts day by day on the most economical footing.[16] Although England and Wales differ from many other European countries (including Scotland) in giving so much escort responsibility to prison staff, it would seem that planning and coordination might yield savings wherever a number of different institutions or police forces make frequent productions to the same courts. Elsewhere, we have suggested that thought might be given to the provision of a separate escort service, a portion or all of which might be privatized.[17]

Security classification. Another means of making better use of resources is to allocate prisoners more efficiently to the different levels of security. The average weekly cost of keeping a person in prison in England in 1984-85 was $358, but this obscures the differences between security levels.[18] At the top end of the scale, the average weekly cost in a dispersal prison (maximum security) was $635. In closed training prisons, the figure was $675; in local prisons and remand centers (also closed, but providing little in the way of work, training, or educational programs), it was $337. Costs in open prisons (minimum security) came a long way below these, at $230 per week. Not only are there great savings in running costs, but the capital investment for open prisons is comparatively modest.

Over the last 20 years there have been several swings in policy regarding the use of open prisons. For a time in the early 1970s, the English prison population appeared to have stabilized. The introduction of a greater range of noncustodial penalities at that time also reduced the supply of prisoners thitherto thought suitable for minimum security, and lent weight to the belief that a person who could be trusted in open conditions could be trusted to get on with his life outside, and should therefore be subject to a noncustodial penalty. In 1978 a Parliamentary Select Committee[19] drew attention to the underoccupancy of open prisons and argued that, notwithstanding diversion through parole and noncustodial penalties, the open prisons, with their low costs and more relaxed and humane conditions, could make a substantial contribution to the prison service. The general tone of the government's response to the Expenditure Committee's recommendation was cool.[20] The burgeoning prison population and the need to find rapid means to reduce pressure on the closed prisons have since encouraged some wiser second thoughts. The *Fourth Report* of the Home Affairs Committee concluded that there was scope for increasing the use of open prisons for men.[21]

Attempts to use the expensive commodity of security should not be restricted merely to a consideration of open prisons. There are different levels of security among closed prisons, and even within prisons there are various zones of security. Because high security is connected with intensive staffing, electronic surveillance, and high-specification plant, costs (both capital and current) are quite high. A prudent and economical use of resources would require, therefore, that prisoners not be given a higher, more expensive security rating than they actually require.

The Home Affairs Committee inquired whether it would be possible to make some savings by more precise security classification and allocation procedures. The committee found that there was little hard information on this subject. Certain groups of staff considered that security levels could be relaxed for some prisoners, while the home secretary was doubtful about whether much could or ought to be done to relax levels of security. On the lack of tangible information on this subject, the committee observed that

apart from the extreme case, there must be a good deal of subjectivity of judgement in the security classification of prisoners. Some of that subjectivity derives from the experience and professional intuition of prison staff; some part of it cannot but be influenced by the consideration that an error in the direction of under-secure classification would, in the event of an absconding or escape, be productive of much criticism both of the service and the staff concerned in the classification decisions.[22]

The committee thought that it was understandable, and to some extent in the public interest, that the prison service should be overcautious in matters of security classification. However, it also suggested that there might possibly be some relaxation in security classification procedures without an increased risk to the public.[23]

An internal review of the problems of security and control in English prisons has also been carried out and reported.[24] The Control Review Committee, as it is called, now recommends a significant shift in the policy of holding category A (high-security) prisoners in dispersal prisons.[25] Impressed by the American experience of new-generation prison designs, which appear to avoid many of the dangers hitherto perceived in the concentration of maximum-security prisoners in one super-security prison, the Control Review Committee urged that the introduction of such new-generation prisons in England and Wales be considered. In December 1985 a full report with plans was published by the Home Office so that all might see what was under consideration.[26]

A change in the policy of dispersing maximum-security prisoners would necessitate a review of the procedures governing the security classification of prisoners. These far-reaching proposals have been welcomed by some prison staff, officials, and ministers, and are seen as providing the Home Office with a positive agenda for action. Since the publication of the Control Review Committee report, it has become clear that the implementation of these proposals will have a domino effect and "ultimately permeate the whole prison system" in a beneficial way.[27]

However, there has also been adverse comment. The Prison Officers' Association (which represents the uniformed staff of the English prisons) has described the proposals as "ill-conceived, woolly-headed and downright dangerous."[28] Prison reform organizations have also expressed their reservations, and point out that the new generation of "high-tech" U.S. prisons has not been entirely successful either in preventing escapes or in developing humane and constructive regimes.

We believe that this development shows clearly that the English prison system is likely to develop along divided lines, since one

regime and set of arrangements will prevail for high-security prisoners and those who present serious control problems, while a different one will apply to the rest of the prison population. We have
argued elsewhere that one way to effect this reorganization would
be to restore the local prisons (what in America would be called
jails) to local management, as was the arrangement before they were
brought under central government control in 1878.[29] The advantages
we see in this would be that these local prisons, which hold 40
percent of the prison population, would come under the control of
local management boards, representing the relevant local interests
in criminal justice administration.

Fiscal constraints and legal and administrative pressures in the
United States have also led to an increased interest in classification.
Solomon and Baird, in an article generally castigating past classification research, note that financial pressures have forced several
penal services to reconsider their classification procedures, and that
"almost without exception, these jurisdictions have found that their
populations were overclassified to a significant degree and that construction costs could be considerably reduced by placing more inmates in less secure (and less costly) environments."[30] This point is
bolstered by an interesting article by Alexander, in the same volume,
dealing with the classification practices of the New York State Department of Correctional Services, from which it would appear that
population pressures have played a significant part in the development and application of classification tests, and that such tests
have proved to be reasonably successful.[31] It is clear that further
progress can be made in this field, and that improved classification
procedures offer considerable scope for an economical use of resources while at the same time maintaining public protection and
avoiding political controversy. Two points must be made, however:
tests, no matter how sophisticated, are only as reliable as the information with which they are fed; and instruments and procedures
should be well understood by those who use their results to make
decisions, if they are to be utilized fully.[32]

Pretrial prisoners. Remand prisoners (as pretrial detainees are
called in England) accounted for nearly 23 percent of the average
daily population of English prisons in 1984-85: 8,861 persons out of
43,618.[33] Following the experience of certain continental and U.S.
jurisdictions, a new Bail Act was introduced in England in 1976. In

essence, this act created a presumption in favor of bail-granting decisions. Despite the new measure, the 1979 Committee of Inquiry into the United Kingdom Prison Services (May Committee) observed that as many as 44 percent of those remanded in custody did not subsequently receive a sentence of immediate imprisonment, and that it was a matter of continuing concern that "remand periods in England and Wales are frequently excessively long and have generally been increasing."[34] Thus, although there had been a 19 percent decrease in the annual number remanded in custody between 1975 and 1979 (much of which would seem to have been due to the working of the Bail Act), there had been a 9 percent increase in the average daily population of remand prisoners over the same period, because of lengthening periods of remand. That there was scope for reducing the amount of time taken by the courts to deal with the cases was shown by the differences between courts in different areas.[35]

In the granting of bail, a balance must be struck between the interests of justice and the safety of the community and witnesses on the one hand, and, on the other, the right of defendants to be protected from the hardship of an unnecessary custodial remand. There seems to be a fair measure of agreement that the 1976 Bail Act has met these different interests in a reasonable manner, and that not much scope remains for a further granting of bail.[36] The Home Office announced in 1985 a limited experiment whereby a time limit would apply to prosecutions (as has existed in Scotland for many years) so as to ensure speedy trial. When this experiment has been evaluated, it may be possible to introduce such a speedy trial law to apply throughout England and Wales.

Two further steps have been suggested that might prove useful in ensuring a modest expansion in noncustodial remands: one could be achieved at little cost, whereas the other would involve much the same costs as imprisonment, but could be justified as costing no more and as being more humane.

The first of these measures involves a better provision of noncustodial facilities for the preparation of social inquiry, psychiatric, and medical reports, and also persuading the courts to make fuller use of them. In 1975 the Home Office issued a circular to the courts urging them to draw up lists of doctors and psychiatrists willing to undertake court work, in order to reduce the necessity of remanding defendants in custody. Although this produced some response, a later Parliamentary Select Committee inquiring into the problems connected with women and the penal system was told that much remained to be done: the courts seemed almost reflexively to remand for medical and psychiatric reports, and in many cases a noncustodial remand would have served just as well.[37]

Another type of person is remanded in custody not because of apprehension about the seriousness of the offenses he might commit, but because of fears of absconding. These are people whose drifting and rather rootless life-styles make them unattractive prospects for bail.[38] For some of this group, there is no alternative but a custodial remand; for others, however, it might prove possible to decrease further the use of imprisonment. This might be done by means of conditional bail, requiring residence (the terms of which could be variously specified) at a bail hostel. In England such hostels are sometimes run by the Probation and Aftercare Service, elsewhere by voluntary organizations. The hostels need not be of an elaborate nature, but obviously supervision is necessary, for which purpose a resident staff of at least three persons would be required. The hostel, to be an economical alternative to a custodial remand, would need to accommodate continuously a sufficient number of persons to keep per capita costs low; for this reason, bail hostels are probably most suitable for larger towns and cities where the volume of court business is sufficient to keep up a steady flow of clients. The possibility of involving a voluntary organization, albeit with the support of grants to cover some capital and most current expenditure, is a major attraction of the bail hostel for criminal justice administration and funding. At the same time, it must be acknowledged that bail hostels can be expected to make only a fairly marginal impact upon the problems under discussion; in 1979 there were only about 350 bail hostel places available in England, and no further great expansion was forecast.[39]

Diverting from Custody

As in America, there has been mounting pressure in England and Wales to divert offenders from custody. The search for alternatives was already well under way when the matter was investigated by the House of Commons Expenditure Committee in 1977-78. That committee's report identified several groups of offenders who are presently more often than not incarcerated, but for whom society should provide an alternative means of disposal for the courts' use.[40] These groups were as follows: (1) petty inadequate offenders; (2) mentally disordered offenders; (3) fine defaulters; and (4) drunks.

Petty inadequate offenders. There is widespread agreement about the futility of sending petty inadequate offenders to prison. Their crimes constitute more of a nuisance than a menace; they reoffend frequently, so one can say they do not learn from experience; and society is put to a great deal of trouble and expense to no purpose. The Home Office has admitted that "if this group could be removed from the prison system it would have a significant impact upon the size of the prison population."[41] There is some difficulty, however, in identifying precisely who these people are. Estimates as to the number of such offenders admitted to prison or currently imprisoned vary widely,[42] and few solutions have been found to alleviate the problem.

Such offenders usually do not have the means to pay a fine and would be unlikely to turn up for community service if such an order were made. Probation does not seem to be indicated, as they might not respond and as probation resources must be husbanded for more serious and difficult cases. A suspended sentence or partly suspended sentence would mean very little to such offenders. A requirement to reside in a hostel might not be practical, as such offenders might either decamp or abuse the facilities and be required to leave. Any way you look at it, the problem seems insoluble, and prison appears to be the only way to cope, notwithstanding that in many cases it is not the first time for the offender to be imprisoned. Policing and controlling the petty, inadequate, rootless, and (usually) propertyless offender remind us of the paucity of sanctions that may be imposed with any effect upon the most marginal members of our society. Perhaps halfway houses along American lines, with overnight and weekend detention, should be tried. There has been no such experiment in England and Wales, and this is one respect in which these countries could benefit from American experience.

Mentally disordered offenders. Over the years there have been repeated denunciations of the practice of keeping the mentally disordered in prison. Many such offenders are not identified by the courts as suitable for a mental hospital order, and they wind up in prison. Some develop their mental illness while in prison, and every year a handful of the most florid and dangerous cases are transferred to secure mental hospitals (known in England and Wales as "special hospitals"). Again, as with petty inadequate offenders, estimates vary concerning the number of prisoners who are suffering from mental disorders including severe subnormality. Most commentators accept that some thousands of prisoners are so affected, although figures supplied by prison medical staff show a much lower number.

The main difficulty arises from the unwillingness of the mental hospitals forming part of the National Health Service to accept transfers from prisoner to patient status. Medical officers and nursing staff appear to be extremely reluctant to take on such patients, who are likely to be troublesome and difficult to manage.[43] One solution that has long been planned is the construction of a number of secure units attached to mental hospitals on a regional basis. However, progress in establishing such units has been minimal. The result is that the prison service has had to provide for such offenders from its own scant resources. One psychiatric prison hospital (Grendon) exists with room for some 200 adult male offenders and 70 young adult male prisoners serving sentences of youth custody. No separate psychiatric prison exists for female offenders, who have to be detained in Holloway prison, London, or elsewhere in the women's prisons. Instances of suicide, self-mutilation, and attacks on women staff and other prisoners have led to an internal inquiry conducted by the Prison Department, but so far there has been little sign of its recommendations being implemented. An advisory group has also reviewed the therapeutic regime of Grendon and made useful recommendations. Opened in 1962, Grendon has been run as a group of therapeutic communities.[44] Research findings have shown a disappointing degree of success even though the population is a highly selected one, consisting only of prisoners thought amenable to the treatment program.

Fine defaulters, maintenance defaulters. Prison is still the last resort for convicted offenders who refuse to pay the fines imposed upon them, and for other civil debtors such as those who are in default over maintenance orders to spouses. There is little doubt that this means of collecting the monies due is quite effective. So far no other means more effective has been devised to take its place.

Suggestions have been made for extending the procedure whereby earnings for wages may be "attached" by court order so that deductions are made by the employer. The present procedure (which can be used for maintenance orders) is cumbersome and not altogether effective. Furthermore, it is of no use when the offender is unemployed or in casual employment rather than in a regular job. Requiring fine defaulters to undertake community service has so far been resisted by the probation service, although the Home Office already has the power to introduce it. The probation service apparently fears that offenders who are so feckless as not to pay their fines may be an unreliable labor force when it comes to being organized for community service.

The extent to which the fine has come to be used as a penalty in England and Wales since World War II is a remarkable feature of the modern English criminal justice system. Almost 90 percent of those sentenced for nonindictable (equivalent to misdemeanor) non-motoring offenses are fined, and about 50 percent of those sentenced for indictable (roughly equivalent to felony) offenses. The fine has proved to be very successful, since well over 90 percent of those fined pay up without further sentence. Nevertheless, improvements in the efficiency of the fine system are overdue. The Home Office has resisted pressure to follow the Swedish "day fine" system, which fixes the amount of the fine in relation to the wage or salary of the offender, on a calculation of daily earnings. The system has great merits, but there are difficulties with introducing it into a country as anarchic as Britain where no accessible central records of earnings exist.

Drunks. Many people are in prison because of offenses of public drunkenness. Although since the 1977 Criminal Law Act the courts may no longer sentence these people directly to imprisonment, drunks find their way to prison indirectly for nonpayment of the fines imposed upon them. No solution to this problem has yet been found. Drunks compose only a small part of the average daily population of prisons, but they make up a substantial portion of the annual receptions into custody, with all the concomitant expense and trouble that involves. In 1984 1,054 males were received into prison in default of payment of a fine imposed for drunkenness. This figure may be compared with that for 1974 (2,217), and we can see evidence of a substantial drop in prison commitments for drunkenness. The same seems to be the case for females, where the decline (from 80 received into prison in connection with drunkenness in 1974 to 25 in 1984) is even more dramatic.[45]

The 1972 Criminal Justice Act, section 34, provided police with the power to take the drunken offender to a medical treatment center instead of instituting a prosecution. This provision was enacted at a time when it was thought desirable to develop a series of detoxification centers to be run in connection with the National Health Service. The development of these centers proved tardy, and there were many hesitations and difficulties. Some probation services developed such facilities, but there is no enthusiasm for such provisions within the hospital service, where other developments appear more attractive and urgent (including recently increasing the provisions for those suffering from drug addiction).

There has been no inclination to provide the more simple overnight tank to which people might be taken simply to dry out. Yet there is undoubtedly a substantial population of males and females sleeping in public places even in the coldest months, and many of these have an alcohol problem that accounts for their destitution. Such people are beyond the reach of the penal system, and indeed the criminal sanction is meaningless because it is so ineffective. It may have to be left to the private sector, by which we mean here the idealism of voluntary agencies, to devise means for dealing with the homeless, of whom a large proportion owe their predicament to alcohol. The recently announced initiative sponsored by H.R.H. the Prince of Wales is to be welcomed in this connection.

Sentencing Reform

Diversion measures have an effect on the number of persons sent to custody. Most knowledgeable commentators would agree that the best prospect for reducing the prison population lies with reducing sentence length as well as the number of commitments. The difficulty is how to achieve this goal when so many factors point in the opposite direction. The rise in crime,[46] including violence, inevitably leads to more prison committals, and the public concern about punishing those who rob, rape, and sexually abuse children is constantly paraded in the media, as though these types of crime were characteristic of all crime. Sentencing takes place against a backdrop of irrationality and powerful emotive demands for more, not less, in the way of punishment. Home Office statistics show an increase in the number of offenders sentenced to immediate imprisonment over the last decade. The increase is steeper in the magistrates' courts than in the Crown courts (where serious offenses are tried, with a jury trial in cases of pleas of not guilty),[47] although there has been some decline in response to the more recent initiatives described below.

Several attempts to influence sentencing choices have been made in recent years in England and Wales. These have emanated from the executive and the judiciary, but so far legislative intervention has been abjured. One effort emanated from the Home Office's Advisory Council on the Penal System. In its two reports, the *Interim Report: The Length of Prison Sentences* (1977) and the major review *Sentences of Imprisonment: A Review of Maximum Penalties* (1978), the advisory council set out its views that sentences were in general too long, and that when courts decided to sentence an offender to immediate imprisonment, they should always pause to consider whether a shorter sentence might not serve equally well.[48] The *Maximum Penalties* report outlined a scheme whereby courts choosing normal sentences would be subject to a downward revision of the maximum penalties available to them; in some cases this would have involved a substantial reduction. Exceptional cases could still be given sentences in excess of the normal maximum, but in that event certain safeguards would apply, such as requiring the court to give reasons for the choice, and automatic review. This initiative failed because the device adopted to fix the new range of normal sentences[49] was too artificial and involved some dramatic and extremely controversial reductions for "normal" cases, such as reducing the maximum penalty for rape from life imprisonment to seven years' imprisonment. It is regrettable that nothing came of this report, even though it contained many interesting and sensible recommendations.

Nothing came either from a Home Office attempt to provide by law for automatic parole for prison sentences of up to three years. This was advanced in the context of the success of parole in England and Wales, and the fact that it had developed to the point that two out of three prisoners eligible for parole had been granted early release on a parole license. It was thought that there would be a substantial gain in making parole automatic for sentences of up to three years; many more prison places would become available as a result. However, the judges felt very strongly opposed to these proposals, and there was a real fear that this would lead to a compensatory increase in sentences if the proposals went through. So they were dropped. Instead, there is provided to the Home Secretary an emergency power to release certain limited categories of prisoner in the event of some disaster such as fire or prison riot rendering prison accommodation unserviceable. The partly suspended sentence was also introduced.

There remain the imprecations from on high of the Lord Chancellor (responsible minister for the judiciary and the lay magistrates) and the Lord Chief Justice, who have continued to preach the gospel of shorter sentences, but without avail. One of the first acts of the new Lord Chief Justice on appointment in 1980 was to utter a series of carefully weighed pronouncements, in the cases of *Upton* and *Bibi*,[50] about the need for courts to make prison sentences for non-violent offenders as short as possible. "Sentencing judges," said Lord Lane, "should appreciate that overcrowding in many penal establishments in this country was such that a prison sentence, however short, was a very unpleasant experience indeed for inmates."

It would seem that there is little disposition on the part of the Home Office to go further than this and ask Parliament to intervene to enforce shorter (or longer) sentences. Some of these matters are addressed in the white paper published in March 1986 announcing the Home Office's plans for legislation during 1986-87. It is now proposed to give statutory recognition to the practice of the Lord Chief Justice in the court of appeal publishing sentencing guidelines, and it is also proposed to make these guidelines more accessible and comprehensive.[51] The experience with the proposals for automatic parole provides a cautionary tale. England may be forced to consider amending the law in other ways, however. For example, there is some pressure in favor of adopting minimum sentences or fixed sentences. This usually arises in connection with expressions of deep concern about the inadequacy of sentences passed in some sensational trial where media attention has been engaged. It should be understood that the prosecution has no means in English law to test the appropriateness of the sentences so chosen, by means of an appeal for a heavier sentence.

One suggestion, emanating from Andrew Ashworth,[52] is that there should be a Sentencing Advisory Council to examine and consider the issues referred to it, and to issue recommendations that might well be embodied in the form of "practice directions" published widely and likely to be obediently followed by the courts. It might be possible by this means to develop a more rational and coherent response to the vexed questions about sentencing that arise from time to time.

A wider proposal was made by the Home Affairs Committee of the House of Commons in its *Fourth Report*. That was to establish a National Criminal Policy Committee whose tasks would be "to construct a comprehensive criminal policy in the light of the most modern administrative knowledge and research findings."[53] The present government declined to accept this recommendation, but in many political, official, and academic circles it is accepted that in one form or another an attempt will have to be made to provide a structural means for planning and coordinating criminal justice policymaking and administration. The recent collection of papers issued by the Home Office Research and Planning Unit, entitled *Managing Criminal Justice*,[54] shows the way the wind is blowing. Of special interest to British observers will be the initiative emanating from the National Institute of Corrections supported by the Edna McConnell Clark Foundation[55] to assist selected states in criminal justice planning and to evaluate that process.

One might add that interest in sentencing guidelines such as those adopted in Minnesota and several U.S. jurisdictions has been slight in Britain. This also applies to other variants of sentencing reform such as presumptive sentences and the like. The results seem not to have been altogether satisfactory. Illiberal and frequently irrational forces have been unleashed in the legislatures, and pressure on prisons has increased to an explosive point as a result of the sentences now being handed down. The furthest Britain has been prepared to go is to recognize the need for guideline judgments on certain selected sentencing questions issued by the Lord Chief Justice with all the authority of the appeal court, and if the recent white paper is adopted with statutory recognition, as has already been mentioned. There may also be something to be said for routinely supplying to the courts a report on the prison resource implications of any sentencing choice made. At the end of the day, however,

Britain still prefers to adhere to its idiosyncratic highly discretionary and loosely structured sentencing procedure and practice.

CONCLUSIONS

In the compass of this chapter it has been possible only to sketch the more important problems and policy issues of recent years. There are many similarities between England and the United States in terms of their common legal heritage and constitutional traditions, and also in the degree of urbanization and social conflict experienced in modern times, when criminal justice has, sadly, become a growth industry on both sides of the Atlantic. One important circumstance favors the United States in the making of criminal justice policy— its extremely decentralized system of lawmaking and law enforcement, which enables experiment and initiative to proceed more easily than in England and Wales. Poor examples can be avoided, while positive and productive ones might be imitated, all with more speed in trial and error.

In this spirit, the following aspects of criminal justice policy and administration might bear consideration by the American reader:

1. The rate of incarceration in England and Wales is much lower than that in the United States: 90 per 100,000 (combined prisons and jails) compared with 270 per 100,000. Given that England and the United States are both industrialized countries with common legal and cultural features, this would suggest that some aspects of English criminal justice policy might profitably be applied to the United States.

2. There is a much stronger tradition in England and Wales of using the fine as a response to both lesser and more serious criminal offenses (although in both countries, gross criminal behavior will attract a sentence of imprisonment). The rate of fine collection is very high, and although England does not have the extra enforcement problems arising from a federal system of administration, neither does it have the highly centralized means that permit other European countries to have easy government access to private earnings.

3. There should be parsimony in the use of imprisonment, and this can be achieved in full consonance with public safety, if more rational means are employed to fix the length of sentences and to decide on the use of levels of security within the prison system.

4. Politics and criminal justice make bad bedfellows. Where possible, criminal justice policymaking should proceed in a noncontroversial manner. Situations should be avoided that pit the powers of the legislature against the authority of the judiciary. It is better to encourage policy leadership within judicial circles.

5. Although the scope for diversion from custody may not be as great now as it was in earlier years, there remain various groups of nuisance offenders for whom, with no great trouble, alternative means of disposal might and should be found.

6. In its promulgation and enforcement, the common law tends to a much more segmented system of administration than the civil law of continental Europe and other parts of the world. This is a heritage in which we take historical and constitutional pride, since it reflects (among other things) a series of determined stands for individual liberty. At the same time, the disadvantages of such an arrangement must be recognized; and without doing violence to the fabric of our traditions, more effective means must be found to promote coordination. Without the various criminal justice agencies and bodies working together to a much greater extent than at present, there can be little effective criminal justice policy, and change will always tend to follow and to engender crisis.

NOTES

1. The jails in England and Wales have been under central government (as distinct from county) control since 1878. The term "prison" therefore includes "jail." Although some English prisons specialize in providing custody for long-term prisoners only, many prisons are omnibus institutions that hold a variety of inmates, from pretrial to medium-and even long-term prisoners. The different classes of prisoners are, however, held in separate wings or blocks of the prison.

2. Speech of Home Secretary, Prison Reform Trust, April 10, 1986.

3. Home Office, *Report on the Work of the Prison Department 1984/85*, Cmnd. 9699 (London: HMSO, 1985), p. 10.

4. House of Commons, *Fourth Report from the Home Affairs Committee, Evidence*, Session 1980/81 HC 412/i and ii, *The Prison Service* (London: HMSO), p. 47. For some types of refurbishment, a loss of 10 percent of accommodation is necessary. See the section "Providing Greater Resources?" later in this chapter.

5. Home Office, *Report on the Work of the Prison Department 1981* (London), p. 3.

6. *Fourth Report from the Home Affairs Committee, Evidence*, p. 17.

7. House of Commons, *Fifteenth Report from the Expenditure Com-*

mittee (*Education, Arts and Home Office Sub-Committee*), *Evidence,* HC 62/I (London: HMSO, 1978), p. 238.

8. Ibid., *Report,* pp. 1, li, passim.

9. Ibid., *Report,* p. 25.

10. See *Report on the Work of the Prison Department 1981,* pp. 14–15, for a fuller discussion of these schemes.

11. See Home Office, *Statistics of the Criminal Justice System, England and Wales, 1968–78* (London: HMSO, 1979), p. 74.

12. Because of planning (zoning) laws, the need to coordinate construction activities in an already crowded system, and the normal delays due to professional consultation and to construction, the time scale for new prisons from planning to completion is around 10 years, and even on minor projects is rarely less than four years. This would seem to be an area where English administrators could profitably study American procedures, which typically result in a much shorter time span between drawing-board and occupation.

13. *Fourth Report from the Home Affairs Committee, Evidence,* p. 23.

14. Ibid., *Evidence,* Q. 71, p. 19.

15. Ibid., *Report,* p. xxviii.

16. Ibid., *Report;* Ibid., *Evidence,* pp. 92–93.

17. Sean McConville and Eryl Hall Williams, *Crime and Punishment: A Radical Rethink* (London: Tawney Society, 1986). However, a recent Home Office statement indicated that no plans for the privatization of English prisons were then under consideration; see *The Times* (London), February 18, 1986.

18. English prisoners are given one of four security classification designations. Category A are those who are a great risk to public safety, and who must be subject to the maximum level of security; category B are those for whom escape must be made extremely difficult (and these are the majority of closed-prison inmates); category C cannot be trusted in open conditions, but are unlikely to try to escape; and category D can be trusted in open conditions. Some C and D prisoners are kept in B prisons to form outside working parties. Category A, of whom there are only a few hundred, are kept in high-security dispersal prisons, where they are a small minority among B prisoners.

19. *Fifteenth Report from the Expenditure Committee, Report,* pp. lviii–lx.

20. Home Office, *The Reduction of Pressure on the Prison System: Observations on the Fifteenth Report from the Expenditure Committee,* Cmnd. 7948 (London: HMSO, 1980), pp. 15–17.

21. *Fourth Report from the Home Affairs Committee, Report,* p. xli.

22. Ibid., *Report,* p. xl.

23. Ibid., *Report.*

24. Home Office, *Managing the Long-Term Prison System*, Report of the Control Review Committee (London: HMSO, 1984).

25. Dispersal prisons are maximum-security prisons to which the few hundred category A prisoners are dispersed, as distinct from being concentrated in one or two super-security institutions. The dispersal prisons mainly hold category B prisoners, and the category A inmates are subject to special restrictions.

26. Home Office, *New Directions in Prison Design*, Report of the Home Office Working Party on American New Generation Prisons (1985).

27. *Report on the Work of the Prison Department 1984/85.*

28. *The Daily Telegraph*, May 24, 1985.

29. McConville and Williams, *Crime and Punishment.*

30. Larry Solomon and S. Christopher Baird, "Classification: Past Failures, Future Potential," in American Correctional Association, *Classification as a Management Tool: Theories and Models for Decision Makers* (College Park, MD: American Correctional Association, 1982), quoted from a draft, Sorin Research Institute, Cooperstown, NY, 1982, p. 8.

31. Jack Alexander, "Security Classification in New York State," in ibid., pp. 93ff.

32. Stephen D. Gottfredson and Don M. Gottfredson, "Screening for Risk: A Comparison of Methods," in ibid., p. 63.

33. See *Report on the Work of the Prison Department 1984/85*, p. 9.

34. Home Office, *Committee of Inquiry into the United Kingdom Prison Services*, Cmnd. 7673 (London: HMSO, 1979), para. 3.66.

35. Whereas on the North Eastern circuit the average time spent awaiting trial was 10.4 weeks for the quarter ending September 1979, for London it was 30.9 weeks. This difference could not be explained either by the nature of the cases or by the speed at which material could be put to juries of the two circuits (see *Fourth Report from the Home Affairs Committee, Report*, p. xxv).

36. Nevertheless, there should almost certainly be benefits in the introduction of a more *systematic* screening for bail in England and Wales, along the lines of a number of pretrial release schemes that now operate in various jurisdictions in the United States. The Home Office has been actively promoting research along these lines in recent years.

37. See *Minutes of Evidence Taken before the Expenditure Committee (Education, Arts and Home Office Sub-Committee) 4th December, 1978*, p. 36.

38. This would also seem to be the case in many jurisdictions in the United States. The procedures for granting bail in Maryland, for example (under Maryland District Rule 721 and ss. 616 1/2 and 638 of the Annotated Code of Maryland), require that in determining the type of release that

will best ensure the defendant's appearance (custody, conditional release, or the posting of bond), the court consider, among other things, family ties, employment, and length of residence in the community; see Martin D. Sorin, "Bail Crime and Pretrial Release in Baltimore, Maryland," p. 10.

39. *Committee of Inquiry into the United Kingdom Prison Services, Report*, para. 3.66.

40. *Fifteenth Report from the Expenditure Committee.*

41. Home Office, *A Review of Criminal Justice Policy 1976* (London: HMSO, 1977), pp. 7–8.

42. S. Fairhead, *Persistent Petty Offenders*, Home Office Research Study no. 66 (London: HMSO, 1981), found that there were about 1,700 "petty inadequate offenders" in English prisons, about 4 percent of the prison population. The British Association of Social Work estimated 10,000 such prisoners in its evidence to the House of Commons Expenditure Committee in 1978 (*Minutes of Evidence Taken before the Expenditure Committee*, pp. 532–33).

43. *Fifteenth Report from the Expenditure Committee*, pp. xxxix–xl, paras. 74–77.

44. *Report on the Work of the Prison Department 1984/85*, p. 43, para. 131, and p. 69, para. 285.

45. Home Office, *Criminal Statistics (England and Wales) 1984*, Cmnd. 9622 (London: HMSO), 1985, table 7.2, pp. 94, 95.

46. England and Wales have not enjoyed the fortunate reduction in reported crime experienced by U.S. jurisdictions over the last four years.

47. *Criminal Statistics (England and Wales) 1984*, pp. 137–38.

48. Home Office, Advisory Council on the Penal System, *Interim Report: The Length of Prison Sentences* (London: HMSO, 1977), and *Sentences of Imprisonment: A Review of Maximum Penalties* (London: HMSO, 1978).

49. The recommendation was to fix the new maximum sentence permitted by law at the point below which 90 percent of the cases decided in the past three years fell.

50. *Upton* (1980), 71 Cr. App. Rep. 102; *Bibi* (1980), 71 Cr. App. Rep. 360.

51. Home Office, *Criminal Justice: Plans for Legislation*, Cmnd. 9658 (London: HMSO, 1986).

52. Andrew Ashworth, *Sentencing and Penal Policy* (Oxford: Clarendon Press, 1983), p. 447.

53. *Fourth Report from the Home Affairs Committee*, p. xlvi.

54. Home Office, *Managing Criminal Justice*, ed. David Moxon (London: HMSO, 1985).

55. As outlined in Robert K. Yin and Betsy Lindsay, *Planning for Action: Phase I of the Prison Overcrowding Project* (Washington, DC: The Case Study Institute, 1982).

7 The Problem of Crowding: A System Out of Control

DON M. GOTTFREDSON

Our legislative and sentencing practices, in relation to resources, are out of control. This is shown by the problem of crowding in jails and prisons that provides the focus for the discussions in this book on the nation's correctional crisis.

There are now more than two-thirds of a million persons in our country in jail or prison.[1] Soon there will be half a million in prison alone. Two-thirds are confined in less than 60 square feet of floor space[2] (the American Correctional Association's minimum standard).[3] In many states, the courts have found that the treatment of offenders is unconstitutional, that is, in violation of the First, Eighth, or Fourteenth Amendments. Usually, the violation has been related to crowding.

The purpose of this chapter is to show how the criminal justice decision processes can be brought back into control and thereby help alleviate this serious national problem. At the same time, the decision can be made more fairly.

THE NEED FOR A RATIONAL MANAGEMENT SYSTEM

The solution requires policy models for the decisions at various steps in the criminal justice process. These models include specific

Author's note: Adapted from a presentation at The Johns Hopkins University Symposium on Prison Crowding March 22, 1984.

guidelines for the decisions that most closely affect jail and prison populations. They must be formulated and implemented in such a way that the consequences of the policy, or of changes in it, for jail and prison populations can be estimated accurately and taken into account in assessments of the desirability of the policy. They require monitoring, to determine whether the policy is being followed and whether it is working as intended by those responsible for it. The guidelines that are a central part of the policy require classifications of persons accused or convicted of crimes.

The general problems surrounding criminal justice decisions include issues of ethics and values as well as scientific and management concerns, but they will be little discussed in this chapter. That omission is made despite the importance of the issues of the choice of purposes and their ethical foundations—issues that are fundamental to any serious examination of these decisions—since they are not critical to the position taken on a method for decision policy and the management of its implementation. This position, with one exception, is atheoretical in respect to the purposes of bail, sentencing, and corrections that provide the context for the criminal justice decisions discussed. The exception is that a high value is placed on fairness and the reduction of disparities in decisions for unknown or unspecified reasons or for reasons that may be acknowledged to be illegitimate.

THE IMPORTANCE OF CLASSIFICATION

Problems of the classification of offenders are central to all criminal justice decision making. The determinations of magistrates about bail or release of an accused person, of judges deciding on a sentence for one who has been convicted of a crime, of correctional administrators determining treatment placements or fixing the degree of custody to be required for an inmate, or of paroling authorities deciding whether or when to release an inmate to parole supervision—all rely on some method of classification of persons.[4] Similarly, administrators of probation or parole supervision programs classify offenders for placement in the type of program thought most likely to meet both offender needs and societal protection.

Since decisions about accused persons or convicted offenders are the stuff of the criminal justice system, the classifications of persons on which decisions are based are critical to attempts to reduce the problems of jail and prison crowding. And since the crowding problem cannot be separated, except for discussion, from the ultimate questions about the purposes of sentencing and corrections, it is important to note that all the traditionally argued aims of sentencing and corrections depend critically for their achievement on classification. That is why the model advocated does not depend upon any particular theory of punishment, sentencing, or corrections. It does, however, require for its formulation to result finally in a more clearly articulated conceptualization of those purposes. It requires that a variety of policy and value choices be made distinctly; but the model itself does not dictate them. It is one of the values of the model that these choices must become more clear, open, and explicit.

All major theories or perspectives on sentencing require the classification of persons. Although each person is unique, concepts of fairness as well as effectiveness require that they be grouped in terms of some similarities, with what are believed to be less important differences ignored. In applying retributive or desert theories,[5] offenders must be categorized, in terms of similarities, according to some classification of the seriousness or harm of the transgression, and perhaps of the prior criminal record.[6] Competing utilitarian theories such as those emphasizing deterrence or incapacitation or treatment also require that offenders be classified: which types of offenders will be deterred by what sanctions; which should be incapacitated for the most crime reduction at acceptable costs; what sorts of persons are to be placed in what kinds of programs for rehabilitative aims? The desert theorist claims that what is right is good, the utilitarian that what is good is right,[7] and the two positions are often regarded as unalterably opposed; but both must rely on classification to achieve the purposes desired. That provides the basis for the claim that the methods advocated in this chapter do not depend upon any particular theoretical orientation about sentencing purposes. The exception, although it reflects a value shared by both retributive and utilitarian positions, is that of fairness—of which equity is a part.[8] Thus, in the policy models to be discussed, equity, and hence fairness, is emphasized as well as the reduction of crowding.

THE AIM OF THIS CHAPTER

This chapter advocates a general method of policy definition and implementation, using guidelines that rely on classification to control jail and prison populations.[9] The model, developed out of other motivations, is believed to have a considerable potential for helping to address the crowding problem in an equitable and rational manner. It will be argued that it compares favorably with currently popular competing proposals for the control of crowding.

Examples are chosen to illustrate promising methods of structuring bail, sentencing, prison placement, and parole decision making in a way that can permit the population control sought. They show how more efficient classification methods have improved the decision-making process and suggest the further potential for reducing jail and prison crowding. The illustrations selected represent different positions on the issue of acceptable bases for the person classifications.[10] In bail decisions, the efficient classification of accused persons has been shown to help not only in reducing unwarranted disparities, but also in applying rational standards to ensure appearance for trial.[11] In sentencing, the appropriate classification of offenders has been demonstrated to help similarly in disparity reduction, for a greater degree of fairness, and also to assist in a more rational allocation of offenders in relation to available resources, including prison program spaces.[12] It is that innovative use of the model, in Minnesota, that stimulates hope for its wider applicability in addressing the crowding problem. In paroling decisions, a classification decision model has been used to structure discretionary decision making with an apparent result of substantial decreases in disparities of punishment for similar offenders.[13] Similar methods, when related to capacity constraints, could be used to help reduce crowding in both jails and prisons.

THE MEANING OF CLASSIFICATION

Person classifications may or may not make use of predictions; and although classification is required by the policy control concept, prediction may or may not be used. They should be distinguished. The concept of classification refers to the assignment of persons to groups in such a way that the members are in some way similar and

the groups are different from one another. [14] (This is a different usage
of the term from that common in correctional agencies, where classification usually refers to the assignment of persons to different
programs or to different levels of custodial supervision.) It is important to differentiate the concept of classification from that of
prediction. The concept of prediction refers to two assessments of
persons, separated over time; the first assessment has to do with
any information about the person, the second to some outcome we
would like to forecast—such as recidivism, parole violation, or the
rate of committing robberies. On the basis of the relation between
these two assessments, offenders may be classified according to
expected values of the outcome in new samples. [15] Thus, classification, which may have many purposes, may or may not be used with
a predictive intent. The importance of classification, and sometimes
of predictive classifications, can be seen in the development and
use of guidelines for decision making at the several critical decision
points already mentioned.

ADDRESSING THE CROWDING PROBLEM

Points of potential solutions to crowding have often been referred
to as "front door" or "back door." [16] Generally, front-door solutions
have to do with sentencing (or with legislation regulating that, or
with prosecutorial policy and discretion), while back-door proposals
concern paroling. This is reasonable, since it is clear that any plans
to decrease crowding must address either who is in confinement
now, or who will be confined, or for how long, or combinations of
these sources of crowding. [17] That is, to be successful in reducing
crowding, we must either reduce admissions, shorten sentences,
accelerate releases, or do more than one of these. No matter what
the more *distal* causes of crowding may be, the *proximal* determinants are in legislation, sentencing, and paroling. [18] It should not be
surprising, therefore, if predictions of prison populations are more
accurate when based on indices of these proximal determinants
rather than on such indices as crime rates, unemployment, or demographic items, even if these distal variables are demonstrably
related to the incidence or prevalence of crime. [19] One writer has
referred also to "trap-door" solutions, [20] and we may add at least
one "side-door" program aimed at alleviation of the problem. The

former refers to emergency release procedures to be implemented when crowding reaches some specified level. The latter refers to a reconsideration for release after the offender has already been sent to jail or prison.

There is a good potential for use of decision-making guidelines at each of these points: front door, back door, trap door, and side door. Guidelines of the type advocated not only may improve fairness in the relevant decisions but also help control populations in a more efficient and effective manner.

ESSENTIAL FEATURES OF GUIDELINES

The word "guidelines" means various things to various people, so it is important to indicate the way in which the term is used in this chapter.[21] These are some interrelated, indispensable attributes of the kind of decision policy and procedures advocated:

1. A general policy for decision making has been articulated in explicit terms, within which individual decisions are made.

2. The criteria for decision making are explicitly defined, and so are the specific weights to be given to them.

3. Within the general policy model, guidelines in the form of a chart (matrix or grid) are used in the process of arriving at a particular decision.[22] The most important policy concerns, decided by those responsible for the decision-making policy, are reflected in the dimensions of the grid. In most models, one axis reflects the seriousness of the offense; the other reflects characteristics of the offender. The intersection of the appropriate columns and rows for the two axes gives an expected decision for usual cases possessing the attributes used in the classifications of persons that form the basis for the chart.

4. The guidelines grid is intended to structure the use of discretion but not to eliminate it. There are two ways in which discretionary judgments are required by the decision maker: (1) Some discretion must be exercised within the cells of the two-dimensional grid. For example, a range of sentence durations may be suggested within which a choice may be made. (2) It is not only permitted but expected that the decision maker may sometimes reach a decision that is a departure from (that is, an exception to) the suggested decision outcome.

5. When departures are made, explicit reasons must be given by the de-

cision maker for the exception to the usual decision for offenders or accused persons in the classification that applies.

6. A system of monitoring is established to ensure compliance with the policy and to provide periodic feedback to the authorities responsible for the decision policies, giving the percentage of decisions falling outside each guideline category and the reasons given for these departures.

7. The authorities responsible for the policy may modify the guidelines at any time.

8. The general policy, including the guidelines incorporated within it, is not regarded as a once-and-for-all statement of a "right" policy; rather, the intent and the procedures developed are both designed to facilitate an evolutionary system of policy development changing in response to experience, resultant learning, and social change.

9. The policy in general, and the guidelines specifically, are open and available for public review, criticism, and debate.

The guidelines policy control methods advocated as having a potential for increased fairness and decreased crowding all share these essential features. Similar models may differ in other respects. They may vary in the emphasis given in their development to a careful description of current decision practices or to an examination of normative judgments about desirable policy.[23] They may differ in the specific structure of the guidelines themselves.[24] The nature of information believed justifiably included as criteria for decision making may vary.[25] Similarly, guidelines models may differ in the relative emphasis given to attributes of the *offense* and of the *offender*.[26] These are important issues, but they are not critical to the use of the policy definition and accompanying procedures that are proposed in this chapter as one means of controlling jail and prison populations.

THE RELATION OF GUIDELINES POLICIES TO CROWDING

Front-Door Guidelines

Experience with policy models using guidelines has demonstrated the utility of the concept at sentencing and at bail decision making. The first example shows how prison populations can be controlled at least to the extent that they do not exceed capacity. The second suggests strongly that a similar utility is to be found at the bail decision—a determination critical to crowding in jail.

The Minnesota Sentencing Guidelines Commission has provided a clear example of the utility claimed.[27] The model and procedures developed and implemented meet all of the essential criteria listed. Moreover—and this gives the particular relevance to the problem of prison population control—the commission determined that its guidelines "were to be written so as not to cause the current rated capacity of Minnesota's state prisons to be exceeded."[28] Thus, the concept of the policy control method using guidelines was linked by the commission to the control of prison crowding. That innovation and its implementation in Minnesota suggest that similar procedures can be effective at other points of decisions that have led to the present crowding problems.

Similarly important to population control was the joining in Minnesota of sentencing policy development to repeated analyses of expected impacts of policy choices on prison population in relation to capacity. A population projection method (which can be adapted for use by other jurisdictions)[29] was used to identify policies that were and were not feasible to implement within the available prison capacity.[30]

The careful monitoring of decisions as required by the guidelines procedures, together with the population projection method, provides the Minnesota Sentencing Guidelines Commission with a powerful tool for examining, in detail, the consequences for crowding of any proposed change in sentencing policy. This has permitted the utilization of available prison spaces, without exceeding capacity, according to reasoned and consistent standards. Besides the contribution to population control, the evidence shows that a greater degree of fairness in sentencing has resulted. (For example, more person offenders and fewer property offenders have been imprisoned; disparities in sentencing—defined as variability in sentences for persons similarly categorized in terms of the offense and offender dimensions of the grid—have been reduced; and an increase in the proportionality of the severity of sanctions to the seriousness of offenses has occurred.)[31]

The system thus far has controlled crowding in the prison system. A 1982 study of the impact of the policy procedures, done by the commission staff, reported that in the period after the first implementation, prison populations remained within the state prison capacity, and that commitments were close to the levels projected. Since the program includes procedures for repeated examination of the impact of sentencing policy on prison populations, it is clear that the program has at least the *potential* for avoiding the crowding experienced by so many other jurisdictions.

This experience suggests strongly that similar procedures could be developed and used to control jail populations—not just at sentencing, but also at the hearings of accused persons when bail, release, or detention is determined. This suggestion is given much further credibility by recent experience with a similar policy model in Philadelphia.[32]

The problems of jail crowding across the country are due to the confinement of persons in two classes of status within the criminal justice system.[33] One, of course, is composed of persons sentenced to jail confinement (in most jurisdictions, some misdemeanants, some felons). The second, usually about equal in size, is made up of accused but not convicted persons awaiting trial, not released on their own promise to appear for trial, denied bail, or unable to make bail.[34]

Application of decision guidelines at either sentencing or bail does not require any new conceptualization, untried technology, or procedures not already found to be feasible in at least one jurisdiction. This is due in large part to the study completed by the Philadelphia Court of Common Pleas in developing and testing, by rigorous experimental methods, a guidelines policy for the bail/release-on-recognizance decision.

That study had two parts. First, about 4,800 bail and release-on-recognizance decisions made by the judges were analyzed to determine what determinations of release on recognizance or of bail were made for what kinds of accused. Then, the pretrial performance of defendants (appearance for trial and pretrial arrests) was analyzed. From these analyses, and from extensive discussions and debates within the judiciary, various guidelines models were developed and examined. Finally, model one was selected for implementation on an experimental basis. This was a matrix: the seriousness of the charge was laid out on one dimension, and the risk (according to an empirically derived scale) that the defendant either would fail to appear for trial or would experience new arrests was set out on the other. The intersections of columns and rows pointed to the expected decision outcomes for the defendants thus classified: release on recognizance, bail, and, if bail, a range for the amount. The experimental implementation was a true experiment. The guidelines were used on a random basis so that their effects could be evaluated rigorously. An important result—besides the major findings of reduced disparities in this decision when the guidelines were used, and a clear positive answer to the feasibility question— was that of the relation of the policy, now for the first time explicitly defined, to the problem of jail crowding. Goldkamp, studying the jail population during the experiment, showed how the guidelines could be used to analyze the pretrial population.[35] The identification of unusual decisions that resulted in pretrial jailing could provide a means for controlling the pretrial jail population without departing from the policy favored by the judges who had responsibility for it. A selective use of bail reductions (still in accord with the policy explicitly favored by the court), with supervised release if deemed warranted, could reduce the pretrial jail population.

Trap-Door Guidelines

At least seven states have adopted some form of emergency release provisions[36] similar to Michigan's 1980 Prison Overcrowding Emergency Powers Act.[37] In the associated procedures, it is usually the case that if the rated capacity of the prison is exceeded for a specified period of time, an emergency is declared such that terms of confinement are shortened for some classifications of inmates. In Michigan, there is a 90-day reduction of minimum terms for those who have them, resulting in earlier parole consideration. If the population is not reduced to 95 percent of capacity by consequent earlier paroles, then another 90-day reduction of minimum terms is granted. In a similar plan in Illinois, the commissioner of corrections reduced population when it exceeded capacity by awarding "administrative good time" reductions of terms for certain categories of inmates with mandatory release dates (and clear disciplinary records for six months).[38] Such procedures thus offer the potential of at least temporary relief from crowding. But why arbitrarily roll back parole eligibility or release dates for those set to be released soon in any case? Would it not be preferable to make use of the advantages of the guidelines policy model at the trap doors? That suggestion is to argue that there is a need for:

1. articulation of a clear, explicit statement of policy governing the release of inmates when a population crisis has occurred;
2. specification of the classifications of inmates eligible;
3. consistent application of the specified criteria in determining release;
4. consideration, in formulating the policy, of the purposes of imprisonment;
5. allowance for the exercise of discretion in unusual cases;
6. requirement that reasons be given for atypical decisions;
7. monitoring the decision process to assess how well and how fairly it works;
8. periodic examination and revision if needed; and
9. a decision process that is open and subject to public review and criticism.

If these are needed or valued, then the application of the advocated models at trap doors is needed. If emergency procedures are needed, as apparently they sometimes are, then they should be administered with equity. This means that similarly classified persons (once the relevant and legitimate bases for the classifications have been decided upon by the authorities responsible) should be treated similarly. The guidelines policy models have been demonstrated to help achieve that.

Side-Door Guidelines

When convicted offenders have already been sent to prison (front door), are not yet eligible for parole consideration (back door), and are not advanced for release or parole consideration (trap door), can procedures be invented to permit some to be resentenced, sending them back into the community? A novel program in New Jersey aims to do that, by providing a new sanction of severity intended to be intermediate to that of probation and prison.[39] It was created by the legislature explicitly in response to prison crowding.[40] Prisoners already serving time in prison may apply for release to an intensive program of community probation supervision and community service. Inmates must apply soon after their imprisonment, and those with sentences for certain crimes (homicide, robbery, sex offenses) and persons with mandatory-minimum terms are excluded. Decisions are made first by a screening board, then by a resentencing panel of three judges. The screening board operates under an explicit policy model using guidelines of the type discussed here.[41] One dimension of the matrix guidelines contains nine categories of crime seriousnesses. On the other, there are seven categories of prior record. A dispositional line sets the usual policy for acceptance or rejection of the application at this stage of a sequential decision process. There is, however, an allowance for discretion by a band adjacent to the dispositional line within which the panel may reject or continue the decision process. Decisions outside those usually expected may be made, but then specific aggravating or mitigating factors must be cited. So far, most cases referred favorably to the judicial resentencing panel after this screening have been returned to the community under the special program.[42]

Back-Door Guidelines

Paroling guidelines are perhaps the best known of the type of guidelines advocated, since they were the first developed. Some related system now exists in a number of states and in the United States Parole Commission, which originated the model. Yet none of the systems in place, so far as known to the writer, has explicitly linked the guidelines to prison capacity. There is no *technical* drawback to doing so; and the Minnesota guidelines solution to crowding is, in theory, applicable at the paroling decision as well as at sentencing. Where parole boards exist, they are in an excellent position to enhance equity and also to help control crowding problems.

COMPETING PROPOSALS

The proposals advanced here for a greater use of guidelines policy models linked to availability of resources, especially of jail and prison capacity, must compete with alternative, quite different suggestions for dealing with the problem of crowding. Several prominent and popular arguments may be noted and compared with the methods advocated. These are proposals to reduce crowding by: (1) adding capacity according to expected need; (2) forcing the budgeting of program space (cell) assignments by restricting sentences to set quotas; or (3) using prisons more for incapacitation and less for other purposes.

The Building Solution

Most popular, it seems, is the proposal to reduce crowding by building more jails and prisons. The arguments against building cannot be rehearsed fully here, although they are discussed elsewhere in this volume.[43] However, it may be asserted that

1. the United States already imprisons a greater proportion of its population than nearly any other country;
2. the costs of building are huge;
3. the arguments typically advanced for building that rest on deterrence and incapacitation are not supported by the scientific evidence; and
4. there are sound ethical reasons to seek a reduction in the use of imprisonment.

Many prisons have been built on the argument of expected need. But that argument must be faulted on two main grounds. First, it requires the questionable assumption either that the present use of institutions is desirable or that use will nevertheless continue much as in the past. If it is assumed, on the other hand, that there are strong scientific reasons to question the utilitarian efficacy of this present use, and that such use cannot be justified on acceptable retributive principles, then there is little to support present practices other than tradition or a desire to maintain the status quo. Minimally, projections of prison space needs ordinarily require the assumption that policy will not change or will change only slowly.[44] The point is that rapid change will invalidate the projections, which we may very well seek to accomplish.

Second, even if these more fundamental challenges should fail, the argument falters on our presently weak abilities to forecast crime and imprisonment.[45] It is surprising to see repeated calls for building institutions on the basis of expected need when demonstrable success in accurate forecasting is so lacking. Yet the absence of forecasting accuracy sufficient to justify policy decisions of such

importance cannot itself occasion surprise. Present abilities to measure the incidence and prevalence of crime (let alone to predict crime
trends); difficulties in estimating shifts in the opinions of various
publics about punishment; problems in forecasting political changes;
the inability to predict accurately economic shifts, including unemployment rates; difficulties in estimating arrest probabilities, in
estimating the probability of conviction given an arrest, and in pre-
dicting the probability of sentence to confinement given conviction
are some of the difficulties in forecasting in the long range.[46] These
problems should do more than give pause to those who would for-
mulate a public policy of institutional building on such a shaky
foundation. Rather, it would seem that those who propose building
on grounds of predicted need must first demonstrate an ability to
make such forecasts with reasonable accuracy.

The Quota Solution

Other proposals assert that existing capacity should be used as a
guide to confinement policy. Examples include the use of "bartering
chips" proposed for use in judicial allocation of confinement spaces
versus relatively lower-cost placements such as probation or other
community programs or fines.[47] Such proposals founder on a failure
to include provision for the assurance of equity. Whose theory of
justice would define fairness in terms of the availability of prison
space, its cost in relation to resources available to the court at the
moment, the rate of crime in the offender's neighborhood, or how
many chips the prosecutor or judge has left for the month?

The policy models using guidelines tied to resources have, as a
central, demonstrable attribute, the potential for increased fairness—at least for increased equity, defined as similar treatment of
similarly situated offenders or accused persons. It is true that the
Minnesota model thus far has used existing capacity as the major
constraint on sentencing policy and prison use. But there is no logical
necessity (from the sentencing policy and management model) for
this. The concept of a programmed, gradual reduction in prison use
combined with development of alternative programs would not be
alien to the general model.

The Retributive Model

Various "philosophical models" are currently advocated in competition with that urged here. One is the retributive orientation or, in more recently debated form, the desert theory of punishment.[48] It may be noticed that if the prior record of the offender is accepted as one legitimate basis for the sanction to be imposed (along with the seriousness of the harm done and the culpability of the offender), then something of the nature of the guidelines system advocated is necessary for implementation. Unless the punishment is to be imposed solely on the basis of harm done (or harm and culpability), some provision must be made for determination of the relation of harm *and* prior criminal history to the level of sanction deemed appropriate. But when the retributive philosophy is imposed as the guiding principle for sentencing (perhaps buttressed by the scientifically weak arguments favoring an emphasis on deterrence and incapacitation, and incorporating none of the advantages argued here for a guidelines model), then the result may be simply an increase in the use of prisons and consequent crowding, accompanied by a shift in uncontrolled discretion from the parole board to the prosecutor and the judge.[49]

The Selective Incapacitation Solution

The arguments for the policy model proposed here must also compete with arguments favoring incapacitation as a major reason for imprisonment. Currently, there are proposals for a variety of incapacitation models. The most prominent of these recently has been that of selective incapacitation.[50] This concept has generated widespread public interest and professional controversy as a result of the promise of the proposal to decrease the crime rate while simultaneously reducing prison populations.[51]

What has been proposed is that sentence lengths for some types of crime such as robbery or burglary should be set on the basis of how much crime the offender is predicted to commit if not in prison. Offenders may be classified into predicted high- and low-rate groups. Those in the first group would serve more time than now required of them, while the low-rate group would serve less. The net result, it is claimed, could be reduced crime *and* prison pop-

ulations. Thus, the aim is a more efficient use of correctional resources (prison space) through appropriate predictive classifications
and a greater selectivity.

A carefully conducted questionnaire survey of jail and prison inmates conducted by the Rand Corporation found large differences
in the rates of crime that the offenders who completed question-
naires reported having committed before their confinement. Most
inmates said that they committed serious crimes infrequently; but
a portion said that they committed crimes such as a burglary at a
rather high rate, requiring a good deal of energy and ambition: 200
per year. One Rand researcher, Peter Greenwood, argued that if
such high-rate offenders could be identified and confined longer,
then an effective crime control policy could be the result. He reported that the high-rate robbers *can* be identified, among those
convicted of those crimes, by using a prediction scale of seven items
measuring the offender's reported prior criminal record, drug use,
and unemployment. Given these results (which seemed to show
that a relatively small proportion of convicted offenders may be
expected to commit many crimes, and that these offenders can be
identified by the prediction method), policies based on a selective
use of incapacitation can, it was claimed, reduce crime rates, incarceration rates, or both.

The proposed selective incapacitation strategy raises issues of two
types. There are questions of science, having to do with the research;
and there are disputes about ethics, focused on issues of fairness
and on the fundamental purposes of sentencing. These issues, of
course, are intricately intertwined.

The research has been criticized on various grounds. All the data
of the study on which the proposal is based are retrospective self-
reports of apprehended, convicted offenders sentenced to jail or
prison, composing a nonrepresentative sample of inmates. Associated with each of these characterizations is a criticism. The instru-
ment intended to be predictive has not been tested on any new
sample, as is necessary for confidence in the stability of the method,
in order to see how well it works with another group of offenders—
let alone on a prospective sample as required by the concept of
prediction. There has been no independent corroboration of the
self-reported rates of committing crimes, even though the research
focuses on those who report themselves to be a troublesome minority

(whose veracity, therefore, might be questioned). The results, based only on the study of jail and prison inmates, cannot be generalized to offenders in the community who have not been caught and sentenced to confinement; and even in regard to prisoners, the samples may not be representative.[52]

There are other objections. Since the research included only confined offenders, it has not been shown to be useful for deciding whether or not to incarcerate.[53] Difficulties in translating the results, based on self-reported past behavior and used in the prediction method, to official record data for use at sentencing have not been resolved. No account was taken, in estimating incapacitative effects, of possible variation in the offender's criminal activity over time, nor were possible "replacement effects" considered (for example, removal of one gang member may not reduce the rate of crimes by the group).[54]

The level of predictive accuracy (not validated on any new samples) is about the same as that found in much recidivism prediction research,[55] and that is modest when it comes to using the predictions in individual case decisions.

The ethical debate about selective incapacitation focuses on the consequences of errors in prediction (and resulting misclassifications) as well as on more basic questions of the purposes of sentencing and corrections. The issue points up a conflict between the values of fairness in sentencing and those of societal protection. In the absence of a perfection of prediction never to be expected, any prediction method (statistical or clinical) used in practice will always result in two types of errors. "False negatives" or "misses" are persons mistakenly identified as good risks; for them, a policy of selective incapacitation will fail to provide the public protection sought. "False positives" or "false alarms" are those mistakenly predicted to be recidivists or to commit crimes at a high rate; for them, a deprivation of liberty will be imposed, under a predictive restraint policy, for anticipated crimes that would in fact not be committed. The resulting dilemma for sentencing policy is posed by the prisoner's right not to be a false positive (that is, to be kept in prison unnecessarily) and the ordinary citizen's right not to be victimized by a false negative.[56]

The false negative problem has received the most attention on ethical grounds. This may be due in part to the relatively low level of validity of prediction that has been achieved thus far. In the Greenwood formulation, the false positive errors could be as high as 50 percent.[57] That is, half the persons for whom terms would be increased would serve longer sentences as a result only of their misclassification. The debate on selective incapacitation of course addresses more fundamental issues of sentencing. These are related to the question of whether persons are sent to prison for deserved punishment or for utilitarian purposes. The selective incapacitation strategy is clearly utilitarian (although not the only one of such purposes), since it is aimed at crime reduction and the more efficient use of correctional resources. From the conflicting ethical theory of just desert, it is unfair to punish for choices expected but not yet made and possibly never to be made—that is, for expected crimes that might never be committed. Moreover, equity requires similar punishments for offenders convicted of similar crimes with similar culpability. And, it is asserted, the present list of items on the prediction scale includes some that have little to do with the blame-worthiness of the offender—unemployment, drug use, and age at first conviction.[58]

This intriguing concept has merit if a utilitarian view of the purposes of sentencing and corrections is accepted. But the strategy depends on reliable, valid classification of predicted high-rate offenders—an ability not yet demonstrated.

If sufficient predictive validity were to be achieved and if the ethical arguments could be overcome and the concept of selective incapacitation accepted, then unless the concepts of desert and proportionality are entirely forsworn, something like the guidelines models proposed would be required for implementation.

CONCLUSION

The competing currently popular models for reducing crowding in the nation's jails and prisons are inadequate to the task. The policy control model advocated here has a number of advantages. It does not rest on any particular theory of sentencing, but it does value fairness and require clarity of other purposes. It demonstrably provides procedures that enhance equity. It does not eliminate discretion in decisions, provided that explicit reasons for departures from usual decisions for like cases are specified. It includes mechanisms to ensure compliance with agreed-upon policy. It provides an opportunity for the learning from experience that is the hallmark of rationality and the scientific method. And it has demonstrably assisted in the control of confined populations, at least to the extent of capacity.

Guidelines policy control methods can help control jail and prison populations. The system now out of control can be reined and managed with increased rationality, more commitment to fairness, and a greater humanity. The methods are available. They should be used.

NOTES

1. This statement is conservative: at the end of 1984, there were 463,866 persons in prison; see *Prisoners in 1984*, Bureau of Justice Statistics Bulletin, April 1985. In June 1983, there were 223,551 persons held in local jails; see *The 1983 Jail Census*, Bureau of Justice Statistics Bulletin, November 1984.

2. J. Mullen, with K. Carlson, and B. Smith, *American Prisons and Jails*, vol. 1, *Summary Findings and Policy Implications of a National Survey* (Washington, DC: National Institute of Justice, October 1980), p. 81.

3. Ibid.

4. For an extended discussion, see M. R. Gottfredson and D. M. Gottfredson, *Decisionmaking in Criminal Justice: Toward the Rational Exercise of Discretion* (Cambridge, MA: Ballinger, 1980).

5. A. von Hirsch, *Doing Justice: The Choice of Punishment* (New York: Hill and Wang, 1976).

6. A. von Hirsch, "Desert and Previous Convictions in Sentencing," *Hamline Law Review* 65 (1981):591.

7. This concise formulation of fundamental premises of, on the one hand, the Kantian view that undergirds the desert argument and, on the other, the utilitarian stance in its generic sense, was used by H. A. Pritchard in "Does Moral Philosophy Rest on a Mistake?" *Mind* 21 (1912), reprinted in A. I. Melden, ed., *Ethical Theories*, 2d ed. (Englewood Cliffs, NJ: Prentice-Hall, 1955), pp. 469–81, at p. 476; he rejected both assertions, invoking motive as critical.

8. This concept is discussed further in relation to guidelines in D. M. Gottfredson et al., *The Utility of Experience in Parole Decision-Making: Summary Report* (Washington, DC: U. S. Department of Justice, Law Enforcement Assistance Administration, November 1974); portions are re-

printed as chapter 75 in N. Johnston and L. D. Savitz, *Justice and Corrections* (New York: Wiley, 1978), pp. 875–90.

9. The original conceptualization for the guidelines policy control model discussed was described in D. M. Gottfredson, L. T. Wilkins, and P. B. Hoffman, *Guidelines for Parole and Sentencing: A Policy Control Method* (Lexington, MA: Lexington Books, 1978), presenting a summary and extension of Gottfredson, et al., *Utility of Experience.* For discussion of extension to parole in seven states, see D. M. Gottfredson et al., *Classification for Parole Decision Policy* (Washington, DC: U. S. Department of Justice, National Institute of Law Enforcement and Criminal Justice, 1978). A study of the feasibility of applications to sentencing was reported in L. T. Wilkins et al., *Sentencing Guidelines: Structuring Judicial Discretion* (Washington, DC: U. S. Government Printing Office, 1978). For discussions of extensions to other criminal justice decisions, see also Gottfredson and Gottfredson, *Decisionmaking in Criminal Justice.* For application to bail decisions, see J. S. Goldkamp and M. R. Gottfredson, *Policy Guidelines for Bail: An Experiment in Court Reform* (Philadelphia, PA: Temple University Press, 1985).

10. Compare the guidelines of the United States Parole Commission (in Gottfredson et al., *Guidelines for Parole and Sentencing*) and the Philadelphia bail guidelines (in Goldkamp and Gottfredson, *Policy Guidelines for Bail*) with those of the Minnesota Sentencing Guidelines Commission (in its report cited below). The paroling and bail guidelines were formulated with an express consideration of the risk of new offenses (or parole violation or failure to appear for trial); the Minnesota Sentencing Guidelines Commission explicitly reduced, as a matter of preferred policy, the importance of utilitarian aims and emphasized retribution. See Minnesota Sentencing Guidelines Commission, *Preliminary Report on the Development and Impact of the Minnesota Sentencing Guidelines* (St. Paul: MSCG, July 1982), p. 5. This document provides a detailed discussion of the policy choices made by the commission; see also A. von Hirsch, "Constructing Guidelines for Sentencing: The Critical Choices for the Minnesota Sentencing Guidelines Commission," *Hamline Law Review* (1982):164–215.

11. Goldkamp and Gottfredson, *Policy Guidelines for Bail.*

12. MSGC, *Preliminary Report*, pp. iii–iv and 12–32.

13. See M. R. Gottfredson, "Parole Board Decision Making: A Study of Disparity Reduction and the Impact of Institutional Behavior," *Criminology* 70, no. 1 (1979):77–88; Gottfredson and Gottfredson, *Decisionmaking in Criminal Justice*, pp. 299–306; J. Cohen and M. Tonry, "Sentencing Reforms and Their Impacts," in A. Blumstein et al., eds., *Research on Sentencing: The Search for Reform I* (Washington, DC: National Academy Press, 1983), p. 438.

14. R. Cormack, "A Review of Classification," *Journal of the Royal Statistical Society* 3 (1971):321.

15. D. M. Gottfredson, "Assessment and Prediction Methods in Crime and Delinquency," in President's Commission on Law Enforcement and Administration of Justice, *Task Force Report: Juvenile Delinquency and Youth Crime* (Washington, DC: U. S. Government Printing Office, 1967).

16. S. D. Gottfredson, "Institutional Responses to Prison Crowding," *New York University Review of Law and Social Change* 12 (1986):259–73.

17. There are, of course, many ways in which these results can be accomplished. For example, there are options at legislative, defense bar, prosecution, sentencing, paroling, and other points of decision. The Minnesota Sentencing Guidelines projection method, however, is based directly on this conceptualization: see K. A. Knapp and R. E. Anderson, *Minnesota Sentencing Guidelines Population Projection Program User's Manual* (St. Paul: MSGC, February 1981). See also A. Rutherford et al., *Prison Population and Policy Choices*, vol. 1 and 2 (Washington, DC: U. S. Government Printing Office, 1977).

18. See K. A. Knapp, "The Etiology of Prison Populations: Implications for Prison Population Projection Methodology" (Paper prepared for the Prison Overcrowding Project sponsored by the Edna McConnell Clark Foundation and the National Institute of Corrections, circa 1983).

19. See Gottfredson and Gottfredson, *Decisionmaking in Criminal Justice*, for an illustration.

20. Gottfredson, "Institutional Responses to Prison Crowding."

21. This listing is abstracted from M. R. Gottfredson and D. M. Gottfredson, "Guidelines for Incarceration Decisions: A Partisan Review," *University of Illinois Law Review* 2 (1984):291–317.

22. Other models, such as sequential ones, have been used; see examples in Gottfredson et al., *Classification for Parole Decision Policy*.

23. For example, the United States Parole Commission guidelines development emphasized the former, and the Minnesota Sentencing Guidelines Commission emphasized the latter.

24. See note 10.

25. Blumstein et al., *Research on Sentencing*.

26. See, e.g., A. von Hirsch, *Past vs. Future Crimes: Deservedness and Dangerousness in the Sentencing of Criminals* (New Brunswick, NJ: Rutgers University Press, 1985).

27. MSGC, *Preliminary Report*.

28. von Hirsch, "Constructing Guidelines for Sentencing," citing Minnesota Sentencing Guidelines Commission Report to the Legislature, January 2–3, 1980, at pp. 13–14.

29. A New Jersey example is given in Gottfredson and Gottfredson, *Guidelines for Incarceration Decisions*.

30. For specific examples of the implementation of this program, see ibid.

31. MSGC, *Preliminary Report*. These proportions began to return to preguidelines levels in 1982–83, however; see discussion below.

32. Goldkamp and Gottfredson, *Policy Guidelines for Bail*.

33. National Advisory Commission on Criminal Justice Standards and Goals, *Corrections* (Washington, DC: U. S. Government Printing Office, 1973).

34. See J. Goldkamp, "Bail Decision Making and the Role of Pretrial Detention in American Justice" (Ph.D. diss., State University of New York, Albany, 1976).

35. J. Goldkamp, "An Analysis of the Population of the Philadelphia Prisons: Working Paper I" (Philadelphia, PA: Department of Criminal Justice, Temple University, 1982); Goldkamp and Gottfredson, *Policy Guidelines for Bail*.

36. J. Galvin et al., *Setting Prison Terms*, Bureau of Justice Statistics Bulletin (Washington, DC: U. S. Department of Justice, August 1983), p. 4.

37. State of Michigan, Public Act 519 of 1980.

38. This discussion of Michigan and Illinois procedures was informed by a personal communication from M. Kay Harris.

39. J. Marzulli, *Intensive Supervision Program* (Trenton, NJ: Administrative Office of the Courts, March 23, 1983).

40. Ibid.

41. Personal observation.

42. Of about 1,000 applicants in the early months of the program, about 10 percent were accepted into the program. F. S. Pearson and J. Toby, *Third Quarterly Progress Report to the National Institute of Justice on the "Controlling Offenders in the Community Research Project,"* April 20, 1984.

43. See Chapter 3, "The Costs of Incarceration," and Chapter 10, "A Brief for Deescalating Criminal Sanctions," in this volume.

44. This is the "postulate of permanence" that is fundamental to science; but science does not require absolute permanence—only slowness. Indeed, rates are often the subject of scientific investigation. See C. W. Brown and E. F. Ghiselli, *Scientific Method in Psychology* (New York: McGraw–Hill, 1955), pp. 18–19.

45. For reviews and examples of recent work, see L. Cohen, M. Felson, and K. Land, "Property Crime Rates in the United States: A Macrodynamic Analysis, 1947–1977, with ex ante Forecasts for the Mid 1980s," *American Journal of Sociology* 86 (1980):90–117; D. Rauma, "Crime and Punishment Reconsidered: Some Comments on Blumstein's Stability of Punishment Hypothesis," *Journal of Criminal Law and Criminology* 72, no. 4, 1772–

98, and the rejoinder by Blumstein et al. and the reply by Rauma in the same volume.

46. See, Knapp, "Etiology of Prison Populations."

47. P. F. Nardulli, "The Misalignment of Penal Responsibilities and State Prison Crises: Costs, Consequences, and Corrective Actions," *University of Illinois Law Review* 2 (1984):384–86.

48. von Hirsch, *Doing Justice*; "Desert and Previous Convictions"; *Past vs. Future Crimes*.

49. See J. Casper, D. Brereton, and D. Neal, "The Implementation of the California Determinate Sentencing Law," Final Report to the National Institute of Justice (Washington, DC: National Institute of Justice, 1981). And although it is not a necessary consequence of an emphasis on desert, it appears that this emphasis *can* lead to increased prison terms readily invoked, and to an increase in the requirement of mandatory terms for selected offenses, and thus it can generally contribute to crowding problems. The evidence suggests that both justice and public safety would be better served by shorter terms consistently, equitably applied. See Gottfredson and Gottfredson. *Decisionmaking in Criminal Justice*, chaps. 7–9. There is very little evidence, given the general absence of relations between time served in prison and recidivism, that public safety would be impaired by shorter terms.

50. P. W. Greenwood, with A. Abrahamse, *Selective Incapacitation* (Santa Monica, CA: Rand Corporation, August 1982).

51. For critiques, see A. von Hirsch and D. M. Gottfredson, "Selective Incapacitation: Some Queries about Research Design and Equity," *New York University Review of Law and Social Change* 12, no. 1 (1983–84); J. Cohen, "Incapacitation as a Strategy for Crime Control: Possibilities and Pitfalls," *Crime and Justice: An Annual Review of Research*, vol. 5, ed. M. Tonry and N. Morris (Chicago: University of Chicago Press, 1983); A. von Hirsch, "The Ethics of Selective Incapacitation: Observations on the Contemporary Debate," *Crime and Delinquency* 30, no. 2 (April 1984):175–94.

52. von Hirsch and Gottfredson, "Selective Incapacitation," extends these arguments.

53. Cohen, "Incapacitation as a Strategy."

54. von Hirsch and Gottfredson, "Selective Incapacitation."

55. Ibid.

56. See J. Monahan, *The Clinical Prediction of Violent Behavior* (Rockville, MD: U. S. Department of Health and Human Services, National Institute of Mental Health, 1981), p. 123.

57. von Hirsch and Gottfredson, "Selective Incapacitation."

58. Ibid.

8 Sentencing and the Prison Crowding Problem

ALFRED BLUMSTEIN

THE GROWING PROBLEM OF CROWDED PRISONS

The mid-1980s statistics regarding crime and imprisonment raise many important questions. Crime rates climbed almost continuously through the 1960s and 1970s, but reached a peak in 1980, dropped a bit in 1981, and declined through 1984. On the other hand, national incarceration rates were at a minimum in 1969; they then began a fairly steady climb in 1972 and were still climbing in the mid-1980s.

Thus, during the last several years crime rates in the United States have declined and prison populations have grown. To some observers this situation is confusing because they expect those two time series to move together—more crime implies more criminals, which should be associated with more arrests and convictions, and that should imply more prisoners. This connection would require the two series to move together, and so their movement in opposite directions is particularly perplexing.

To other observers, the interpretation of these opposite series is deceptively simple. If more criminals are in prison, then there are fewer criminals on the street, and so the incapacitation effect is greater, and that should give rise to less crime. Furthermore, if judges are tougher about sentencing policy, as the larger prison populations presumably reflect, then a stronger message of general deterrence is sent to all potential criminals, and that has an additional effect on crime reduction. Thus, these observers interpret the relationship between the two time series as a causal one, with the greater use of imprisonment causing the reduction in crime. In reaching that conclusion, they ignore the possibility of a third common cause.

Still others interpret the opposite trends in the rates of crime and of incarceration to be a direct consequence of the changing age mix of the population associated with the post-World War II baby boom. First, they recognize that the peak age for criminal activity is rather different from the peak age of imprisonment. Crime is predominantly committed by young people shortly past their midteens; most of those people never get to prison because they stop committing crime in their late teenage years. Prison, on the other hand, is reserved for adults rather than juveniles, and indeed only for adults who commit the most serious crimes or who accumulate a reasonable number of convictions for the less serious. By the time they are ready for prison, most such offenders have moved into their twenties, so that the peak imprisonment ages are in the twenties, rather later than the teenage years that characterize the crime peaks.

Thus, the interaction of these fairly stationary age patterns of crime and of incarceration with the movement of the population bulge known as the baby boom through those age groups can explain much of the divergent movement of crime and prison population statistics.

The leading edge of the baby-boom generation was the cohort born in 1947, and the largest cohort of the generation was the one born in 1961. Following 1961, there was a general decline in birth rates, reaching a trough in 1976 after which the "echo boom" (the children of the baby-boom generation) began to appear as a new growth factor in the population.[1] Thus, the 1947 cohort reached age 16 in 1963, just about at the beginning of the rise in crime rates that continued until 1980, when the 1961 peak cohort reached age 19. The prison population rise did not begin until about 1972— when the 1947 cohort reached age 25—and has continued to climb since then. By 1990, the 1961 cohort will reach age 29, past the peak incarceration age.

Thus, even in the 1970s, careful demographic analysis could have anticipated a peaking of crime in about 1980 and a continued growth of prison populations until well into the 1980s, with a subsequent decline after about 1990. Indeed, this was the suggestion proposed by Blumstein, Cohen, and Miller in a paper published in 1980 based on data from Pennsylvania in the 1970s.[2] Their projection, invoking data on the changing demographic composition, suggested that crime rates would peak in about 1980, as they indeed did. Of course, that fact could not be discerned until the data for 1981 were collected and analyzed, and that could not occur until well into 1982. Furthermore, since no single point can establish a new trend, confirmation from 1982 data was necessary, and additional confirmation from 1983 data was desirable. It turns out that index crime rates did decline by 1.7 percent in 1981, 4.3 percent in 1982, 7.7 percent in 1983, and 8 percent in 1984.[3] These results are certainly consistent with the demographic hypothesis and the demographically based projections, and this confirmation of the anticipated turnaround (especially after almost 20 years of continuously climbing crime rates) lends support to the underlying theoretical presumption of the strong influence of the age composition.

Demographic factors also influence the prison problem. The age-specific rates of incarceration are less steep than age-specific crime rates, but there is still a very sharp difference across age groups in their incarceration rates. The peak imprisonment age is 23, and the rates decline from there.[4] It is this difference between the peak crime age (about 16–17) and the peak imprisonment age (about 23) that gives rise to the important lag between the peaking of crime rates in 1980 and the anticipated peaking of imprisonment rates somewhat later, approximately in 1990, due to the movement of the baby-boom population bulge.

These demographic factors, of course, cannot alone explain crime rates or imprisonment rates, but they do represent an important projected baseline from which other factors can still move prison populations up or down. It is important that they be considered because they clearly have a strong effect; for example, the age-specific arrest rate for robbery reaches a peak at age 17, falls off with age to a level of half the peak by age 23, and continues to decline exponentially with increasing age.[5]

Furthermore, that effect is significant because the age composition of the population is changing rapidly; the largest cohort of the baby-boom period, the 1961 cohort, passed through the peak crime age group in the late 1970s and is moving through the peak imprisonment age groups in the mid-1980s. Also, it is important to account for the demographic effect because it represents one of the very few windows through which one can have any reasonable vision of the future for the criminal justice system; of the many candidate causal factors influencing crime (for example, family structure, economic conditions, unemployment, social mores) or prison populations (for example, crime rates, political and judicial mood, resources), the large majority are no less difficult to anticipate for the future than are crime rates and prison populations themselves. With demography, however, we can know the future much better. Virtually everyone of interest to the criminal justice system until the end of the twentieth century has already been born; even beyond that, demographic trends are reasonably forecast. The U.S. Census Bureau, for example, has a detailed population forecast by age, sex, and race to the year 2080.[6]

These demographic factors have been emphasized because of the considerable difference in the appropriate policies under different expectations of growth of prison populations. In 1985, there were 505,037 people in federal and state prisons in the United States,[7] representing a compound average annual growth rate since 1972 of 8 percent per year. An aggressive commissioner of corrections could present those data to his governor or budget bureau director and argue that prison populations are continuously increasing, that even the current population is well in excess of capacity, and that a major new building program to provide additional prison capacity must be launched.

The argument would be based on an extrapolation of the growth from 1972 through 1985. The projection should extend at least to 1990, the earliest year in which a budget decision made in 1985 would result in making additional capacity available because of the time lags associated with the decision process itself, enactment of the necessary legislation and appropriations, the design process and its bureaucratic requirements, the letting of construction contracts, and finally construction. More properly, the projection should go well beyond 1990 to cover the expected population needs throughout the expected life of the institution, which is likely to be 50 to 100 years.

A budget director seeing the extrapolation of the 13-year growth, and being unaware of the demographic considerations, would undoubtedly squirm at the prospect of paying an initial $50,000-

$75,000 per cell of additional capacity, and at a gross annual operating cost of about $10,000-$15,000 per prisoner. (See Chapter 3, "The Costs of Incarceration" in this volume for more detailed compilations of net costs.) But in a political environment where vulnerability to charges of being "soft on crime" is extremely dangerous, the request for additional capacity might well be granted, even if reluctantly.

A very different picture emerges, however, if the changing demographic composition is taken into account. Since the baby-boom wave can be blamed for much of the growth in the prison population, and since that group will soon be passing out of the age groups of high imprisonment, one can anticipate that the prison population will begin to decline some years after the 1961 cohort (the peak of the baby boom) passes age 23 (the peak imprisonment age) in 1984. Obviously, other factors relating to shifting attitudes toward punitiveness could shift those effects somewhat. But the major demographic shifts of the baby-boom cohort—a 35 percent rise from 1946 to 1947, a 16 percent rise from 1947 to 1961, and a 30 percent decrease from 1961 to 1976—represent a very powerful influence that is virtually certain to have an effect, to which other factors will add or subtract. Thus, a budget director armed with knowledge about these demographic considerations—as well as a responsible corrections commissioner—would recognize that the incessant growth of prison populations since 1972 will taper off before long. Thus, he could conclude that a major building program to accommodate current overcrowding is inappropriate in light of the long interval between a decision to build and the availability of operational capacity. He would also conclude that additional prison capacity is not the solution to the short-run problem because of the expected turnaround in prison populations by the time the new capacity becomes available.

This is certainly not to argue that new prison construction is not desirable. First, many states, especially those in the Sun Belt, are experiencing significant population growth, and there clearly would be a need to expand their prison capacity in accord with the states' population growth; this simply reflects the fact that the aggregate conditions that apply to the United States as a whole are not shared equally by each of the individual states. Even in the states of the industrial Northeast and Midwest, where the phenomenon of a steadily aging stable population is much more characteristic, a substantial proportion of existing prison accommodation was built in the nineteenth or early twentieth centuries, and could very properly be replaced with more modern facilities. These, however, are more appropriate reasons for new construction than simply accommodating the recent growth in prison populations.

THE SENTENCING RESPONSE

In light of the seriousness of the current prison crowding problem and the inappropriateness of additional construction to accommodate that problem, more immediate approaches are needed. These can be found in the sentencing decision, broadly defined.

Viewed narrowly, sentencing is something that a judge does in a courtroom. A more appropriate view of that process, however, recognizes that the essence of sentencing involves, first, a decision as to whether a particular convicted offender goes to prison and, second, how much time he spends there. Many people in addition to the judge contribute to those decisions. Most important among them are the prosecutor, who decides on charges and, in conjunction with a defense counsel, most often reaches a final disposition charge that is associated with a defendant's plea of guilty. The parole board also influences the time-served aspect of the sentencing decision by deciding when a prisoner is to be released from prison. All of these work within the rules and limits established by the legislature: the crimes code, statutory-maximum sentences, mandatory-minimum sentences for certain offenses, habitual-offender laws, and, increasingly, determinate-sentencing laws.

In contrast to prison capacity, sentencing policies and practices are much more amenable to rapid change to accommodate the current prison crowding crisis. Indeed, the state of Michigan passed legislation—its Emergency Powers Act—that authorizes revision of the prisoners' sentences to accommodate the prison population to the available capacity. When a condition of prison overcrowding is declared, the governor is mandated to reduce every prisoner's minimum sentence by 90 days, thereby increasing the pool of prisoners eligible for parole. The parole board still retains its discretion in the sentencing process, since it can refuse to release an eligible individual whom it considers to be dangerous. Thus, a sentencing response to the crowding problem can be enacted quickly if necessary, can provide short-term relief, and need never involve a judge.

Part of the growing problem of prison crowding is attributable to the shift in sentencing policy over the 1970s. The early 1970s saw a decline in the commitment to rehabilitation as a result of a succession of evaluations that brought into question the effectiveness of corrections programs in influencing offenders' subsequent behavior. Since the indeterminate sentence—with its emphasis on a subsequent assessment of when an offender was "rehabilitated"—represented a central aspect of the rehabilitative strategy, this led to a significant shift toward determinate sentences.

This shift to determinacy prevented the parole board from serving as a safety valve to relieve prison crowding when it occurred. Traditionally, when prisons became overcrowded, the parole board could shift the threshold of the criteria by which it decided whether to retain or to release prisoners; the board might decide to take a marginally greater risk by expanding the conditions under which it was willing to offer parole or by reducing its propensity to reimprison a technical violator. The movement toward determinate sentencing was thus accompanied by a movement for "abolition of parole." Actually, this movement was primarily for abolition of the parole release decision, and generally involved retaining the other parole functions of support and supervision within the community and of enhanced vulnerability to reimprisonment. This shift to determinacy has thus served to limit the ability of the corrections system to accommodate the problem of prison crowding.

Thus, the increased numbers of people in the prison-relevant age groups, the diminished flexibility of the corrections system to accommodate those larger numbers, and public pressures for a more punitive response to crime through greater use of imprisonment have all combined to generate the current prison crowding crisis. Only the sentencing system can provide relief from the problem. In particular, it is necessary to introduce some form of constraint on sentencing policy that is responsive to the current and anticipated state of prison congestion. This, of course, conflicts with the view that a sentencing decision should be made on each case in isolation from all others, and is a matter that involves only a judge and his conscience. It invokes concern for the aggregate impact of all sentencing decisions, and bringing that concern to bear on each individual decision.

We will consider here five somewhat different approaches to a population-sensitive incarceration strategy: (1) a planned policy that uses sentencing guidelines and links those guidelines to prison capacity; (2) a policy that links the provisions of a mandatory-minimum sentencing law to its impact on prison populations; (3) a policy that employs a population-responsive safety valve to release prisoners when overcrowding becomes excessive; (4) a modified safety valve that mobilizes available public facilities as extra minimum-security institutions; and (5) a strategy that allocates the limited number of prison spaces to each court and its judges or prosecutors, who must take their limited allocation into account in making their own decisions.

Capacity-Constrained Sentencing Guidelines

The best example of a planned population-sensitive incarceration policy is the sentencing guidelines matrix developed by the Minnesota Sentencing Guidelines Commission.[8] The commission's work followed from an explicit legislative mandate to "take account of prison capacity" in developing its sentencing guidelines, and used prison capacity as a specific constraint on the sentencing schedule that emerged. Thus, if some commission member wanted to increase the mandated sentence for robbery, he had to identify the offenses for which he would like to reduce the sentences in exchange. Such a procedure requires a technology (such as some kind of simulation or estimation model) that enables the policy group to calculate for each possible sentencing schedule the prison capacity it would consume. This in turn requires information on the expected number of convicted offenders in each category within the sentencing schedule (based, in Minnesota's case, on an offense severity score and on the length of the offender's prior conviction record) in order to estimate the prison capacity that the schedule would consume.

The existence of this prison capacity constraint imposes a rare discipline on the policy debate. In most settings where sanction policies are debated, advocates of tougher sentences gain political benefits without having to consider the costs of their actions. The methods developed by the Minnesota Sentencing Guidelines Commission deserve much credit for the fact that in 1981, when the U.S. prison population as a whole increased 12.1 percent from 1980, Minnesota had one of the lowest rates of increase, only 1.1 percent.[9] There remains the important question of whether the willingness of the Minnesota criminal justice system—and especially its judges—to accept the discipline of sentencing guidelines is likely to be replicated in other jurisdictions where the commitment to rational government may be less strong.

Capacity Considerations and Mandatory-Minimum Sentencing Laws

Whereas the Minnesota legislature and sentencing commission decided to develop their sentencing policies within the available capacity, some states may choose to develop policies that call for additional prison capacity. Indeed, most legislative actions on sentencing do imply a need for additional capacity, but it is rare for legislatures to address that need. It is much more common for them to derive the political benefits of toughness, leaving the prison impact as an issue to be addressed at some indefinite time in the future.

One striking exception to this general practice of separating sentencing policy from its prison population implications was the development of the mandatory-minimum sentencing legislation submitted to the Pennsylvania legislature by Governor Dick Thornburgh in September 1981. His legislative proposal replaced a mandatory-minimum bill already in the legislature that covered a broad range of offenses. A prison impact analysis indicated that the prison capacity needed to house the extra prisoners would be excessive. Using the impact analysis in negotiation with the previous bill's sponsors, Governor Thornburgh got them to join him in endorsing a revised legislative package. The new bill called for five-year mandatory-minimum sentences for a narrowly limited group of offenses: crimes committed with a gun, the most serious robberies and assaults by recidivists, and crimes on public transportation. These provisions were combined with a request for legislative authorization of a $134 million bond issue to provide 2,880 additional prison spaces to accommodate the anticipated increase in the prison population. In addition, the bill specified the sites on which the additional capacity was to be located—often a more difficult political question than even the financing. The governor let it be known that approval of the sentencing legislation without the bond issue would risk a veto. Both components were passed with virtually no opposition.[10]

An Automatic Safety Valve

Both the Minnesota and the Pennsylvania approaches require analysis to develop impact estimates associated with any policy choice being considered. Fortunately, a rich array of analytical tools exist to help in that estimation, even though any such estimate is inherently only a rough approximation. Michigan has responded to its prison crowding by providing a safety valve through the Emergency Powers Act adopted by the Michigan legislature in 1981.[11] This act charges a corrections commission with monitoring the population of the state's prisons in relation to their capacity, and with reporting to the governor when the population of the prisons exceed their capacity for longer than 30 days. Upon receipt of such a report, the governor is then required to reduce the minimum sentences of every prisoner by up to 90 days, thereby increasing the population eligible for parole. This does not represent an automatic release of all these prisoners, because they still have to appear before the parole board, which can still retain the dangerous convicts until their maximum sentences expire.

This approach diffuses the political cost of reducing the prison population to stay below the available capacity. The legislature enacts the law; the independent corrections commission declares the condition of overcrowding; the governor orders the reduction of minimum sentences; and the parole board orders the actual release. This approach provides all participants with a politically palatable means of acting in ways that avoid the consequences of prison overcrowding. It is, however, limited in its applicability, since the prisons become increasingly populated by prisoners with long sentences. After several occasions in which the safety valve is invoked, the supply of eligible candidates for release is diminished, and so more basic solutions are required.

Providing Emergency Capacity

An alternative to the Michigan strategy that accommodates the concern over releasing convicted offenders directly to the community would involve the rapid creation of backup facilities that are less restrictive than regular prisons. Such minimum-security institutions could be converted from public institutions that are currently vacant or sparsely occupied. These would include mental hospitals, which have been emptied by the deinstitutionalization of the mentally ill over the past two decades. They could also include educational institutions or juvenile institutions that are currently closed because of diminished enrollments, due largely to a decreased number of juveniles in the relevant age groups.[12]

This approach recognizes the fact that any classification of a prisoner in terms of the necessary security level must involve some degree of ambiguity around any threshold (between minimum and medium security or between medium and maximum security). The Michigan approach leads to release into the community, but this variation generates more intermediate gradations. When an institution is found to be overcrowded, the lowest-risk individuals can then be transferred to a backup institution of a lower-security classification. Of course, if that prisoner were to violate the security conditions of that institution, he would then be vulnerable to being returned to the higher-security institution from which he came. The threat of this response should enhance the likelihood of successful performance at the lower-security level.

This kind of spare capacity should be readily available in any state with crowded prisons. It offers a means of relieving the overcrowding conditions and still avoiding direct release. Any state whose prison populations are at or above capacity should begin to plan to convert some of its available surplus institutions to such backup functions.

Allocation of Prison Capacity to Courts

A particularly provocative approach to assuring that sentencing take account of limited prison capacity was proposed by the late John Manson when he was commissioner of corrections for Connecticut.[13] In his proposal, prison cells are allocated directly to each individual court within a state, or possibly even to the prosecutors. Then, a court that has used up its ration and wants to send an additional convicted offender to prison is required to identify which cell from among its allocation should be vacated. The judge must then release a current occupant in order to obtain the needed space for the new one. This approach forces the judge (or the prosecutor before him) to take into account the political costs of prison crowding in making sentencing decisions.

Of course, if such an approach were adopted, it would require careful consideration of the appropriate allocation rules. If a court's ration were based on last year's usage, that would reward the more punitive. If it were based on a weighted number of convictions, then that might represent too difficult a shift for the courts that had previously made relatively greater use of prison. Some form of gradual shift over a number of years from current inequitable usage to an equitable allocation would probably be required.

Other problems are raised by the year-to-year chance fluctuations in a court's needs for prison space. In a large urban court, the law of large numbers can accommodate those fluctuations, but a small court that found a large organized crime network operating in its jurisdiction might find its ordinary ration seriously inadequate. This problem might be addressed by retaining part of the total supply of cells at a central office (say, the state's court administrator) to be used only in cases of emergency.

These and other major operational problems (some of which are addressed in more detail by Blumstein and Kadane)[14] make it very unlikely that the Manson proposal will ever be implemented. It is particularly valuable, however, because its seeming reasonableness helps focus attention on the inherent allocation issue and the need to address it in some way. It also thereby makes the Minnesota approach seem most attractive.

Defining Capacity of a Prison

All of the approaches to population-sensitive flow control require an explicit formulation of the excessively flexible concept of prison capacity. As long as double or triple celling is a possibility, capacity remains a very poorly defined notion, and could represent no constraint whatsoever on any of the policymakers or decision makers within the criminal justice system. When considerations such as excessive prisoner density become more explicit and are taken into account, then capacity does become a more meaningful limit, and explicit policy statements can be formulated to define it. This can be done by a commission including representatives of the legislature, the judiciary, the correctional administration, and prosecutors.

THE RACIAL DISPROPORTIONALITY IN PRISONS

One of the most distressing aspects of the crowded prison situation is the gross disproportionality of the racial composition of American prisons.[15] Although blacks represent roughly one-eighth of the U.S. population, they represent about one-half of the prison population, and this results in a ratio of black-to-white incarceration rates (prisoners per capita) of about 7 to 1. Perhaps even more troublesome is the fact that while the aggregate incarceration rate in the United States is slightly less than 2 per 1,000 population in prison on any day, among black males in their twenties the rate is over 30 per 1,000. That is, over 3 percent of those young men are in a state or federal prison on any given day; adding local jails raises this figure to almost 5 percent in prison or jail.

These disturbing figures generate a strong concern that the disproportionality may be directly attributable to sentencing discrimination, and the criminal justice system has indeed been attacked on those grounds. Of course, this then raises the question of the degree to which that racial disproportionality in prison is attributable to sentencing discrimination and how much of it is attributable to differential involvement in criminal activity, and particularly in the kind of serious criminal activity that is most likely to lead to imprisonment and to longer sentences.

The sex ratio in prisons, for example, is far more disproportionate than the race ratio. Ninety-six percent of prisoners are male and only 4 percent are female, so that the sex-specific incarceration rates are in the ratio of 24 to 1, more than three times the ratio between the races. There are very few who would argue, however, that this disproportionality results primarily from discrimination in favor of females—even though there might well be some such discrimination. It is generally accepted that males do engage in a disproportionately larger amount of crime and of the more serious crime. If that differential representation of males in prison were fully explained by their differential involvement in crime, then attempts to reduce the disproportionate representation in prisons would have to focus on the causes of that differential involvement rather than on sentencing discrimination.

Of course, isolating discrimination from other factors that might be associated with sentencing is an extremely difficult task. Many investigators have tried using fairly crude multiple regression techniques to accomplish such analysis. The general conclusion from most such investigations is that it is extremely difficult to discern a significant discriminatory effect,[16] although when samples are large enough a statistically significant effect can sometimes be isolated. Such methods are always subject to concerns about adequate specification of the statistical model and about the selection effect of the individual cases entering the analysis (that is, if the prior stages exhibited discrimination against blacks, then the black offenders who appear for sentencing would be disproportionately less serious cases, and that selection bias could mask discriminatory treatment).[17]

One approach that attempts to surmount these problems involves examining the race of arrestees at arrest by crime type, and then weighting the crime types in accordance with their representation in prison. Such an analysis allows one to estimate the racial composition that would prevail in prisons based only on the crime type of arrest and if there was no discrimination following arrest. That analysis accounts for 80 percent of the racial disproportionality in prisons,[18] thereby suggesting that the racial disproportionality in prison is much more attributable to differential involvement in serious crime (or, at least, to arrest for serious crime) than to discrimination. For example, 60 percent of those arrested for murder and robbery are black, and these two crime types account for 40 percent of state prisoners.

These results are certainly not intended to suggest that there is no discrimination; there is still considerable room left for some. The possibility is suggested by the fact that the fraction of the racial disproportionality accounted for through arrest diminishes for the less serious offenses. It is highest for murder and robbery, suggesting that the seriousness of these offenses is the dominant consideration associated with imprisonment. On the other hand, it is least for the more discretionary offenses like burglary, larceny, auto theft, and drugs. For these, more discretion is involved in making incarceration decisions and on establishing time served. That discretion could be used to take into account differences in prior record, employment status, or other factors that are at least arguably relevant and may be correlated with race; it could also be used to invoke racial discrimination with no legitimacy. Nevertheless, even if all of the unexplained differences were eliminated and the race distribution in prison were made the same as at arrest, it would have only a small effect on the racial composition of prisons. That happens because the people charged with those lesser offenses make up only a small fraction of the prison population, and adjustments in their racial composition do not have a strong influence on the total racial composition of prisons.

Another potential problem in the analysis is the use of the race of those arrested to infer the race of offenders. Those results could be distorted if there is serious discrimination in arrest. Studies have addressed this issue by comparing the race distribution of those arrested as reported by the police with the race distribution of offenders as reported by their victims. These studies have found a strong similarity in the two distributions.[19] Thus, while there may be considerably more police patrol in minority neighborhoods, and while police may be more willing to arrest a minority person they encounter for a public-order offense, these results suggest that there is no indication of significant police discrimination in arresting for the serious offenses that result in imprisonment.

These results certainly do not argue that discrimination is absent in sentencing or even that the amount of discrimination is negligibly small or unimportant. Nor should they provide an excuse for impeding any efforts to discover and to eliminate discrimination wherever it exists. They do suggest, however, that a finding of racial disproportionality does not by itself demonstrate the existence of discrimination and, further, that attacks on discrimination in the criminal justice system to redress the disproportionality in prison are not likely to have the desired effect on prison populations. Any significant impact on racial mix in prisons will have to come from addressing the factors in the society that generate the life conditions that contribute to the different involvement between the races in serious personal crimes.

SUMMARY

The considerations developed in this chapter suggest strongly that the prison crowding of the mid-1980s, while a serious problem, is not inherently one that is likely to continue far into the next decade. This expectation derives largely from a recognition that a major factor contributing to the current crowding is the large number of people in the age groups most vulnerable to imprisonment. Recognition of this fact casts strong doubt on the wisdom of additional construction to accommodate the current overcrowding; the time needed to complete the construction would make it available just about the time the problem begins to recede. Construction may well be necessary, however, to accommodate growing populations or to replace obsolete institutions. The immediate need is one of finding short-term approaches that could be implemented quickly to alleviate the current crowding. These approaches generally involve some form of population-responsive control over the flow of prisoners into or out of prisons. The major possibilities to be considered include capacity-constrained sentencing guidelines such as Minnesota's; capacity-triggered emergency valves such as Michigan's; or a variant that uses minimum-security institutions converted from available public facilities (such as vacated mental hospitals or schools) as backup capacity.

Also, consideration of any new sentencing legislation should be accompanied by a "prison impact statement" that assesses the magnitude and timing of the anticipated effect of the legislation on prison populations. If that impact would exceed the capacity of the existing institutions, then any such sentencing legislation should be accompanied by appropriations and site commitments for providing the additional capacity required. This was the approach followed in Pennsylvania in developing a mandatory-minimum sentencing law that increased penalties, but also provided the additional prison capacity to accommodate the extra prisoners.

Fortunately, methods developed in recent years provide a reasonable basis for estimating the impacts of sentencing policy. Additional research is still needed, however, to develop improved methods and improved data bases in various jurisdictions to develop their own impact estimates. A valuable federal role would involve the support of such developments as well as technical assistance to states intending to use such methods for developing impact estimates.

NOTES

1. These observations are apparent from the data presented in "Projections of Populations of the United States, by Age, Sex, and Race: 1983 to 2080," *Current Population Reports*, Series P–25, no. 952, (Washington, DC: U.S. Department of Commerce, Bureau of the Census, May 1984). The numbers in table 6 for July 1, 1984, were used to develop the 1984 age distribution, and the sizes of the birth cohorts were approximated from the age distribution in 1984.

2. See A. Blumstein, J. Cohen, and H. Miller, "Demographically Disaggregated Projections of Prison Populations," *Journal of Criminal Justice* 8, no. 1 (1980): 1–25, for the detailed analyses, and A. Blumstein, J. Cohen, and H. Miller, "Crime, Punishment, and Demographics," *American Demographics* (October 1980):32–37, for a shorter summary.

3. The rates of decline of the index crime rates were obtained from the *Uniform Crime Reports* for 1981, 1982, 1983, and 1984, respectively, published by the Federal Bureau of Investigation, Washington, DC.

4. The age-specific incarceration rates were derived from the age distribution of prison inmates presented in "Profile of State Prison Inmates: Sociodemographic Findings from the 1974 Survey of Inmates of State Correctional Facilities," *National Prisoner Statistics Special Report SD-NPS-SR-4, August 1979* (Washington, DC: U.S. Department of Justice, 1979). The 1974 population was inferred from the 1984 projection in "Projections of Populations of the United States," lagged by 10 years.

5. The age-specific arrest rates were estimated using age-specific arrest numbers presented annually in the FBI *Uniform Crime Reports* and corresponding estimates of the age distribution of the general population available from the U.S. Bureau of the Census.

6. See "Projections of Populations of the United States."

7. Prisoners in 1985, Bureau of Justice Statistics Bulletin (Washington, DC: U.S. Department of Justice, Bureau of Justice Statistics, June 1986).

8. Minnesota Sentencing Guidelines Commission, *Preliminary Report on the Development and Impact of the Minnesota Sentencing Guidelines* (St. Paul: Minnesota Sentencing Guidelines Commission, 1982).

9. The effects of the sentencing guidelines are addressed by Kay Knapp,

"What Sentencing Reform in Minnesota Has and Has Not Accomplished," *Judicature* 68 (1984): 181–89.

10. Pennsylvania Act 54 of 1982, the Mandatory Minimum Sentencing Act, became effective on June 6, 1982.

11. Michigan Comp. Laws Ann. 800.71.79 (Supp. 1981).

12. In the 1990s, as the baby boom moves out of the high-imprisonment age groups and the "echo boom" moves into the relevant age groups, those facilities may no longer be needed for prison purposes, and they could then be converted back to their original use.

13. See John R. Manson, "The Prison Overcrowding Dilemma: A New Approach" (Unpublished manuscript, Connecticut Department of Corrections, Hartford, CT, 1981).

14. See A. Blumstein and J. Kadane, "An Approach to the Allocation of Scarce Imprisonment Resources," *Crime and Delinquency* 29 (October 1983):546–60.

15. A. Blumstein, "On the Racial Disproportionality of United States' Prison Populations," *Journal of Criminal Law and Criminology* 73, no. 3 (1982):1259–81 provides a detailed analysis of the disproportionality and of the factors contributing to it discussed in this section.

16. Much of this research has been reviewed by John Hagan and Kristin Bumiller in "Making Sense of Sentencing: A Review and Critique of Sentencing Research," in A. Blumstein et al., eds., *Research on Sentencing: The Search for Reform*, vol. 2, Report of NAS Panel on Sentencing Research (Washington, DC: National Academy Press, 1983), pp. 1–54.

17. The problem of selection bias is discussed in S. Klepper, D. Nagin, and Luke-Jon Tierney, "Discrimination in the Criminal Justice System: A Critical Appraisal of the Literature," in *Research on Sentencing*, pp. 55–128.

18. The details of this analysis are presented in Blumstein, "Racial Disproportionality."

19. See M. Hindelang, "Race and Involvement in Common Law Personal Crimes," *American Sociological Review* 43 (1978):93–109; and M. Hindelang, *Criminal Victimization in Eight American Cities: A Descriptive Analysis of Common Theft and Assault* (Cambridge, MA: Ballinger, 1976).

9 Structuring the Development of Alternatives to Incarceration

ALAN T. HARLAND
and
PHILIP W. HARRIS

Dissenting in *Abrams v. United States*, Justice Holmes observed that "The best test of truth is the power of the thought to get itself accepted in the competition of the market."[1] By this criterion, it might appear that recent advocacy of alternatives to incarceration has failed to capture some essential truth, or has been based on thoughts that are woefully deficient in persuasive power. For despite the gallons of printer's ink, innumerable conference hours, and millions of tax dollars that have been devoted ostensibly to promoting and discussing "alternatives," the conclusion of most reviewers remains consistently disheartening. We have heard a great deal about the wisdom of pursuing alternatives to incarceration, but we have seen almost no indication that they have gained any significant acceptance, at least in the competition of the market frequented by policymakers and practitioners.[2] According to Austin and Krisberg, "A careful review of the research literature on alternatives to incarceration suggests that their promise of reducing the prison population has remained largely unmet."[3] Similarly, Harris notes that "There is a growing consensus that programs which were intended to serve offenders who otherwise would be incarcerated have generally failed to reach that population."[4]

Unfortunately, the popular wisdom about the failure of recent policy and programs aimed at reducing reliance on imprisonment has not been matched by a useful explanation for that failure. Few of the reform efforts initiated as alternatives to incarceration have produced case studies to supply descriptive data on the ways in which they were developed and implemented. As one recent review of alternatives research concluded, "A major flaw in virtually all the studies is the absence of process descriptions of program conceptualization, context, implementation and demise. Most studies are, instead, narrowly preoccupied with evaluating program outcome."[5] As a result, we are largely forced back on speculation in trying to understand why so many suggested alternatives to imprisonment have failed to gain acceptance, or have mainly affected offenders other than those in prison or jail or headed in that direction.

Where accounts of specific alternative ventures are available, they most often take the form of agency self-studies, in which accounts of how the measures were implemented tend (if included at all) to be highly particularized descriptions of local politics, personalities, and resources.[6] The task of generalizing from such specific descriptions and circumstances, to begin developing theories and strategies of implementation, has been undertaken to advantage in other areas of criminal justice reform,[7] and in the field of organizational change in general.[8] It has received little attention, however, in the literature on alternatives to incarceration.[9]

In describing what has been identified as the "implementation approach" to introducing innovation, Schlossman, Zellman, and Shavelson note that key to this approach is the idea that successful innovation may be more closely associated with characteristics of the adopting organization and its implementation strategies than with the innovation itself.[10] In contrast to this prescription for successful innovation, the literature on prison alternatives has largely focused on the structure and content of various sentencing and other alternative mechanisms. Consequently, there is abundant information on a wide variety of substantive and procedural aspects of alternatives to custody.[11] The list includes intensive community supervision, home arrest, restitution, fines, and community service as well as various procedural options such as client-specific planning, decision guidelines, mediation, arbitration, and reconciliation; it could equally well include technological and other advances aimed at speeding up the processing of offenders, especially those being held pending trial or sentence.[12]

In comparison with the copious body of materials advocating and describing specific alternatives to incarceration, far less emphasis has been placed on strategies for implementing alternatives that might successfully reduce widespread dependence on incarceration.[13] Similarly, little attention has been paid to the complexities of the organizational context in which alternatives must be developed and implemented.[14] Yet it is self-evident that continued emphasis on devising and tinkering with the content of laundry lists of sanctions and procedures that might, under certain circumstances, lead to reduced or even different reliance on incarceration is a destructively incomplete approach to reform. It is incomplete insofar as sanctions and procedures are not self-implementing; and experience so far demonstrates that merely increasing the options available to decision makers, without more systematic and rigorous attention to the circumstances under which such options are likely to be implemented, leads either to their being ignored, or to unintended and undesired changes in direction. It is destructive to the extent that public and professional dissatisfaction with either outcome results in unwarranted criticism and premature rejection of the specific sanction or procedure per se, when the explanation rests more significantly in flaws in the particular approach to implementation that was followed.[15]

Our objective, therefore, is to examine the issue of alternatives to incarceration as a problem of implementation. More specifically, this discussion focuses on the feasibility and potential advantages of one particular approach, in which decisions about adopting and implementing alternatives are the routine and continuing task of an organizational entity such as a specially constituted commission or an "alternatives authority." Framing our assessment of such an approach around some of the key features and practical implications of what has been called the "implementation approach" to reform, we shall focus on the importance of process considerations in improving our ability to introduce and repeat innovations that will work successfully as alternatives to incarceration.

PERCEIVED NEED FOR CHANGE

A central theme in the implementation literature dealing with criminal justice, and with other fields such as educational reform, has been the importance of understanding change as a process and not merely an event.[16] Self-evidently, such a process begins with a perception of a need for change, either because existing prac-

tices develop general or specific problems, or because new alternatives arise that were previously unknown or unavailable. One
type of reform impulse has arisen from humanitarian desires to reduce incarceration in order to diminish gratuitous suffering,[17] and
to promote the rehabilitation of offenders.[18] More recently, concern to save souls has been overshadowed by a desire to save
money, as current incarceration rates and consequent overcrowding have led to astronomically priced construction plans.[19] Further pressure to consider alternatives has come from court orders
to reduce crowding within a space of time that is too short to allow
for prison building.[20] Forced to reduce confinement levels or face
further court action, even the most reluctant politicians and officials may view the need to consider alternatives of their own fashioning as preferable to a loss of control over the reduction of
prison populations.[21]

If traditional reform arises from principled dissatisfaction with
existing practices, pragmatic concerns may be based on the much
more qualified perception that existing practices, although perhaps
preferable to alternatives in some ideal sense, are no longer finan-
cially or legally viable. Between these two approaches there may
arise a situation in which new awareness of an innovation, such as
a sentencing or parole option, stimulates a belief that change is
needed where none was previously thought necessary. It is undoubtedly with this latter possibility in mind that so much descriptive and prescriptive information on sentencing options has
been disseminated.[22]

Although the continued expansion of such lists of options is obviously not without merit,[23] it is axiomatic that they will be of little
use unless decision makers are also given the necessary incentive,
skills, and resources to implement the new measures. Without attention to how such options are operationalized, moreover, it is
possible that one individual's or group's perceived need for
change may be quite different from the intentions of the original
promulgators. A description of community service sentencing, for
example, might trigger a rethinking of short-term jail sentencing
practices in some circles, but it might equally strike others as an
alternative to fines for traffic violators or as a way of "toughening
up" dispositions for offenders who were "getting off with just
probation."[24]

STRUCTURING THE PROCESS

A sine qua non of any successful reform process, therefore, is that it be introduced by means that allow the reason for change to be aired and pursued to best advantage; that is, the process must promote a dialogue that will define more completely the problem or opportunity giving rise to the need for change, identify problem sources, specify the goals of change, and develop and implement appropriate solutions.[25] Several familiar responses spring to mind, including professional publications, articles and letters to newspaper or magazine editorial pages, legislative debate, and informal idea and information exchanges within and between interested parties. Although each of these might well contribute to one or another phase of the process of adopting or implementing a particular innovation, they may also be viewed as merely subcomponents of an overall forum or process; the success of this supraprocess will depend on its ability to promote, coordinate, monitor, and sustain the participation, support, and competence of its key actors.[26]

The type of forum most likely to facilitate the process between perceiving a need for change and bringing alternatives to imprisonment into operation will have two characteristics. These are, first, the skills and resources needed to conduct an informed evaluation of different innovations, and to develop and execute appropriate implementation strategies; and, second, the administrative and authority structure required to maximize the availability and impact of such skills and resources. The first of these characteristics can be termed the "resource requirements" of an ideal reform forum; the second is its "structural requirements." Both requirements must be determined by two frames of reference. The first frame of reference is the environmental context within which the change process will take place, a context we shall refer to as the "implementation milieu." The second is the phase of the change process, and thus requires an analysis of the process of reform.

Implementation Milieu

As already noted, a key element of what has been called the implementation approach to reform has been its emphasis on the idea that successful innovation may depend more on the characteristics of the adopting organization than on those of the innovation itself. In particular, "theorists stress that an effective implementation process rests crucially on the adopting organization's capacity to mobilize and build participant support, cooperation, and competence."[27] An immediate difficulty in applying this insight to criminal justice innovations, however, is that there is no single "organization" within which reforms take place. This is especially true in areas such as alternatives to incarceration involving sentencing options that are shaped by the policies, procedures, and practices of a wide variety of actors across the entire criminal justice system and beyond it. Although it is common to hear of a particular alternative as being a "probation" program, a "public defender's" program, or even a "courts" program, the nature of the criminal justice process guarantees that few reforms of any substance can hope for success unless the adopting "organization" incorporates a variety of other agencies and outside parties whose interests might be affected.

Numerous writers have commented on the unique structure of the criminal court system,[28] concluding that it is not only an organization in which deviations from the status quo will encounter strong resistance,[29] but also one in which change is unlikely to be considered at all.[30] Three dimensions of organizational structure—complexity, formalization, and centralization—have been identified by Zaltman and Duncan as affecting the change process. Complexity refers to the number of occupational specialties and levels of professionalization in the organization; formalization is the extent of emphasis on conformity to rules; and centralization refers to the negatively correlated dimensions of authority and participation. Obviously, the fragmented complex of interdependent agencies that make up the criminal justice system—with their diversity of values and goals, and with their independent power bases, largely unconnected by any form of hierarchical authority—scores high on complexity and low in terms of centralization, a combination considered least conducive to a successful implementation process.[31] Similarly inauspicious is the observation that the need to maintain smooth case flow, professional power, and existing resources—in the absence of hierarchical authority, and in a politically vulnerable setting in which external pressures from the public, media, and politicians are a constant threat to stability—all promote an organizational climate characterized by informal accommodations and relationships that are consistently and tenaciously protected and enforced.[32] To the extent that open dialogue on the need for change might undermine such a system of accommodations (by highlighting for the system's critics sources of internal conflict), tolerance is unlikely to be high for a process in which such a dialogue may perhaps be the most critical element.

Because of its high complexity, low centralization, and high emphasis on rule compliance, therefore, the criminal justice system is certainly not an ideal organizational context for a process of reform. Several writers have suggested that where existing organizational structures are ill suited to the task, an alternative one should be created. Zaltman and Duncan and Hudzik and Cordner, for example, have argued that where dominant organizational attributes are an impediment to innovation, a separate decision-making structure should be established for the purpose of initiating and developing innovations—or, in other words, for strategic planning.[33] This response is consistent with the observation by Lawrence and Lorsch that decentralized organizations frequently develop formal coordinating units, or what they refer to as "integrators."[34] This practice has long been reflected in the creation of state and local criminal justice planning agencies or coordinating commissions in the United States; in standing law reform commissions used in Britain and other Commonwealth countries, and advocated in the United States;[35] and, more recently, in the formation of very specialized entities such as sentencing guidelines commissions and prison overcrowding task forces.

Both the need for and the difficulty of creating a distinct entity for dialogue and action concerning the implementation of alternatives to incarceration stem from the broad array of actors who play a role in the way the criminal justice system operates. In other words, the interdependence of the system's different components and the ability of actors in one part to nullify or redirect changes made in another virtually guarantee that successful alternatives reform must be a group process. Such a process should be constrained by, and mutually adaptive to, the organizational context in which it must function.[36] In the absence of explicit recognition and analysis of the complexities of such a process, what little progress has been recorded toward implementing alternatives may be attributed to the adventitious political, professional, and personal skills and influence of individual innovation entrepreneurs.[37] In their recent examination of factors influencing the level of implementation of community corrections in Oregon, for example, Palumbo, Maynard-Moody, and Wright state:

> The literature on implementation also stresses the importance of "fixers," small numbers of persistent advocates who push for programs. The most successful counties [in Oregon] had a prominent individual or several individuals who took a leading role in getting the program started and in keeping it running once it was in place.[38]

Although the energies and skills of influential or charismatic change agents may obviously play an important role in any reform undertaking, exclusive reliance on their infrequent and serendipitous appearance, and on their having at least an intuitive sense of some of the fundamental elements of implementation theory, is obviously an unsystematic, ultimately unstable basis for progress. Rather, dependence on such individuals constitutes a prescription for faddish, sporadic, and transient emphasis shifts that in the long run may do more to detract from than enhance the development of rational, consistent incarceration (or any other criminal justice) policy and practice in which the role of alternatives is clearly and systematically considered.

It might be helpful, therefore, to consider the potential advantage and feasibility of moving away from a hit-or-miss reform scenario toward one in which decisions about adopting and implementing alternatives might become the routine undertaking of an organizational vehicle such as an alternatives authority. Such a consideration may be informed by reference to the limited documentation on the experiences of similar efforts in the past, and confidence in the generalizability of those experiences may be enhanced by comparing them with prescriptions for successful change derived from the more general implementation literature.

Phases of the Reform Process

Whether the potential utility of a specially constituted alternatives authority is assessed against theory or against prior experience, the assessment task may be clarified by considering the role of such an entity and its ability to enhance the likelihood of success at different phases of the reform process. The view that planning and analysis of the reform process may benefit from a "stage" or "phase" perspective has received widespread support in the general literature on planned change and criminal justice, and more recently in works specifically addressing correctional overcrowding problems. Kaufman, for example, has categorized the work of participants in the Philadelphia-based Prison Overcrowding Project—which attempts to address crowding problems with carefully selected "policy groups" in Oregon, Michigan, Colorado, and South Carolina—as a process involving six phases; these range from defining the problem and identifying factors that have led to population increases, to adopting and implementing options to control overcrowding.[39]

Going beyond such very basic descriptive accounts, other authors have suggested different process models that utilize a phase approach. Yin, for example, has proposed a model that progresses through four phases that he labels policy development, program development, project design, and project implementation.[40] Similarly, in their discussion of alternatives to incarceration, Mathias and Steelman suggest a model that divides the process of change into three stages of development, enactment, and implementation.[41] Even more generally, Zaltman and Duncan divide the process into two stages of initiation and implementation, including in the former the steps of developing an awareness of a need for change, exploring alternatives, and deciding to adopt particular solutions.[42]

Although each of the various models embodies slightly different insights, their shared emphasis on viewing the process in terms of separable stages or phases has several advantages. Most important, it helps to anticipate and identify some of the sources and types of intense resistance to change that are likely to occur at different points in the process. Resistance to change is one of the most extensively documented phenomena in the planned change literature, with an abundance of illustrations from the field of criminal justice, especially in situations in which the particular innovation involved may radically affect the distribution of power within and between different agencies in the system.[43] A phased task orientation permits better categorization and management of sources of resistance for a number of reasons. Recognition that different phases of the process will require the support and cooperation of different decision makers, for example, allows an opportunity to diffuse resistance by involving key actors in stages preceding the one in which their participation begins to be particularly crucial. Similarly, just as key decision makers and sources of resistance may be isolated for attention at different stages of the process, so obviously can the strategies, resources, levels of authority, administrative structure, and procedures needed to accommodate them.

INITIATING THE PROCESS

As we have noted, the seeds of change are sown with the perception on the part of an individual or group that problems with existing practices and the availability of potentially superior options make reform desirable or necessary. Indeed, the strength of the motivation to change has been categorized in the implementation literature as one of the three major determinants of successful innovation,[44] and a variety of factors have been identified as most crucial to the strength or weakness of the motivational impetus for reform. In assessing the potential utility and composition of a body such as an alternatives authority, therefore, a first step would be to consider how such an entity might enhance or detract from such factors.

In general, two sometimes related variables have been specified as playing a major role in enhancing the motivation for change, and thereby the likelihood of successful initiation and implementation of reform. To use Justice Holmes's expression again, one factor, to which we shall return later, is "the power of the thought," or the persuasiveness of the logical and empirical rationale behind the perceived need for change. A second dimension, which has been a dominant theme in the literature of planned change, consists of factors defining the locus of the perceived need for change; foremost among these are the status or relationship of the change promoters with respect to the target organization and the extent to which their motivation is shared by significant others.[45]

On the question of status, several writers have emphasized the advantage of having the perceived need for change originate with or be strongly endorsed by insiders of the target organization.[46] Carroll and Galegher and Feller and Menzel have noted the increased probability of successful implementation when the change process is initiated by an organization's leaders.[47] Similar importance has been attached to the fact

> that the initiation come from a respected and, ideally, a trusted source. The persons being influenced need confidence that the change can, in fact, be effected, and a large part of this confidence comes initially from their confidence in the power and judgment of the influencing agent.[48]

Still further emphasis on the significance of the high status of those promoting change is found in works by Rothman, Erlich, and Teresa and by Dalton,[49] who goes so far as to say that "prestige and power on the part of the initiator seem to be a necessary if not sufficient condition for introducing large-scale change in any system."[50]

In addition to the emphasis on the status of the change promoter, a central theme of the implementation literature has been that organizational support is strongly enhanced by a broadly shared dissatisfaction with existing practices. Broad participation in the initial process of defining the problem, specifying the goal, and deciding to adopt a particular reform, although often cumbersome and not without potential drawbacks, is widely held to improve the probability of successful implementation.[51] Participation increases ownership in the process and commitment to the decisions that result from it.[52] From this perspective, whether the triggering mechanism behind the initial perceived need for change is the result of self-analysis of personal practices and values, or an inspirational insight gained from the professional or popular media or from a social or professional exchange, the task of responding to that motivation by initiating a planned process of change toward greater reliance on alternatives to incarceration (or some other innovation) can be seen as one of progressively broadening a constituency within the target organization, among whom the perceived or felt need for change becomes shared.

In weighing the utility of a standing body such as the alternatives authority, along the dimensions of providing the degree of status, opportunity for constituency building, and broad participation, the assessment must take into account the dual role of such an entity: such a body would not only generate and promote innovations but would also serve as gatekeeper or broker for change entrepreneurs seeking recognition by the organization. If the ultimate target organization is seen as the criminal justice system as a whole, then on each criterion specified obvious advantages accrue from having in the role of change promoter a broadly based alternatives authority, composed of influential system, political, and community leaders. The probability of successful innovation improves with the high status of its individual members within and between their respective home agencies, their attendant ability to secure the cooperation and participation of subordinates in different phases of the process, and their collective advantage in securing additional sources of influence such as political and media support or external funding.

In addition to the role of an alternatives authority as the collective promoter of change, it is also possible to view such a body as a sort of intermediate target organization available to individual change entrepreneurs as a bridge of communication and influence to the system as a whole. Its strength in this capacity can be measured by its ability to provide a conveniently centralized point of access and audience for individual change promoters who may be outsiders to the system or occupy only subordinate positions within it. When the likelihood of successful implementation is jeopardized by such status difficulties, the situation can be improved by locating and securing the support of high-status allies within the target organization. To the extent that formal and informal provisions for access to the standing alternatives group facilitate such a task, the burden of initiating reform may be lightened accordingly.

At a minimum, routinizing at least the contemplation of alternatives to incarceration by a standing body may constitute an important step toward inducing reform, insofar as it signifies that these alternatives are to be taken more seriously than they have been to date. As Harris has recently noted,

It is reflective of the dominance of imprisonment in the imagery of punishment in America that the bulk of significant changes in sentencing and correctional law, policy, and practice over the last decade have focused almost exclusively on modifying how imprisonment is used....Often they have dealt to some extent with the question of which offenders would be imprisoned and which not (the in/out decision), but most of the new schemes are relatively indifferent as to what happens to persons who are not incarcerated at all or who are released from confinement early but kept under correctional supervision....[T]he fact is that we have little clear sanctioning law or policy except with respect to imprisonment. As a result, there is widespread public and official ignorance about and disenchantment with sanctions not involving confinement.[53]

Granting as much importance and opportunity to the consideration of alternatives as we have hitherto reserved for regulating the conditions and length of confinement suggests a vital symbolic catalyst toward promoting the eventual value clarification and specification necessary to secure greater acceptance of alternative sanctions.

ASSESSING ALTERNATIVES: INFORMATION AND RESOURCES

Turning from the general significance of the collective and individual status of members of an alternatives authority, its potential utility and composition can be explored further through a more specific examination of its role. As noted earlier, such an assessment involves questions of the resources needed to inform dialogue and decisions about adopting and implementing alternatives, as well as questions of the appropriate authority structure and administrative procedure to maximize the availability and impact of such resources.

Information Needs

Whether the task is weighing the validity of arguments for change or a particular alternative as a prelude to reaching policy decisions, or whether the concern is for subsequent management control and assistance to field staff during implementation, the scope and complexity of the logical and practical issues to be resolved are daunting.[54] Success or failure in each undertaking will hinge critically on an ability to develop and utilize information ranging from programmatic goals and outcomes to technical capacity and political feasibility. In the absence of any clear hierarchical control structure among and even within components of the criminal justice system, the importance of a comprehensive information strategy becomes acute:

After all, the absolute ruler needs little or no information to command and expect compliance....Information[, however], looms as a critical factor in sophisticated games involving bargaining (leveraging) and fixing....[T]he emerging information strategy will be our best early indicator of the extent to which an agency has begun to adopt the implementation perspective. If we continue to see the same rhetoric about final outcomes and the same kind of unrealistic reliance on management information systems of the past, this surely is good evidence of game playing or of basic misunderstanding. Information demands take on a concreteness not found in other areas, and so can tell us a great deal about the seriousness of the agency in pursuing the implementation perspective.[55]

Information demands in the area of alternatives to incarceration are most generally shaped by requests by and to criminal justice policymakers for alternatives that "work"; more specifically, the entrenched status of prison and jail dispositions has cast the prospect of change as a task of finding alternatives that "work as well as" incarceration. In order to operationalize a mandate as vague as the delivery of alternatives that are "as good as" incarceration (or at least not appreciably worse), information needs present themselves at several levels.

First, more specificity must be provided concerning the variety of possible meanings implied in the term "work." If alternatives are to be advocated or opposed on the basis of whether they are "as good as" incarceration, a necessary starting point for rational dialogue must be to make explicit answers to the implied question, "As good at doing what?"

Accommodation versus Specification of Goals

Given a wide variety of motives for considering alternatives to incarceration, criteria for evaluating the success of any particular innovation will also vary. That is, goal consensus cannot be assumed even when many key actors are voicing support for similar alternatives. Some may define success, for example, as reducing the prison population, while others may define it as avoiding court intervention or as seeing probationers actively paying for their crimes through community service.

In the reformers' haste to bring about desired changes, there is a temptation to accommodate as many of these goals as possible. Emphasis is placed on obtaining support rather than on establishing a common ground for supporting, or at least accepting, the adoption of a particular innovation. Inherent in such broad accommodations are several dangers with respect to both the implementation process and the innovation's effectiveness.

First, it is well established that innovations undergo modification or adaptation during implementation,[56]a process necessitated by the interaction between an innovation and the personal preferences of those implementing it, as well as by the unique nature of each organization's environment. Cultural norms, political traditions, and current power struggles are among the factors that will define the shape of the innovation. The success of this adaptation process is to a great extent determined by the structure provided by setting clear and specific goals for the innovation. Lacking this specificity, the innovation as implemented may only faintly resemble what was originally intended, thus making likely a view that the innovation "doesn't work."

Implementation involves translating abstract ideas into concrete actions. Although vague or multiple goals may facilitate the initial acceptance of an innovation, unclear or contradictory goals greatly hamper the ability of program directors to communicate expectations and standards of behavior to staff who will be working directly with offenders, and this in turn reduces the clarity of expectations communicated by staff to offenders. Lack of specificity at this level of implementation, therefore, may lead to confusion, frustration, and dissatisfaction with the program.

A third and more critical consequence of attempting accommodation of a broad array of goals is its impact on future innovation efforts. Once an innovation is in place, conflict is likely to arise as to its effectiveness.[57] After all, different goals imply different effectiveness criteria, and while success may be indicated on some measures of effectiveness, other measures may indicate failure. Supporters of the goals that are not being achieved will judge the program a failure, and if confronted with other supporters who view the program as a success, they are likely to mistrust not only the program's proponents but also the implementation process itself. This mistrust and newfound reluctance to participate in future projects are a most damaging consequence of sacrificing goal specificity for broad support.

Specification of goals, then, is a crucial step in the implementation of alternatives to incarceration as well as other criminal justice reforms. While extensive dialogue will be necessary to arrive at a satisfactory level of agreement as to what those goals should be, the value of specification must not be underestimated. Furthermore, such dialogues are likely to increase the capacity of criminal justice systems to develop and implement innovations and to communicate clearly its success to other systems.

Goal specification in the alternatives debate, or clarifying demands for alternatives that "work" or are "as good as" incarceration, typically expands into concerns that they must "protect society" and see that "justice" is done. The former criterion envelops the variety of traditional utilitarian, crime-control issues of incapacitation, rehabilitation, and deterrence. Comparing incarceration with the alternatives on the "justice" dimension most typically translates into retributive, desert, or (less charitably) vindictive concerns that an appropriately severe penalty be imposed (that the punishment fit the crime). Although this latter demand most often reduces to a sense that offenders should "pay their debt to society" and should not "get off" too lightly, it is increasingly supplemented nowadays by support for compensating crime victims in various ways.[58]

For both utilitarian and retributive goals, a further comparison dimension that has assumed heightened importance in recent years is that of equity. Although the standards of vital "similarity" will vary considerably depending on the broader utilitarian or retributive goal being pursued, the basic challenge to alternatives advocates on this level is to show that their approach is no worse than incarceration at guaranteeing that similarly situated offenders will be handled similarly.

Further probing of the meaning behind demands for alternatives that "work" reveals a variety of more functional goals that must be factored into the balance. Included at this level are concerns such as costs, personal and organizational convenience, impact on public and professional relations and image, and political feasibility.

The range and importance of possible goals against which incarceration and the alternatives might be compared will inevitably fluctuate over time. Consequently, specification of goals must be accomplished not only for an elite cadre of policymakers but also for those practitioners who will exercise front-line control over whether a particular alternative is successfully implemented. As a result, systematic identification and weighing of the initial and continued salience of the various comparison dimensions will be essential throughout the entire reform process. Demonstrating even the most overwhelming advantage of an alternative over incarceration will obviously be to little avail if the evaluation criterion stems from a goal that is of little interest to key actors in the process.

Assuming the specification of goals and their salience as a basis for developing a working level of consensus about criteria for demonstrating the relative advantage of alternatives over incarceration, still a further information gap remains. Performance data in the form of input, output, and outcome information are required for responding to questions about the ability of alternatives to satisfy the specified assumptions and expectations of key participants in the change process. An adequate information strategy at this level requires sensitivity to the unique climate of the target jurisdiction, demonstrating any advantage of a specific alternative under specific social, economic, cultural, and political circumstance.

Resource Needs

The adoption and implementation of alternatives to incarceration in a continuing process of dialogue driven by the foregoing types of information obviously constitute a major departure from the relatively serendipitous approach that has produced so little progress thus far. Equally apparent should be the necessity for a sizable commitment of support and resources for the work of any entity such as an alternatives authority, as well as a significant level of involvement by its members. Most of the empirical questions raised by the comparison demanded between incarceration and the alternatives, whether along normative or functional dimensions, cannot be answered from available data to any significant degree. Comparisons in terms of traditional utilitarian punishment goals, for example, are hindered by the twin problems that our understanding of the crime-reduction effects of incarceration is very hazy,[59] and that none of the options typically referred to as "alternatives" has yet been shown to have actually been applied to any sizable offender population that would otherwise have been incarcerated. Similarly, little empirical foundation exists to indicate the relative weight that should be afforded to retributive considerations in formulating and implementing policy about alternatives to incarceration.[60] Comparisons in terms of functional goals, such as public and professional approval and political expedience, are thwarted by comparable information deficiencies, perpetuating what may be a pluralistic ignorance that may impede risk taking.[61]

To remedy these information deficiencies and to make the implementation of alternatives a continuous extension of the correctional policymaking process, provisions must be made in the composition of an alternatives authority for an action-research staff authorized to coordinate the systematic collection, analysis, and feedback of information on which planning and implementation decisions can be based. The carefully planned interaction of research scientists and practitioners/policymakers that characterizes the action-research model of organizational change[62] stands in sharp contrast in many ways to the attitudes toward information needs, ranging from casual lip service to open contempt, that too often pervade the deliberations of legislative bodies, task forces, and commissions dealing with criminal justice issues. It requires substituting as a foundation for reform a dynamic, long-term information strategy instead of the rote parroting of vaguely articulated, untested assumptions and opinions that so often passes for rational debate and justification for actions in the above forums. It is neither inexpensive nor often conducive to quick-fix solutions to complex problems. Its strengths, however, are well documented in the general literature on organizational change, and its effectiveness as a reform strategy is receiving increasing attention and recognition in the field of criminal justice.[63] Recent efforts to reform commitment policies and practices in the areas of bail release, sentencing, and parole decision making, for example, all show encouraging signs of the value of systematic application of the collaborative elements of an action-research approach to implementing change.[64]

CONCLUSION

Obviously, it has not been our intent to offer a detailed blueprint for an "ideal" alternatives authority. Beyond the general principles we have touched on, issues of authorization, funding, composition, and administration will all require far more extensive jurisdiction-specific consideration than is possible here. Although alternatives to imprisonment might best be considered by a state-level organization, for example, consideration of alternatives to jail might proceed to most advantage on a local or regional basis. If so, the systemwide focus we have emphasized clearly requires further planning to coordinate the activities of authorities operating at different levels. In either case, a more detailed assessment of the feasibility and utility of any alternatives authority would have to include attention to numerous other concerns such as variations in political structure from site to site, and ways of securing stability and continuity of operation in the face of periodic changes in the key actors involved.

Nor are we unmindful of the remote possibility of success from even the most well-conceptualized and operationalized efforts. Organizational entities such as an alternatives authority, while not a common feature of the criminal justice landscape, are obviously not entirely without precedent. Commissions such as those recently established in a number of jurisdictions to develop and implement decision guidelines schemes, and to respond specifically to prison and jail overcrowding, have many of the attributes of composition or process assumed to be important to successful implementation. Undoubtedly the same could be said over the years of a wide variety of special and standing task forces, councils, and commissions formed in response to fleeting crises or as more stable vehicles for continuing system planning and coordination activities. The dearth of well-documented success stories from such groups would appear to weigh against a too-ready willingness to embrace the strategy we have discussed. Closer scrutiny, however, precludes on a number of grounds its too-ready rejection.

With few exceptions, there is no account of what changes the efforts of these bodies may have actually effected, and, more important, of the ways in which their impact (or lack thereof) might relate to variations in the conditions under which they were constituted and operated. Research to address these questions remains a neglected priority, especially with respect to those groups claiming success in developing and implementing alternatives to incarceration. At the same time, even during times of heightened fear of crime and intolerance for "coddling" criminals, competing concerns for human dignity, individual liberty, and the social and economic evils of incarceration remain compelling motives to entertain the possibility of alternatives. Equally, concern for crime prevention and restoring confidence in the justice system would seem to demand that such possibilities be entertained methodically, experimentally, and at a level of visibility that allows a degree of scrutiny and accountability that has hitherto not characterized the activities launched in the name of alternatives.

Having decisions about adopting and implementing alternatives to incarceration be the routine responsibility of an alternatives authority will not necessarily lead to greater reliance on alternatives to incarceration in the long run. To the contrary, it is conceivable, although to us unlikely, that the resulting understanding of existing practices could lead in the opposite direction. The need for change has not been in the direction of supporting or criticizing any particular alternative to incarceration; rather, our focus has been on an alternative way of approaching the consideration of alternatives as a whole. Regardless of one's preference for ultimate outcome, however, perseverance with the alternatives authority would appear to have much to commend itself as a way of achieving a greater, more informed political and public awareness of the criteria and data that should enter into assessments of the relative safety and justice of incarceration and the alternatives, and as a way of systematically advancing our knowledge of the dynamics of the process by which criminal justice innovation occurs and reforms are successfully implemented.

NOTES

1. U.S. (1919).
2. For research suggesting that U.S. policymakers may underestimate the public's tolerance for nonincarcerative options, and that they may be erroneously attributing excessively punitive attributes to their constituency, see S. D. Gottfredson and R. B. Taylor, *The Correctional Crisis: Prison Populations and Public Policy* (Washington, DC: National Institute of Corrections, 1983). See also T. Flanagan and S. L. Caulfield, "Public Opinion and Prison Policy: A Review," *Prison Journal* 64 (1984): 31.
3. J. Austin and B. Krisberg, "The Unmet Promise of Alternatives to Incarceration," *Crime and Delinquency* 28 (1982): 374.
4. M. K. Harris, "Strategies, Values and the Emerging Generation of Alternatives to Incarceration," *New York University Review of Law and Social Change* 12 (1983–84):141–70, at 145.
5. Austin and Krisberg, "Unmet Promise," p. 377.

6. See, generally, A. T. Harland and P. W. Harris, "Developing and Implementing Alternatives to Incarceration: A Problem of Planned Change in Criminal Justice," *University of Illinois Law Review* 1984 (1984): 319, 327–29.

7. See, for example, P. Ellickson and J. Petersilia, *Implementing New Ideas in Criminal Justice*, R-2929-NIJ (Santa Monica, CA: Rand Corporation, April 1983). See also J. Galegher and J. S. Carroll, "Voluntary Sentencing Guidelines: Prescription for Justice or Patent Medicine?" *Law and Human Behavior* 7 (1983): 361; C. W. Grau, "The Limits of Planned Change in Courts," *Justice System Journal* 6 (1981): 854; and M. Morash, ed., *Implementing Criminal Justice Policies* (Beverly Hills, CA: Sage, 1982).

8. For extensive citations to this body of literature, see Harland and Harris, "Developing and Implementing Alternatives to Incarceration," p. 328, notes 36–38.

9. But see S. Martin, "The Politics of Sentencing Reform: Sentencing Guidelines in Minnesota and Pennsylvania," in A. Blumstein et al., eds., *Research on Sentencing: The Search for Reform* (Washington, DC: U.S. Department of Justice, 1983), p. 36. See also C. Baird, "Report on Intensive Supervision Programs in Probation and Parole" (Unpublished report on file, Department of Criminal Justice, Temple University, Philadelphia, PA, 1983).

10. S. Schlossman, G. Zellman, and R. Shavelson, *Delinquency Prevention in South Chicago*, R-3142-NIE (Santa Monica, CA: Rand Corporation, May 1984), p. 5.

11. See, for example, Harris, "Strategies, Values."

12. Expediting the review and processing of paperwork on pretrial detainees being considered for conditional release, or reducing preparation time for presentence reports or trial transcripts needed for drafting appeals, could speed release from confinement in some cases. The number of offenders being detained longer than necessary because of processing delays varies significantly from one jurisdiction to another, as does the precise nature and cause of those delays. Even if the number may not be thought to be large by most practitioners, however, this group of offenders is at least a relatively noncontroversial starting point in any discussion of alternatives to incarceration; even the most fervent law-and-order advocates will generally recognize the injustice of detaining people longer than necessary because of avoidable bureaucratic or technological bottlenecks in processing their cases.

13. For an exception, see G. Kaufman, response to R. S. Singer, "Desert Sentencing and Prison Overcrowding: Some Doubts and Tentative Answers," *New York University Review of Law and Social Change* 12 (1983–84): 125. See also G. Kaufman, "The National Prison Overcrowding Project:

Policy Analysis and Policies, A New Approach," and J. Mullen, "Prison Crowding and the Evaluation of Public Policy," *The Annals* of the American Academy of Political and Social Science 478 (March 1985):161–72 and 31–46.

14. See P. W. Harris and A. T. Harland, "Sentencing Alternatives: Development, Implementation Issues, and Evaluation," *Judicature* 68 (1985): 210.

15. See, for example, the discussions of failures in the context of sentencing guidelines reforms in Galegher and Carroll, "Voluntary Sentencing Guidelines," and in M. R. Gottfredson and D. M. Gottfredson, "Guidelines for Incarceration Decisions: A Partisan Review," *University of Illinois Law Review* 1984 (1984): 291.

16. Galegher and Carroll, "Voluntary Sentencing Guidelines," p. 395.

17. N. Morris, "Impediments to Penal Reform," *University of Chicago Law Review* 33 (1966): 627.

18. See, for example, National Advisory Commission on Criminal Justice Standards and Goals, *Corrections* (1973): 1–2: "[T]he failure of major institutions to reduce crime is incontestable. Recidivism rates are notoriously high . . . They change the committed offender, but the change is more likely to be negative than positive." See also G. S. Funke, "The Economics of Prison Crowding," *The Annals* of the American Academy of Political and Social Science 478 (March 1985): 86–99.

19. E. W. Zedlewski, *The Economics of Disincarceration*, NIJ Reports (Washington, DC: National Institute of Justice, 1984).

20. For a thorough discussion of the courts' attempts to deal with crowding, see R. Smolla, "Prison Overcrowding and the Courts: A Roadmap for the 1980's, *University of Illinois Law Review* 1985 (1984): 389.

21. The most reluctant actors, of course, may abdicate control over the situation entirely, electing instead the politically safe and irresponsible tactic of condemning court-imposed mandates without offering any workable alternative suggestions, and, more important, without participating in any meaningful dialogue with those in the system who might be open to try to construct and implement them. The difficulty and essential importance of promoting and sustaining such a dialogue among key actors in the criminal justice system, as a prerequisite of successful change, is a theme to which we return repeatedly in our assessment of the potential utility of an alternatives authority.

22. An example of foundation-supported organizations devoted exclusively to such activities is the National Institute for Sentencing Alternatives, Brandeis University, Waltham, MA.

23. See, for example, remarks of Judge B. J. Fried, Criminal Court of the City of New York, in *New York University Review of Law and Social*

Change 12 (1983–84): 201: "I think we need more of these alternatives. Frankly, I think it's an outrage that the community does not provide judges with the kind of flexibility that a range of sentencing options would provide; we just do not have the options."

24. The widely reputed professional and public view that current probation amounts to little more than a "slap on the wrist" for most offenders, and the corresponding belief that it should be made "tougher," gains impetus from reports of ludicrously unmanageable case loads and the impossibility of meaningful supervision under such circumstances. See K. Krajick, "Probation: The Original Community Program," *Corrections Magazine* (December 1980): 7; S. Gettlinger, "Intensive Supervision: Can It Rehabilitate Probation?" *Corrections Magazine* (April 1983): 7.

25. In describing the type of forum utilized (1983–84) in the Philadelphia-based Prison Overcrowding Project, Kaufman ("Desert Sentencing and Prison Overcrowding," pp. 127–28) states.

For policymakers to take responsibility for controlling the size of the prison population, there must be a structure which facilitates decision-making . . . This structure provides the forum to cut across the traditional organizational lines which frequently act as impediments to communication and effective action. It enables these decision-makers to take a "systems" approach to collectively examine, adopt, and implement particular policies to control crowding. To be effective, the policy group members must not only represent the broad range of criminal justice decision-makers but must also be people of power and influence so that they can implement changes once they decide what those changes should be.

26. "The implementation issue most straightforwardly concerns how to bring together communications, commitment, and capacity so as to carry a decision into practice." W. Williams, *Reports of the National Juvenile Justice Assessment Centers: Implementation Issues* (Washington, DC: National Institute of Juvenile Justice and Delinquency Prevention, July 1981), p. 3. For a methodological review of measurement problems associated with assessing degrees of implementation, see M. A. Scheiner and E. L. Rezmovic, "Measuring the Degree of Program Implementation: A Methodological Review," *Evaluation Review* 7 (1983): 599.

27. Schlossman, Zellman, and Shavelson, *Delinquency Prevention*, p. 5.

28. See, for example, Grau, "Limits of Planned Change."

29. Galegher and Carroll, "Voluntary Sentencing Guidelines," p. 386.

30. M. Feeley, *Court Reform on Trial: Why Simple Solutions Fail* (New York: Basic Books, 1977), p. 192.

31. G. Zaltman and R. Duncan, *Strategies for Planned Change* (New York: Wiley, 1977), pp. 261–70.

32. See Feeley, *Court Reform on Trial*. See also C. Baar, "The Scope and Limits of Court Reform," *Justice System Journal* 5 (1980): 274; C. Burnstein, "Criminal Case Processing from an Organizational Perspective: Current Research Trends," *Justice System Journal* 5 (1980): 258.

33. Zaltman and Duncan, *Strategies for Planned Change*, p. 266; J. Hudzik and G. Cordner, *Planning Change in Criminal Justice Organizations and Systems* (New York: Macmillan, 1983).

34. P. Lawrence and J. Lorsch, *Developing Organizations: Diagnosis and Action* (Reading, MA: Addison-Wesley, 1969).

35. See, for example, M. E. Frankel, *Criminal Sentences: Law without Order* (New York: Hill and Wang, 1972).

36. For further reference to the inevitability of mutual adaptation of innovation and organization, such that the former is changed to respond to idiosyncrasies of the local organizational context, while the latter alters to accommodate the innovation, see the section "Accommodation versus Specification of Goals" later in this chapter.

37. See, for example, the account of how Project 20, one of the nation's first community service programs, came into being, in M. K. Harris, *Community Service by Offenders* (Washington, DC: National Institute of Corrections, 1979).

38. D. J. Palumbo, S. Maynard-Moody, and P. Wright, "Measuring Degrees of Successful Implementation: Achieving Policy versus Statutory Goals," *Evaluation Review* 8 (1984) : 64.

39. Kaufman, "Desert Sentencing," pp. 128–30.

40. R. K. Yin, *Planning for Implementation* (Washington, DC: Case Study Institute, 1982).

41. R. Mathias and M. Steelman, *Controlling Prison Populations: An Assessment of Current Mechanisms* (Washington DC: National Council on Crime and Delinquency, 1981).

42. Zaltman and Duncan, *Strategies for Planned Change*.

43. See Harland and Harris, "Developing and Implementing Alternatives to Incarceration," pp. 339–41.

44. The other two are the strength of obstacles and the availability of resources for overcoming them. J. Mohr, "Determinants of Innovation in Organizations," *American Political Science Review* 3 (1969): 111, 114.

45. Zaltman and Duncan, *Strategies for Planned Change*, pp. 16, 24; Galegher and Carroll, "Voluntary Sentencing Guidelines," p. 385; J. Rothman, J. Erlich, and J. Teresa, *Promoting Innovation and Change in Organizations and Communities: A Planning Manual* (New York: Wiley, 1976), p. 24.

46. Rothman, Erlich, and Teresa, *Promoting Innovation*; Galegher and Carroll, "Voluntary Sentencing Guidelines," p. 385.

47. Galegher and Carroll, "Voluntary Sentencing Guidelines"; Zaltman and Duncan, *Strategies for Planned Change*, pp. 262, 276–77.

48. G. Dalton, "Influence and Organizational Change," in O. R. Negandhi and J. P. Schwitter, eds., *Organizational Behavior Models* (Kent, OH: Kent State University Press, 1970), p. 84.

49. Rothman, Erlich, and Teresa, *Promoting Innovation*.

50. Dalton, "Influence and Organizational Change," p. 86.

51. Harland and Harris, "Developing and Implementing Alternatives to Incarceration," pp. 334–35.

52. The theme of broad participation as a means to reduce resistance to change and to gain support for decisions that have been made permeates much of the change literature. See, for example, C. Argyris, *Intervention Theory and Method: A Behavioral Science View* (Reading, MA: Addison-Wesley, 1970); W. Bennis, *Changing Organizations* (New York: McGraw-Hill, 1966); K. Levin, *Field Theory in Social Science* (New York: Harper and Row, 1951); for a more recent example in the criminal justice literature, see H. Toch and J. Grant, *Reforming Human Services* (Beverly Hills, CA: Sage, 1983).

53. M. K. Harris, "Nonincarcerative Sanctions and Reduction of Prison Crowding" (Draft mimeo on file, Department of Criminal Justice, Temple University, Philadelphia, PA, June 1984), p. 11.

54. See, for example, M. McLaughlin, "Implementation as Mutual Adaptation," in N. Williams and R. Elmore, eds., *Social Program Implementation* (New York: Academic Press, 1976).

55. Williams, *Reports of the National Juvenile Justice Assessment Centers*, pp. 80–81.

56. McLaughlin, "Implementation as Mutual Adaptation." See also S. Barrett and C. Fudge, "Examining the Policy-Action Relationship," in S. Barrett and C. Fudge, *Policy and Action* (London: Methuen, 1981).

57. J. D. Casper and D. Brereton, "Evaluating Criminal Justice Reforms," *Law and Society Review* 18 (1984): 126, 130.

58. Although compensating crime victims can be argued for as a requirement of justice, philosophers have long distinguished restitution and punishment as very distinct concepts. See A. T. Harland, "Monetary Remedies for the Victims of Crime: Assessing the Role of the Criminal Courts," *UCLA Law Review* 30 (1982): 52.

59. See sources cited in Harland and Harris, "Developing and Implementing Alternatives to Incarceration," p. 349, note 173.

60. Ibid., pp. 350–58.

61. See Gottfredson and Taylor, *Correctional Crisis*.

62. For a succinct discussion of the action-research model, see M. L. McConkie, *The Correctional Application of Change Theories* (Athens, GA:

Corrections Division, Institute of Government, University of Georgia, June 1977), pp. 117–22.

63. See, for example J. Goldkamp and M. Gottfredson, *Judicial Guidelines for Bail: The Philadelphia Experiment* (Washington, DC: National Institute of Justice, 1984), esp. pp. 5–11.

64. See Harland and Harris, "Developing and Implementing Alternatives to Incarceration," pp. 360–62, text at notes 229–45.

10 A Brief for De-escalating Criminal Sanctions

M. KAY HARRIS

Throughout the 1960s, the adult prison population in the United States was either stable or decreasing in size.[1] In the early 1970s the population began to rise dramatically, growing from 196,183 in 1972[2] to 503,601 in 1985.[3] This more than doubling of our prison population is partially a reflection of growth in the size of the teenage and young adult populations, but there is little doubt that it can be attributed in large measure to growing punitiveness and sterner sentencing and release practices.[4]

Dramatic changes in laws governing sentencing and release decisions have occurred across the country in recent years. Twelve states have adopted determinate sentencing structures and eliminated the discretionary power of a paroling authority to release prisoners before their full sentences have been completed.[5] A number of states have adopted or are developing sentencing guideline systems.[6] Given that other legislatures are considering adoption of similar major changes in sentencing practices, attention has begun to focus on whether or not the tremendous growth in prison populations is related to the restructuring of sentencing systems.

The Panel on Sentencing Research of the National Academy of Sciences recently concluded that the "substantial increases in prison populations in jurisdictions that have adopted sentencing reforms continue preexisting trends in sentencing and do not appear to be substantially caused by these sentencing reforms."[7] The panel noted that these "sentencing reform efforts, rather than stimulating prison population increases, may themselves reflect a broader shift in public sentiment regarding criminal justice policies."[8] However, these findings were based only on experiences of states that have "systematically altered sentencing laws and practices," excluding assessment of the impact of such nonsystematic changes in law as passage of mandatory sentencing provisions for a range of offenses and types of offenders.[9]

In any case, the fact is that whether punishments have become harsher and prison populations so much larger because of changes in sentencing laws or whether changes have been made in sentencing laws because of a shift in public sentiment, our prisons are crowded and our sanctioning practices have grown harsher. The growth of the punishment system is not limited to increases in the prison population: "Throughout the 1980's the probation population in this country grew faster than the prison population did."[10] At year-end 1984, more than 2.3 million men and 323,000 women were under the control of correctional systems, with 1.7 million people on probation, 268,500 on parole, 464,000 in state and federal prisons, and about half that number in local jails.[11] These numbers mean that about 1 out of every 35 adult men in the United States is under correctional control.[12]

As policymakers assess proposals for change in sentencing and dispositional practices, it is important to question whether continuing the recent trend toward making punishment more severe really makes good policy or good sense. To date we have been lamentably uncritical in evaluating the public statements made in support of "cracking down" and "getting tougher." Serious reconsideration of the direction in which sentencing reform should be moving is sorely needed. A central issue concerns the relative merits of choosing either to escalate or to de-escalate the severity of criminal sanctions.

THE PRESUMPTION SHOULD REST ON THE SIDE OF DE-ESCALATION

In determining the overall direction in which sentencing reforms should be moving, certain principles fundamental to a free society require adoption of a presumption in favor of lesser punishments. Care must be taken to see that concern about crime does not lead to acceptance of practices that are inconsistent with respect for the individual liberties and civil rights that we prize so highly. Governmental intrusions into the lives of citizens need to be justified by a clear showing that such intervention is necessary to achievement of a legitimate governmental purpose and that no lesser intervention will serve as well. Those trying to justify the status quo or urging an escalation of punishments should bear the burden of proving that their schemes are necessary. This is the opposite of the current situation, in which it seems that calls for getting tougher are accepted almost without question, while those seeking to reduce the severity of punishments are challenged to provide hard proof of the value of their proposals.

The case for reducing the harshness of criminal penalties is multifaceted, involving philosophical, moral, empirical, and pragmatic arguments. This chapter highlights some of the major propositions on which that case rests. Some research findings are summarized, but greater emphasis is placed on ways of thinking about these issues. The aim is to encourage those who think there is a strong case for making sanctions tougher to think again, and to provide support for those who recognize that when it comes to punishment, more is not necessarily better.

ESCALATION OF CRIME CONTROL AND THE BURDEN OF PROOF

Many people interested in reform of sentencing are seeking ways to increase the effectiveness of sanctions in achieving utilitarian goals. That is, they believe that sentences should be designed to serve broad social goals, especially prevention of future crime. Among utilitarian goals, incapacitation and deterrence are most frequently offered as bases for escalating punishment levels in the interest of achieving greater crime control. Advocates of incapacitation theory argue that crime can be reduced by more effectively restricting opportunities for offenders to commit new crimes, as by incarcerating them for longer terms. Advocates of deterrence theory argue that if punishments are made more severe, both the individual being punished and the rest of the population will be less likely to commit crimes in the future because of fear of the punishment.

Given that incapacitation and deterrence are both utilitarian theories, those who would escalate punishments on these grounds should be expected to satisfy the requirements of utilitarian philos-

ophy. Unfortunately, utilitarian theory has been widely misconstrued as being concerned only with what is useful or "what works."
This misinterpretation as applied to criminal justice questions is
taken to mean that the only concern is what works best to control
crime. Debate then centers on whether future crime can best be
prevented by more rigorously controlling and disabling identified
offenders or by more effectively threatening and scaring potential
offenders, and on the best means of controlling, disabling, threatening, and scaring.

In trying to capture the essence of utilitarianism, John Stuart
Mill, who brought the term into use, said, "in the golden rule of
Jesus of Nazareth, we read the complete spirit of the ethics of utility.
'To do as you would be done by,' and 'to love your neighbor as
yourself,' constitute the ideal perfection of utilitarian morality."[13]
Utilitarian theory holds that the best course or act is the one that
makes for the best whole or that results in the greatest good or the
least dissatisfaction. Punishment, in inflicting pain or harm, must
be regarded as an evil. Thus, whenever some punishment is deemed
to be necessary—necessary in the sense of avoiding greater harm—
careful assessment of its effectiveness in doing more good than harm
is required. A utilitarian orientation requires avoiding inefficacious,
needless, or excessive intrusions on individual liberty, autonomy,
and dignity. Punishing to achieve deterrent or incapacitative results,
then, is justified under utilitarian theory only to the extent that it
can be established that resulting benefits outweigh resulting harms.

Over the last decade or so, a substantial body of knowledge about
the deterrent and incapacitative effects of sanctions has been produced. Notable in this regard are reports published by the Panel
on Research on Deterrent and Incapacitative Effects and the Panel
on Sentencing Research of the National Academy of Sciences. For
the panel on deterrence, Nagin reviewed more than 20 analyses
directed at testing the deterrence hypothesis for noncapital sanctions. He cautioned that

despite the intensiveness of the research effort, the empirical evidence is
still not sufficient for providing a rigorous confirmation of the existence of
a deterrence effect. Perhaps most important, the evidence is woefully
inadequate for providing a good estimate of the magnitude of whatever
effect may exist...

This is in stark contrast to some of the presentations in public discussions that have unequivocally concluded that sanctions deter and that have made sweeping suggestions that sanctioning practices be changed to take advantage of the presumed deterrent effect. Certainly, most people will agree that increasing sanctions will deter crime somewhat, but the critical question is, By how much? There is still considerable uncertainty over whether that effect is trivial . . . or profound. . . . Policy makers in the criminal justice system are done a disservice if they are left with the impression that the empirical evidence, which they themselves are frequently unable to evaluate, strongly supports the deterrence hypothesis.[14]

In a review of research on incapacitation effects, Cohen distinguished between schemes involving collective incapacitation and those involving selective incapacitation. Under collective strategies, standardized sentences would be developed on the basis of information about rates of reoffending associated with various offenses. Under selective strategies, individualized sentences would be prescribed based on predictions as to whether specific offenders would commit serious offenses at a high rate if not incarcerated. Cohen's overall conclusions regarding the effects of each type of strategy were as follows:

Collective incapacitation policies have only modest impacts on crime but can cause enormous increases in prison populations. Selective incapacitation strategies offer the possibility of achieving greater reductions in crime at considerably smaller costs in prison resources, but their success depends critically on the ability to identify high-rate offenders early in their careers or prospectively. As yet, this has not been accomplished.[15]

Numerous ethical objections have been raised to basing sanctions on deterrent or incapacitative aims. Without even reaching such issues, however, existing knowledge simply does not provide clear guides to policy formulation. Furthermore, available scientific information does not offer much support for escalating sanctions for crime reduction purposes. Deterrent effects, when found, seem to be tied more strongly to the certainty of sanctions than to their severity, and the relative benefits of incapacitative effects from incarceration generally seem to drop markedly as terms are extended.[16]

DE-ESCALATION AND JUST DESERTS

Not all "get tough" measures are advanced on crime control grounds. The argument is often made that penalties for various offenses should be increased simply because the crimes in question merit more severe punishment than is commonly imposed. Thus, even if available evidence does not support escalating penalties to achieve crime reduction aims, it might be argued that harsher sanctions would be justified on just-deserts grounds.

In fact, however, many proposals advanced under the banner of "giving offenders their just deserts" reflect fundamental inconsistencies with just-deserts philosophy. Just as utilitarian theory has been widely misconstrued, desert theory often has been confused with unmitigated harshness. Viewed as a compelling drive to see that offenders are made to suffer, a desert label is used to fuel efforts to make penalties increasingly severe.

In many cases, calls for making penalties harsher reflect confusion of desert philosophy with deterrent and incapacitative aims. Advocates of mandatory prison terms or mandatory-minimum sentences often reveal more interest in frightening potential offenders or keeping offenders regarded as dangerous off the streets than in honoring the principles central to desert theory. It is especially objectionable from a just-deserts perspective to determine how much someone will be punished on the basis of guesses or predictions about what that person or others might do in the future. Opposition to treating persons as objects as a means of attaining social goals is the distinguishing feature that attracts many adherents to just-deserts philosophy.

Just-deserts theory emphasizes equity and proportionality, stressing that similar offenses should be punished similarly and that the penalty in a given case should be in balance or commensurate with the seriousness of the crime. This requires that standard penalties of varying severity be available that allow clear distinctions to be made as to the relative seriousness of the crimes they are used to punish. If all offenses are treated harshly, important distinctions among categories of crimes deserving different amounts of blame may be blurred. If only selected offenses of current public concern are singled out for stiffer penalties, the result may be harsher treatment for those offenses than for others of similar seriousness.

Harshness also invites avoidance, as actors in the criminal justice process seek ways to mitigate penalties that seem unjust in individual cases or unrealistic in terms of available resources. Faced with laws mandating severe penalties, prosecutors, juries, and judges may find means to avoid pressing charges, convicting, and sentencing under those provisions. However, the vagaries of such adjustment processes are apt to result in inequities, with some defendants bearing the full brunt of the tougher laws and others escaping their reach. Similarly, as general escalation of penalties leads to backlogged courts and crowded jails and prisons, additional inequities may well result as pleas and sentences are bargained and emergency prison release mechanisms are triggered erratically.

There is another important way in which a just-deserts orientation supports the need for de-escalating penalties from current levels. A principle central to desert theory is that punishment, if undeserved, is unjust. Given that courts across the country have found conditions in prisons and jails to violate the consititutional rights of prisoners,[17] subjecting people to confinement under such conditions could be regarded as just only if the untenable position were accepted that some people deserve to be deprived of the protections afforded by the Constitution. As discussed in the following section, there are overwhelming practical difficulties in trying to eliminate overcrowding and other illegal conditions without also greatly reducing the resort to imprisonment. Thus, those interested in avoiding confinement under conditions that result in injustice would be well advised to support a significant de-escalation of penalty levels, placing special emphasis on decreasing the use of incarceration.

Review of the literature on just deserts provides additional support for the position that desert theory does not imply a preference for harsh punishment. The Committee for the Study of Incarceration, which played a significant role in repopularizing desert theory, interpreted the values central to a desert orientation as calling for an overall reduction from the current severity of punishments. "Under our conception," the committee said, "less severe alternative punishments will have to be devised for the not-so-serious offenses that constitute the bulk of the system's caseload."[18] The committee argued that incarceration must never be used except for that narrow range of offenses that qualify as serious and that the length of confinement ought to be "stringently rationed."[19] Indeed, in the introduction to the committee's report, Gaylin and Rothman asserted that it "would be better to ignore the recommendations of the Committee entirely than to accept any part of them without that focus on decarceration about which all its other arguments pivot."[20]

DE-ESCALATION AND PRAGMATIC CONSIDERATIONS

Review of a few facts about the current situation reveals why de-escalation of punishment practices is strongly supported on pragmatic grounds. Since 1925, the U.S. prison population has undergone an overall annual growth rate that is twice that of the general population.[21] The dramatic growth in recent years has placed an unbearable burden on already inadequate penal facilities. A 1978 national survey of American prisons and jails found that two-thirds of all prisoners were being held in less than 60 square feet of space.[22] Since that time, the confined population has grown by at least 260,000 people on a given day.[23] Although approximately 165,000 beds have been added at the state prison level alone since 1978,[24] even such dramatic expansion has not come close to closing the gap between populations and necessary space.

This situation has led to increasing judicial examination of the operation of correctional institutions in light of the Eighth Amendment's prohibition against cruel and unusual punishment. As of February 1986, courts had ordered sweeping changes in the entire state prison systems of Alabama, Arkansas, Florida, Michigan, Mississippi, Colorado, Oklahoma, Kentucky, Tennessee, Louisiana, New Mexico, South Carolina, Rhode Island, and Texas. One or more facilities in 20 other states were operating under a court order as a result of inmate crowding or unconstitutional conditions of confinement. In all, 34 states, the District of Columbia, Puerto Rico, and the Virgin Islands were operating under court orders because of violations of the constitutional rights of prisoners, and legal challenges to major prisons were pending in 9 other states.[25]

The economic impact of attempting to build our way out of overcrowding is staggering. As many as 700 new county, state, and federal prisons reportedly have been constructed in the last few years or are in the offing, with estimated capital costs totaling $8 billion.[26] Yet those costs represent only the tip of the economic iceberg. One economist has estimated that a decision made in 1982 to build a 500-bed prison in compliance with the standards of the Commission on Accreditation for Corrections would represent a commitment of approximately $350 million (not considering inflation) over a thirty-year period.[27] At that rate, the 100,000 cells reportedly being added to state prison systems alone represent a commitment of $70 billion over 30 years (in 1982 dollars).

The response of some officials to questions about the wisdom of such massive expenditures on more prisons and jails is that this is the direction the public wants to go. They cite the results of public opinion polls showing substantial majorities of citizens agreeing that judges are too lenient. Yet, as Rosett and Cressey have noted, it is important to consider what the pressures for making sanctions harsher reflect about our society and to ask if the consequences are ones that we desire:

Harshness breeds harshness as everyone involved, including the potential criminal, becomes accustomed to the idea that crime is punishable by a ridiculously long prison term. Penalties escalate as sensibilities to the consequences become deadened. Proposals to reduce penalties across the board to a more reasonable level are seen as depriving the punishment of any impact. Yet it is only because society, like drug addicts, has built up high tolerance through habitual overdose, that it needs such increasingly massive injections to get the desired jolt.[28]

DE-ESCALATION AND HUMANITARIANISM, ETHICS, AND RELIGION

The adage that the level of civilization a society has reached can be measured by entering its prisons should have a disquieting impact on Americans today. Development of a more humane, caring, and benevolent society requires more than the elimination of cruel and unusual punishments; it involves a continuing quest for higher standards of decency and good will and an ever-decreasing resort to harsh, brutal, debilitating, and degrading sanctions. As noted above, however, the courts are finding that prisons in many jurisdictions have yet to reach standards that can pass minimum muster constitutionally.

It is important to bear in mind that, as Conrad has stated, "We live in a century when inhumanity administered by governments upon persons under total control has reached a nadir of barbarism."[29] After citing Solzhenitsyn's description of life at the north Siberian facility at Kolyma in *The Gulag Archipelago*, Conrad goes on to say,

This excerpt from Solzhenitsyn's numbing recital of horrors is most easily digested as an example of the hideous brutality of the Soviet regime and peculiar to the contemporary phenomenon of totalitarianism. But comparable degradation has been too frequent in too many other cultures to allow the assumption that it is somehow peculiar to Siberia. In any country, the descent to barbarism starts in its prisons. A country that can tolerate Kolyma or Auschwitz can learn to adjust to many other social controls that are violently inconsistent with civilized relations between the state and the citizen. The conclusion made by Dostoyevsky in the nineteenth century, after his prolonged exposure to the tsarist penal regime is suggestive of a truth that we can ignore at our peril.

"A society which looks upon such things with an indifferent eye is already infected to the marrow."[30]

A review of religious and secular ethical traditions in America will reveal a number of consistent themes that lend support to reducing the harshness of sanctions. Among the themes that stand out are those that relate to respecting the human dignity of all persons, guarding the poor and weak from injustice, exercising humility and restraint in rendering judgments, assuring equal rights for all persons, and practicing loving-kindness, forgiveness, and mercy.[31] Such principles have contributed in significant ways to the lives and aspirations of Americans throughout our history; they should be weighed in the calculus when changes in punishment practices are being considered.

DE-ESCALATION, EQUALITY, AND RACIAL JUSTICE

It is impossible not to notice the glaring color contrasts with respect to who experiences criminal sanctions in the United States. On a given day in 1984, about 1 in 12 adult black males were under the custody or control of the correctional system, a ratio almost four times higher than that for adult white males.[32] The incarceration rates for both black men and black women are approximately seven times higher than those of white men and women.[33] In 1979, blacks composed 10 percent of the adult male population of the United States, but 48 percent of state prison inmates.[34] Hispanic men make up about 3 percent of the total population, yet they represented 10 percent of confined men in 1978. Hispanic women, who also represent about 3 percent of the total population, made up 7 percent of the confined women.[35]

Race and class are highly interrelated in American society, with minorities significantly overrepresented in the most disadvantaged economic statuses. In 1960, about three-fourths of white and black men in the United States were working. In 1982, the figure for white men was about the same, but only 54 percent of black men had jobs.[36] In 1983, 38 percent of blacks and 23 percent of Hispanics fell below the official poverty level, compared with 14 percent of whites.[37]

In 1982, the incarceration rates per 100,000 males between the ages of 16 and 64 were 405 overall, 356 among those employed, 442 among those not in the labor force, and 933 among the unemployed.[38] Almost half of all male inmates in local jails in 1978 reported that they had annual incomes below $3,000 prior to arrest. The median income for those reporting any income at all was roughly a third of that of the general population. About 40 percent of all males in jail had been unemployed at the time they entered jail. Among the others, 12 percent were working only part-time.[39] Our current harsh practices fall most heavily on minorities and persons who are economically disadvantaged.

The United States Civil Rights Commission has pointed out that racism

is not just a matter of attitudes: actions and institutional structures, especially, can also be forms of racism . . . Racism can occur even if the people causing it have no intention of subordinating others because of color, or are totally unaware of doing so . . . Racism can be a matter of result rather than intention because many institutional structures in America that most whites do not recognize as subordinating others because of color actually injure minority group members far more than deliberate racism.[40]

Our prisons are the glaring embodiment of institutional racism in American society. They symbolize, both for Americans and for the rest of the world, the unequal distribution of benefits and burdens in our social and economic systems. In areas such as housing, employment, public accommodations, and education, most Americans have come to understand that practices, structures, or actions that are discriminatory in effect must be changed. While controversy persists as to the most appropriate *means* of eliminating segregated schools or racially skewed voting districts, there is little argument about the *goals* and principles involved. Why then do we seem to have blindfolds that keep us from seeing that it is unacceptable that the most extreme domestic application of state force, the criminal sanction, falls so disproportionately on minorities?

Most of the attention focused to date on the gross overrepresentation of minorities in American prisons has been devoted to assessing the extent to which racial bias may be operating within the criminal justice system. This is an important area of inquiry, but it is a perversely backward form of logic to argue that those concerned with issues of criminal justice should restrict their focus on racial disparities to identifying racial bias within criminal justice decision making because the criminal justice system "merely" reflects racial and social inequities in the larger society. Although it is true that no change in criminal justice practices would be sufficient to eliminate the structural inequalities in our society, it is also true that changes in criminal justice practices can do a great deal to make matters worse. Every movement toward stronger repression through the criminal justice system widens and deepens the gulf between our stated commitment to overcoming racism and inequality and the realities of our current social and economic practices.

Criminal justice issues cannot be separated from issues of social and distributive justice. It is crucial to acknowledge that given current realities, punishment designed to protect and affirm the existing social order also reinforces inequalities in opportunity and status. Honoring our commitment to true justice requires that we stop acting as if the goal were just to get tougher, when those who will feel the sting most are those who already suffer the most from the absence of broader social justice.

CONCLUSION

Despite persistence of conventional wisdom that Americans are soft on crime, the reach of American punishment systems has expanded to startling dimensions. About three-quarters of a million people are being held in the nation's jails and prisons, and nearly three times that number are under correctional supervision in the community. By 1984, approximately 1 in 65 adults, 1 in 37 adult males, 1 in 47 white adult males, and 1 in 12 black adult males were subject to correctional control on a given day. We have increased the capacity of our state prisons by nearly two-thirds in the last seven years,[41] while also acting to make probation and parole increasingly punitive, restrictive, and controlling.

To date, the implications of such a vast punishment and control system for a society that professes to value liberty have received little serious attention. Nor has there been much effort to scrutinize the arguments and rationales offered in support of continuing to get tougher and tougher. For the most part, the recent sharp increases in correctional populations seem to have taken place with little public notice and with those aware of the extent of the growth evidencing casual acceptance, if not vocal approbation. Yet, as this chapter has argued, the course on which we are embarked has little basis in evidence and is strikingly inconsistent with some`of our most deeply cherished values. It is clearly time to reverse course and to begin a rapid de-escalation of the sanctioning system.

NOTES

1. J. Mullen et al., *American Prisons and Jails*, vol. 1, *Summary and Policy Implications of a National Survey* (Washington, DC: U.S. Department of Justice, 1980), pp. 12–15.

2. Ibid., p. 152.

3. *Prisoners in 1985*, Bureau of Justice Statistics Bulletin, June 1986. An additional 223,511 persons were confined in local jails as of June 1983 (*The 1983 Jail Census*, Bureau of Justice Statistics Bulletin, November 1984), from 141,588 in 1972 (Mullen, et al., *American Prisons and Jails*, p. 152).

4. See, e.g., A. Blumstein, "Prisons: Population, Capacity, and Alternatives," in James Q. Wilson, ed., *Crime and Public Policy* (San Francisco: ICS Press, 1983), pp. 229–31.

5. *Probation and Parole 1984*, Bureau of Justice Statistics Bulletin, February 1986.

6. *Setting Prison Terms*, Bureau of Justice Statistics Bulletin, August 1983.

7. A. Blumstein et al., eds., *Research on Sentencing: The Search for Reform*, vol. 1 (Washington, DC: National Academy Press, 1983), pg. 31.

8. Ibid.

9. Virtually all of the states have adopted new mandatory sentencing laws in recent years. Prison terms are mandatory for specified violent crimes in 43 jurisdictions, for habitual offenders in 30 jurisdictions, for drug offenses in 30 jurisdictions, and for violations involving firearms in 38 jurisdictions. *Setting Prison Terms.*

10. Steven R. Schlesinger, Director of the Bureau of Justice Statistics, as quoted in "Probation, Parole Being Used More," *Philadelphia Inquirer*, February 24, 1986, p. 12–A.

11. Ibid.

12. Ibid.

13. J. S. Mill, "Utilitarianism," in *The Utilitarians: An Introduction to the Principles of Morals and Legislation* (Garden City, N.Y.: Dolphin Books, Doubleday, 1961) p. 418.

14. D. Nagin, "General Deterrence: A Review of the Empirical Evidence," in A. Blumstein et al., eds., *Deterrence and Incapacitation: Estimating the Effects of Criminal Sanctions on Crime Rates* (Washington, DC: National Academy Press, 1978), p. 135.

15. J. Cohen, "Incapacitating Criminals: Recent Research Findings" *Research in Brief* (Washington, DC: National Institute of Justice, December 1983). See also J. Cohen, "The Incapacitative Effect of Imprisonment: A Critical Review of the Literature," in Blumstein et al., eds., *Deterrence and Incapacitation.*

16. See, generally, the works cited in notes 14 and 15 above.

17. See text related to note 25 below.

18. A. von Hirsch, *Doing Justice: The Choice of Punishments* (New York: Hill and Wang, 1976), p. 118.

19. Ibid., pp. 113.

20. Ibid., pp. xxxix–xl.

21. *Criminal Justice Newsletter*, January 17, 1983, p. 5.

22. Mullen, et al., *American Prisons and Jails*, p. 81; "No standard setting body has recommended less than 60 square feet of floor space per inmate" (p. 80).

23. Local jail populations increased from 158,394 in 1978 to 223,552 in 1983, and prison populations rose from 307,276 in 1978 to 503,601 in 1985, according to Bureau of Justice Statistics reports.

24. *Prisoners in 1985.*

25. "Corrections Digest," March 12, 1986, pp. 3–6 (citing the Annual Report of the American Civil Liberties Union Foundation, which was released February 20, 1986).

26. *Philadelphia Inquirer*, October 14, 1982, pp. 1A, 28A–29A.

27. G. Funke, "Who's Buried in Grant's Tomb? Economics and Corrections for the Eighties and Beyond" (Mimeo, Institute for Economic and Policy Studies, Alexandria, VA, April 1982).

28. Rosett and Cressey, *Justice by Consent: Plea Bargains in the American Courthouse* (1976), pp. 153–54.

29. J. Conrad, "What Do the Undeserving Deserve?" in Johnson and Toch, eds., *The Pains of Imprisonment* (1982), p. 323.

30. Ibid.

31. See, e.g., V. Mackey, "Punishment in the Scripture and Tradition of Judaism, Christianity, and Islam" (1981); L. H. DeWolf, *What Americans Should Do about Crime* (1976); K. Madigan and W. Sullivan, "Crime and Community in Biblical Perspective" (1980).

32. This estimated rate and the estimated rates in the conclusion of this chapter were calculated by the author and must be regarded as rough, preliminary calculations. The data collected for the various correctional populations included in the estimates were not standard for all populations. Most of the data were drawn from bulletins published by the Bureau of Justice Statistics, but some unpublished, preliminary data were used that were supplied to the author by BJS with the understanding that they had not yet been verified. Bureau of the Census data used on racial, sex, and age distributions were from 1980. In addition, the calculations involving gender and race were estimates made from incomplete data. The major sources relied on were the BJS bulletins *The 1983 Jail Census*; *Probation and Parole 1984*; and *Prisoners in 1984*, April 1985; also the BJS special report, *The Prevalence of Imprisonment* July 1985, by Patrick Langan with the assistance of Lawrence Greenfeld.

33. Bureau of Justice Statistics, *Report to the Nation on Crime and Justice* (Washington, DC: U.S. Department of Justice, October 1983), pp. 31, 36. See also A. Blumstein, "On the Racial Disproportionality of U.S. Prison Populations," *Journal of Criminal Law and Criminology* 73, no. 3 (1982): 1259–81.

34. Blumstein et al., eds. *Research on Sentencing*, p. 13.

35. Bureau of Justice Statistics, *Report to the Nation on Crime and Justice*, pp. 31, 36. Data on minorities in confinement are scarce. Sometimes Hispanics are added to the "white" and sometimes to the "other" category when counts are taken. Counts seldom report information on American Indians, Eskimos, Asians, and other racial and ethnic groups.

36. The other 46 percent of black men were unemployed, no longer looking for work, in correctional facilities, or unaccounted for. *The Flip Side of Black Families Headed by Women: The Economic Status of Black Men*, (Center for the Study of Social Policy, April 1984).

37. *Social Stratification in the United States* (Social Graphics Company, 1983).

38. Bureau of Justice Statistics, *Report to the Nation on Crime and Justice*, p. 38.

39. Ibid.

40. Cited in Christianson, "Disproportionate Imprisonment of Blacks in the U.S.: Policy, Practice, Impact and Change" (Unpublished draft on file with the author, prepared for the National Association of Blacks in Criminal Justice, March 1982), p. 65.

41. Bureau of Justice Statistics, *Prisoners in 1985.*

11 Aid from Industry? Private Corrections and Prison Crowding

SEAN McCONVILLE

As prison populations have soared, the voting public has displayed customary sagacity by clamoring for yet more imprisonment together with unchanged or decreased taxation. Some harassed administrators and politicians have therefore looked to private enterprise for solutions.[1] And for the first time in many generations the political climate is conducive to some revival of privately run imprisonment: a generalized skepticism about the scope, potentialities, and efficiency of public administration has replaced 40 years' more or less uninterrupted and thoroughly optimistic expansion of government duties and services. The Reagan administration both has been the tangible expression of this political mood and has legitimized, celebrated, and encouraged it.

Within the narrower sphere of penal ideas and prison administration, the notion of privatization has not provoked the immediate and vigorous rejection that could have been expected 10 years ago. Criminal justice agencies have been passing through a period of declining public respect and confidence,[2] and the prisons and related "treating" institutions took a body blow from the adverse program evaluation studies of the late sixties. These findings knocked the wind out of prison professionals' defensive rhetoric and undercut the political posturing that might have provided an insuperable initial barrier against privatization.

In various forms, therefore, private sector corrections has come to be considered as one possible solution to the nation's prison and jail crisis. No one has suggested a total takeover by private enterprise of the penal responsibilities of the various levels of government, but some services have already been delegated to private concerns, and more contracts are under consideration. These new relationships raise several important questions. What penal and detention responsibilities might properly be taken on by entrepreneurs? To what extent might they assist in solving current problems? And what practical and theoretical difficulties are associated with the development of private correctional institutions?

HISTORICAL BACKGROUND

The private administration of prisons is, of course, of much greater antiquity than their public administration. And, indeed, although there was a major shift from privately run penal institutions in the late eighteenth and early nineteenth centuries, vestiges of private interest survived until comparatively recent times—with convict leasing by private contractors continuing in Florida until 1923 and in Alabama until 1928.[3] Since private penal management is again a matter for practical decision, what, if anything, might be learned from past experience? Which abuses should most be guarded against? Does the profit motive intrinsically and irremediably tend toward abuse of authority and corruption of administration? Can privatization be humane, efficient, and accountable? Can it stimulate new departures?

Those who seek answers to these questions must be careful not to give an overgilded account of publicly run imprisonment. The last two centuries have scarcely been an uninterrupted success for federal, state, county, and municipal prisons and jails. Thorsten Sellin points out, for example, that even the shift from private convict leasing to public administration did not greatly improve the condition of the convict laborers in the southern U.S. prisons.[4] The catalogue of scandals, defects, and abuses in publicly run prisons and jails is so voluminous and so well documented by legislative, executive, and judicial inquiries, by scholars and journalists, and by staff and prisoners' memoirs, that undoubtedly many of the difficulties that the early prison reformers thought arose exclusively from the entrepreneurial interest in prisons can now be demonstrated to inhere in prison systems of any complexion, given the presence of certain conditions.

It must also be remembered that many of the earlier entrepreneurial prisons (especially those in urban areas) were of a particularly extreme kind: these institutions were expected to be largely or wholly self-financing (as were many public services at that time). It was not merely a matter of public authority contracting on a capitation basis with a private individual or concern to run a prison or jail; rather, the intention was that both costs and profits would be realized by user-fees: the prisoners were expected to pay for their own confinement and the financial well-being of their jailer.

In its "pure" form the entrepreneurial system charged prisoners for their admission to the jail and for the multitude of other transactions and needs that lay between entry and discharge. The granting of credit was no problem, since the prisoner would not be released until he found the wherewithal to pay the jailer. Although the county, the town, or a local charity might provide some assistance for the utterly indigent, food, clothing, warmth, and all other necessities had to be found from the prisoner's own resources.

By the late eighteenth century, both in the newly independent United States and in Britain, entrepreneurial imprisonment had become increasingly unacceptable to an important section of public opinion. The reasons for this distaste with arrangements that had endured for centuries are complex, but two may be noted in the context of our present discussion: there had arisen a great number of what had come to be seen as intolerable cruelties and abuses; and there was a desire to use the prisons for reformatory purposes.

The complaints of the reformers were many, but chiefly they concerned the desire of the jailer to squeeze as rich a living as possible from his charges. Not only did the jailer seek to maximize income, but so also did his various employees; not only were there standard fees for the various rites of passage through the prison, but every possible need and indulgence was bartered between jailer, turnkeys, and prisoners. The prisoners themselves leeched on each other for any tiny remnant of property or possible service that escaped the rapacious jailer and his staff. For a poor person, even moderately prolonged imprisonment meant certain degradation, near starvation, and possible death from disease, hunger, or illtreatment. The fate of those with a little wealth and property was rapid impoverishment and, should their confinement last, the same doom as the poor.

The late-eighteenth-century move to change the prisons was two-fold: steps were taken to curb the jails' grosser abuses and corrupting influences; and the notion gained support that an improved and tightly controlled prison environment could turn the prisons into institutions for the reformation of offenders. The two developments were soon seen as being interdependent: an entrepreneurial jailer and his staff who, to paraphrase a contemporary reformer, "wrung their emolument from misery," could not be expected to administer a reformatory prison. Conversely, how could the public authorities interfere with a man's enjoyment of his property? (And whether a jail lease had been brought or not, the income that arose from the fees and associated trading were generally seen as private property.) To impose a reformatory program meant that the range of goods and services offered by the jailer in pursuit of profit had to be replaced by activities directed only to the safe, secure, sanitary, and proper maintenance of the prisoners, and the reformation of their character.

These were the circumstances in which the entrepreneurial prisons passed away. Of course the change did not occur overnight. The relative strength of central government in Britain made the shift from private to public prison administration speedier and more thorough than in the United States; even so, it was not until 1865 that the last franchise (privately owned) prison ceased to be used in England. In the southern United States the practice of farming out prisoners, by means of the lease of their labor or contracts for their maintenance, continued throughout the nineteenth and well into the twentieth century.[5]

The antecedents of privately run prisons are, at first sight, far from favorable to the case for their late-twentieth-century revival. But the notion of history repeating itself is an overused and misleading cliche. Heraclitus is to be preferred: "You can't step twice into the same river." What has changed in public administration, in prisons and our penal aspirations, and in private enterprise that might prompt us to set aside the ignoble history of private imprisonment? And what lessons and cautions remain valid?

WHAT HAS CHANGED?

Public Administration

What often is overlooked is that during the period of flourishing entrepreneurial imprisonment, public administration was rudimentary. It was not only the jails that were largely user-financed: the courts, sheriffs, county and municipal clerks, and customs and excise all drew incomes from user-fees. It was not simply that such few regulatory and inspectorial agencies that existed were thinly staffed, but the rights of the localities and property owners were paramount. The assumption by government of criminal justice regulatory obligations began in England in the 1830s, and in the United States at a later point in the nineteenth century. The creation of investigatory and regulatory agencies followed thereafter.

The scope and powers of public regulatory bodies have grown enormously in the last century and a half. There now exists government expertise of the highest order not only in fiscal and financial matters, but in a plethora of the activities of our daily life—from the mechanism of elevators and automobiles to the operation of atomic reactors. Some may bemoan the swarming of government inspectors and the host of forms, powers, and requirements that is their milieu—but their existence and frequently high level of activity and competence are a fact of modern life. Certainly there is nothing in the administration and life of the prison that is so complicated that it is beyond the inspectorial abilities and expertise of government at one or another of its various levels, provided that the necessary staffing and support are made available. This competency clearly has implications for the safe and controlled revival of entrepreneurial imprisonment.

Prisons

In the last century and a half there have been many policy, administrative, and physical changes in the prisons. Basic sanitary and health-preserving facilities have been provided (still very basic in some institutions). No longer are prisoners congregated promiscuously in large day and night rooms: elementary (albeit often quite defective) classification procedures have been implemented. The expectation is universal that prisoners will be provided with the necessities of life—food, clothing, heating—and even some of the frills, such as education, work, and recreation. Sometimes, of course, there are considerable gaps between expectation, rhetorical prescription, and daily reality. No one should doubt that according to the economic possibilities and civic standards of the late twentieth century, some prisons and jails are disgracefully deficient. But equally, conditions have changed from the minimal provision of shelter and the disease-ridden dungeons of our ancestors.

Drugs, alcohol, weapons, and sex are all traded or facilitated by prison guards in many of today's prisons. But such activities are illegal, rather than customary, and for the most part are pursued by a tiny minority of rogue staff, who constantly fear detection and the retribution of the law. At basic levels the prison officer's job carries a pitiful salary, small prestige, and not a little social opprobrium. Nevertheless, the modern prison guard is far removed from the eighteenth-century "mercenary Cerberus," and the senior levels of prison administration have none of the stigma that made a pariah of the jailer until the mid-nineteenth century.

And what of our penal aspirations? The seventies and eighties (and maybe nineties) have been and will be marked by great confusion in penal objectives and methods. The decline and virtual eclipse of the reformatory ideal have thrown penal philosophy into disarray. But disarray is the normal state for philosophy, and a smug and unquestioning acceptance of an unrealistic dogma can produce as much social dislocation as uncertainty in policy objectives. In general, however, no penal administrator would embrace (or admit to embracing) as minimal a relationship to his charges as would his predecessor of the early 1800s. Prisons, at the very least, share in what has become the twentieth-century Western democratic expectation of public administration—that they will present a benevolent rather than malevolent, or even neutral, posture toward the citizen. Academics and administrators may wrestle with the formulations, but it is difficult to dispute that imprisonment in our society is wrapped around with some of the elements of a moral endeavor.

Private Enterprise

Accurate general statements about private enterprise are as difficult to make as those about any other sector of modern society. The range of activities is as great as it was 200 years ago, as is the gamut of social reactions. Between the great manufacturing concern or merchant bank and the side-street pornography empire or joint-stock brothel, there looms an enormous chasm of social standing and respectability. But the commercial concerns that provide hostel or community corrections services, or that have begun commercially to operate prisons, are not to be compared in terms of respectability with the trading jailer of the 1790s. Scandal may repeatedly visit a publicly run penal establishment with (regrettably) minimal consequences to administrators and staff. Scandal that touches a commercially run penal establishment may provoke a breach-of-contract suit or a failure to renew a contract. Probity and efficiency are prerequisites for commercial survival to these concerns—and since the utilitarians first taught us the benefits of harnessed self-interest in the ordering of public affairs, a contractually regulated commercial interest has frequently been preferred to a moral one in securing a constant achievement of desired outcomes.

"PANOPTICON": THE UNTRIED ADMINISTRATIVE EXPERIMENT

This last point was taken up by Jeremy Bentham at a critical juncture in the development of English prison administration. In 1810 a parliamentary committee of inquiry was making recommendations for the management of the country's first national penitentiary, and the alternatives were either Bentham's regulated private enterprise model—his "Panopticon"—or a new form of publicly financed and politically accountable bureaucratic administration. Bentham called his scheme "contract-management" and contrasted it point by point most favorably with the publicly financed system, which he called "trust-management." His argument was that material interest should be joined with duty, in order to provide the most substantial guarantees that the penitentiary's objectives would be achieved:

By whom ought a business like this to be carried on? By one who has an interest in the success of it, or by one who has none? By one who has a greater interest in it, or by one who has an interest not so great? By one who takes loss as well as profit, or by one who takes profit without loss? By one who has no profit but in proportion as he manages well, or by one who, let him manage ever so well or ever so ill, shall have the same emolument secured to him?[6]

Bentham proposed that he should be paid by the central government a per capita allowance for each convict received into his penitentiary.

He was to have total authority over the convicts. He would guarantee (by means of a contractual financial penalty) against premature death, escape, or recidivism, and would make the prison available for the inspection of magistrates at all hours, and for all members of the public at specified times.

Within the constraints of his contract, therefore, Bentham considered that the public welfare, the welfare of the prisoners, and the financial interest of the entrepreneur would be united, since for the entrepreneur-warden,

The more orderly and industrious the prisoners, the greater the amount of his profits. He will, therefore, teach them the most profitable trades, and give them such portion of the profits as shall excite them to labour. He unites in himself the characters of Magistrate, Inspector, Head of Manufactory, and of a family; and is urged on by the strongest motives faithfully to discharge all these duties.[7]

Bentham's was to be the last philosophically based, but nevertheless the most ingenious and thoroughly argued, attempt to promote a private enterprise penitentiary for some 170 years. The reasons why the British government decided against his approach were many, but essentially Bentham's timing was wrong. For more than 30 prior years, since John Howard's meticulous 1777 catalogue of the neglects and abuses arising from entrepreneurial imprisonment had captured the sympathy of Europe's educated and powerful classes, the money-grubbing jailer had been identified with a system that irremediably would lead to corruption, degradation, exploitation, and a continued manufacture of the most depraved and hopeless souls in the community. Bentham's ideas had been formulated in the full knowledge of all the evils that private enterprise jails had produced,[8] and it was to meet those evils rather than to ignore or justify them that he proposed more private enterprise, but in the contractual setting that he believed would most effectually resolve them. Though the tide was flowing against him, and though his contract approach was doomed by the stigma attached to the jailer-entrepreneur, who can contemplate the last 175 years of what Bentham termed "trust-management" and say that abuse and scandal have been remedied so effectually by public finance and bureaucratic control that Bentham's scheme was not deserving of a trial?

And who can say that if tried it would not have proved at least as successful as its alternative?

WHAT PRINCIPLES GUIDE THE CUSTODIAL TASK?

The most basic duty of those who administer jails and prisons is to provide safe custody. This requires that the sentence or order of the court should be faithfully followed, as to time of confinement. It also means that the retributive intent of the court, inherent in the length of sentence, should not be exceeded, and that whether deliberately or by default, the life, health, and well-being of the prisoner should not needlessly be put at risk. Safe custody is secure control: prisoners must be protected from each other, as from abuse by prison staff.

Custody is enforced by both physical and organizational means. The former includes such impediments to escape as secure cell houses and impenetrable perimeter walls, and barriers that divide the prison to avoid the mixing of certain classes of prisoner and to prevent unauthorized assembly, riot, and other forms of concerted action against authority. Organizational security measures include a well-supervised and alert staff, an efficient collection and collation of intelligence, and the necessary inspections, searches, routines, and regulations.

Underlying both the physical and the organizational apparatus of prison administration is an implied threat of force. Should a prisoner attack another prisoner or a guard, he must be restrained with all necessary force. At times (for example, should a prisoner lose all control of himself in a fit of murderous rage), such force may have to be used that the inmate is rendered unconscious. *In extremis*, should the life of a fellow inmate or member of the staff be put at risk by the action of a prisoner, deadly force may be used. Similar considerations may apply to an escape attempt. The maintenance of a state of captivity ultimately rests on the threat and imminent presence of deadly force. That remarkably few occasions arise when this threat is realized does not alter this basic fact.

Can this entitlement to use deadly force be delegated by the state to a private concern? Clearly it can be, but it must be exercised by the agency and person to whom it is delegated in the same manner as if it were delegated to an officer of the state—that is, within the law. Moreover, as a recent American Bar Association review of the legal issues surrounding privatization pointed out, the state cannot by delegation evade its own legal liabilities.[9] Rather than being an impediment to the extension of the private sector role in corrections, this inescapable responsibility of the state provides assurance that the fabric of law and order that rests upon the commitment and capabilities of the state would not be undermined by delegation of custodial responsibility to a private concern. Neither does the state's inalienable liability in the matter affect the individual and corporate legal obligations, duties, and liabilities of the contractor and his agents.

Legal liabilities and accountability apart, it might be argued, there is something intrinsically obnoxious in the notion of a private employee using force upon a prisoner. When all the various arguments against private corrections have been considered, one suspects that this apparently instinctive repugnance is the core issue. The American Bar Association review of prison privatization described the symbolism involved as "the most difficult policy issue of all for privatization," and dilated thus upon the matter:

When it enters a judgment of conviction and imposes a sentence a court exercises its authority, both actually and symbolically. Does it weaken that authority, however—as well as the integrity of the system of *justice*—when an inmate looks at his keeper's uniform and, instead of encountering an emblem that reads "Federal Bureau of Prisons" or "State Department of Corrections" he faces one that says "Acme Corrections Company"?[10]

It is perhaps not completely satisfactory to respond to questions about symbolism with observations about practicalities, yet a discussion of symbols may never be resolved unless we introduce some more mundane considerations. How do prisoners now see the badges of their guards? It is probable that few abstract philosophical or political speculations enter their perceptions. More likely, the prisoner wonders whether the wearer of the badge is available when needed, will want to help him, and is fair, knowledgeable, competent, and a decent human being. Conversely, the malign prisoner might wish to know if his guard is lazy, weak, timid, stupid, corruptible, and likely to be an aid or hindrance to his illegitimate scheme. These are practical—indeed, too often life-and-death—matters. It is likely that the vast majority of prisoners are completely indifferent to symbolism, and wholly concerned with what happens and with the quality of the officials with whom they come in contact, rather than with the organizational affiliation of such persons.

Even allowing that the symbolism of a cap-badge or uniform had an effect, it is implausible, from what we know of the dynamics of prison life, that a private rather than public cap-badge would affect one iota a sentenced prisoner's attitude toward the criminal justice system. As for unsentenced prisoners, such is the stigma of the correctional system that being in the custody of a private rather than a publicly run jail may even be marginally comforting. Surely the point does not have to be labored that the grossly crowded, malodorous, dangerous, lawless, and unlawful jail or prison far more undermines the dignity of the state and the law than all the jibes of the political purist or any possible theoretical affront that might arise from decent prison conditions being provided under private auspices.

This is not to argue that no broader philosophical and political issues arise from the private enforcement of custody. Even when acting as a custodian, the state has a moral relationship with the prisoner. That relationship sets some limits to expedience. One does not have to be a fervent interventionist to recognize that in a democratic society, where the promotion of the common good is the basic justification for public administration and political life, public institutions have an obligation not to make things worse for the citizen—either directly or indirectly. We may not feel obliged to strive to make a prisoner better, but he is a human being and we must do something with him: we cannot do nothing.

But the state is an abstraction. Powers are delegated and duties assigned to human beings. There is little moral difference whether one furthers the obligations of the state through private or through public channels. The practical organizational problems of accountability, recruitment, training, supervision, communication, evaluation, and responsiveness are much the same. The symbol becomes flesh and the policy becomes action in much the same way, whether one is dealing wholly with a public bureaucracy, a private corporation, or a combination of the two.

None of this is to argue that the introduction of private enterprise into the administration of corrections is without problems. A number of commentators[11] have itemized issues and putative tendencies that must be prevented or resolved in any furtherance of private corrections. These include:

1. A slowness to recommend prisoners for release because of a profit-driven desire to ensure maximum occupancy of available space.
2. The development of a private corrections lobby that would seek to influence legislators to prescribe a greater amount of imprisonment.
3. Attempts to maximize profits by improper cutting of costs, to the detriment of prisoners' living conditions and staff working conditions.
4. The development of prisoner selection and classification criteria that would result in state institutions being assigned the most troublesome inmates, with the privately run concerns gleaning those whose management is easiest.

Yet we could, without too much trouble, provide parallel issues for publicly run corrections:

1. The overhasty release of prisoners who are a public danger, in order to ease crowding; or the "hoarding" of prisoners with institutionally desirable skills or attributes, rather than downgrading their classification and moving them toward earlier release.
2. A lobbying of legislators for staff and other resource increases without a concomitant demonstration that existing funds are being used efficiently.
3. Fiduciary negligence, recklessness, or indifference: a failure to control costs and to prevent inmate and staff pilferage, to the detriment of the majority of prisoners and staff, and of the taxpayer.
4. The passing off of troublesome prisoners as being reasonably behaved or not presenting special problems, and their removal from one institution to another under false colors.

There would appear to be few, if any, problems associated with private corrections that do not have a counterpart in publicly run institutions. The issues in both types of prisons revolve around well-educated and committed administrators, efficient management, cost control, and staff supervision, and a clear formulation of the goals of the institution.

Nevertheless, there are worries about the development of private corrections to which it is difficult to give reassuring or hard-and-fast answers:

1. Can departments of corrections, many of which have a history of not being successful in the control and inspection of their own establishments, provide the expertise necessary to monitor effectively the delivery of service by private contractors? Should the scrutiny of correctional contracts be handled by a special department of government?

2. Will politicians show the steadfastness and bipartisanship necessary to distinguish between an "acceptable" failure in a private corrections contract and an "unacceptable" failure? An unscrupulous desire to scapegoat or to score political points will surely doom private corrections.

3. Will existing staff and management campaign against private corrections, or will there be an acceptance of the new ventures and some movement between the two sectors?

4. Will private corrections be able to establish a staffing ethos favorable to the recruitment of dedicated and able professionals, a substantial part of whose motivation is public service?

TO WHAT EXTENT IS PRIVATIZATION A SOLUTION TO OVERCROWDING?

In answer to the foregoing and related questions, it seems customary for articles on privatization to counsel that developments should proceed with great caution. The warning would seem to be redundant, since developments in privatization have been comparatively few and of a limited nature. Of the nation's several hundred prisons and 3,000 or so jails, a National Institute of Justice survey, conducted in the spring of 1984, found only 8 adult prisons being operated by the private sector—and 7 of these were being operated for the Immigration and Naturalization Service and U.S. Marshalls' Service and were therefore more in the nature of jails.[12] Only one truly penal adult institution was then under private management. In Hamilton County, Tennessee, the Correctional Corporation of America took over the operation of the 325-bed Silverdale Detention Center.[13] At the time of writing (June 1986), the best estimate of the number of adult prisons corresponding to state-level institutions being operated by private enterprise was 2, and of those equivalent to county facilities, 13. In addition, 5 detention centers were being run by private contractors for the Immigration and Naturalization Service. Given that the nation's prison population in mid-1986 exceeded 503,601 and its jail population (as of June 30, 1984) was 234,500, the private sector involvement in corrections can be seen to be tiny—less than 1 percent.[14]

Although there is a sympathetic political climate, the respectable and relatively trouble-free private sector start in corrections has not yet gained much momentum. If private enterprise corrections is to be tried fairly and is to make a contribution of any significance to the resolution of current penal problems, the pace of development must be increased appreciably. How might this be done? One incentive, above all others, would be to increase the profit possibilities that venture capital might expect from correctional investment. A critical component in this is the tax advantages that investors may expect from a correctional investment. At the very least, these must be comparable to investment in tax-free government bonds. Where it is thought desirable that the contract should take the form of leasing of premises provided by the contractor, with or without a purchase option, state law varies as to tax-exempt status. A state that decided to seek entrepreneurial participation in corrections would be well advised to make that option as attractive as possible, in order to obtain competitive bids from a range of contractors, and should therefore make the necessary legislative changes.

It must be recognized, however, that in this nascent field of investment—which is fraught with all the extra risks of any new development—it may be in the public interest to concede additional profit incentives. This might more easily be done with operational costs, rather than with investment capital interest. Government might be satisfied, at least in the development stages of private corrections, with a smaller saving on daily maintenance costs, in order to stimulate a greater private sector interest, the advantages of which would be expected to accrue in full at a later date.

What Type of Operation Might Be Privatized?

Pretrial Detention

The case for an extension of private pretrial accommodation is strong, even were crowding and a shortage of public resources not factors so urgently to be considered. Despite repeated experiments in many jurisdictions—such as the renaming of jails and other cosmetic changes, and more emphatic internal division to separate convicted and pretrial prisoners—it has remained difficult to see jails as other than penal institutions. This necessarily has had adverse consequences for persons remanded in custody to await their trials. The disadvantages of the confusion of penal and detention services are general and fiscal. (How can a legislature be persuaded that jails for pretrial prisoners should offer amenities at least comparable to those of a modest motel, when legislators think of jails in terms of short-sentence prisoners?) The disadvantages are also personal and immediate. (How can a person properly prepare himself for trial given the emotional, physical, hygienic, and other pressures and constraints of the jail?).

In short, there is a strong argument for relieving crowding pressures by providing privately run pretrial accommodation. This would go a long way to separate a penal service from a detention service, to the considerable advantage of persons who are awaiting their trials and who are legally presumed to be innocent.

Nor should there be any objection to providing a range of accommodation, from the fairly basic to the rather more comfortable and spacious. The abolition of entrepreneurial imprisonment in the nineteenth century led to the standardization of all pretrial accommodation, and in retrospect this can be seen to have been a mixed blessing. The previous practice had been to allow persons with means to purchase some extra comfort while in detention. In the context of a user-fee relationship, and given the desire of the entrepreneurial jailer to maximize revenue, the selling of comfortable jail accommodation undoubtedly led to abuses. The most objectionable practice of the entrepreneur-jailer was to provide a basic level of accommodation of such appalling filth, discomfort, and dangerousness that he could extort unreasonable fees for any mitigation. [15]

One would wish to see a good basic standard of accommodation in a privately run pretrial institution. It would be clean, reasonably spacious, and equipped with a small bathroom, television, writing desk, and, possibly, refrigerator and hot plate. No charges would be levied for the room, and food would be free. Families and friends who were willing to submit themselves to the type of personal search considered appropriate by the jail manager would be permitted extensive private visiting facilities. For persons who could afford the extra charges, more comfortable and agreeable accommodation could be provided together with a greater choice of food and a private telephone. The services of a cleaner would be available to those who desire them. A realistic and fair rent would be charged for those extra facilities. It is extremely hard to find any justification for preventing a person who is in custody awaiting his trial from using his private legitimate means to provide himself with a higher standard of accommodation. The democratic ideal does not insist on an unnecessary equality in the distribution of miseries. Why should an unconvicted person be prevented from spending his money as he wishes?[16] Moreover, the more generous type of accommodation described would permit some pretrial detainees to carry on their lawful businesses, to their personal advantage and that of the community.

There are some objections to the provision of a range of types of pretrial detention accommodation. Steps would have to be taken, for example, to ensure that the proceeds of crime were not used to purchase more comfortable conditions. A person wishing to obtain a higher standard of pretrial detention should not object to some verification of the legitimacy of sources of funds. One would also wish to ensure that unscrupulous prisoners do not exploit the meager resources of their families in order to provide more comfort for themselves. Again, a fairly simple verification procedure could be established to check family income, and a jail rule enacted that would prevent more than a portion of such income being available for pretrial jail accommodation. Finally, it might be desirable to stipulate that, in the event of conviction, the sentencing judge would be informed that while in pretrial detention a prisoner had exercised his right to purchase extra amenities and more comfortable accommodation. The judge could then decide what allowance of pretrial detention to grant against sentence. This last provision is probably necessary to prevent frivolous delays in coming to trial by persons who, knowing that conviction and a prison sentence were inevitable, would wish to prolong the comparative ease of privileged pretrial detention if such detention were automatically to be deducted day for day from their prison sentences.

Those who find their way to pretrial detention include a high proportion of persons from the lowest social classes, and also some whose behavior is irrational. Additionally, some pretrial detainees must be expected to behave in a manner that, for reasons of good order, discipline, and hygiene, is unacceptable. Such persons would be ejected from hostel or motel accommodation were they at large in the free world, and private prison management must be authorized to remove them to whatever type of accommodation is necessary to prevent damage, to cope with filthy and unhygienic ways of living, or to punish and deter destructive behavior. Persons who are mentally ill should have special accommodation and a special regime of treatment, for which the contractor should receive appropriate compensation.

The differential provision of pretrial detention accommodation according to means and wishes would have two helpful side effects. It would enable investors to produce a slightly greater return on capital by increasing the range of services on offer, and by providing a purchaser other than the contracting public authority. Such differential services should also go a good way to promote in the public mind a new image of the pretrial detention center as a secure hostel or hotel, rather than as a penal institution, confinement wherein is necessarily prejudicial to trial chances.[17]

Typically, pretrial detainees account for 40 to 50 percent of jail populations,[18] so any private sector expansion of pretrial accommodation would be very helpful in easing jail crowding. For the political and economic reasons given above, entrepreneurs might find it prudent to venture first into pretrial detention services. An obstacle of some significance is the attitude of some senior corrections and law enforcement officials. Two experienced commentators note, in a report prepared for the National Institute of Corrections, that resentments about "loss of turf" may be a greater barrier to an expansion of private sector corrections than any actual loss of public employment.[19] And, especially pertinent when considering investment possibilities in jails, the National Sheriffs' Association has expressed strong opposition to the development of a private corrections industry.[20]

Accommodation for Sentenced Prisoners

About half of those in jails are sentenced medium- and maximum-security prisoners. In order to be taken seriously as a force in the penal system, private correctional concerns must provide institutions suitable for these inmates. This is partly because of the numbers involved, and partly for political reasons. It would considerably harm private corrections were it to succumb to the accusation that profit was being sought by a process of skimming off the more easily handled prisoners, leaving the government with a residue of the more difficult prisoners—rendered indeed even more troublesome by the removal from their midst of the leavening of better security risks and behaviorally more stable inmates.

In providing jail accommodation for convicted persons, private enterprise might seek initially to provide special services. Many small jurisdictions have to face high per capita costs for their jail populations because, although sometimes crowded, their jails are small institutions and cannot take advantage of economies of scale. Sometimes local political considerations might hinder the construction and use of a regional jail serving several counties and small municipalities. A privately run institution offering flexible and mutually beneficial contracts to the various parties could assist in bypassing political roadblocks.

Similarly, private corrections might provide specialist jail facilities, either attached to or completely independent from existing jails. Regionalization might, for example, enable several jurisdictions to take advantage of economies of scale by making joint use of a private jail for sentenced women. Other specialist jail facilities that could be provided regionally by private enterprise include units for substance abusers, compulsive sexual offenders, and the mentally and physically handicapped. The flexibility and innovative frame of mind associated with venture capital could result in some novel institutions and procedures emerging from such specialist operations. Not only could provision of this kind have an educative effect on conventional corrections, but it would assist in relieving pressures in the public sector institutions, since in a conventional prison setting the mentally and physically ill and substance abusers present difficulties that are quite disproportionate to their numbers. Moreover, since at least one of the new corrections corporations has links (through a parent company) with hospital management, some thought might be given to attaching specialist jail units to private hospitals. Indeed, this might be a venture that some enterprising hospital management might wish to initiate itself, since a specialist jail unit on or near a hospital site could benefit greatly from access to medical staff and support facilities.

Nor should private corrections shrink from becoming involved in the provision of prison space. While a specialist role could also be envisaged for the private sector in providing for these longer-term prisoners, crowding problems could significantly be addressed by institutions for run-of-the-mill general population medium- to maximum-security inmates. New management methods, programs, and types of building should be encouraged in the consideration of bids for contracts, and correctional firms should carefully consider in which areas of management and programming they have distinctive services to offer. Clearly one type of venture that would be welcomed would be a prison run on industrial lines, with full-time employment and market or at least minimum-rate wages being paid to prisoners. Experience has shown time and again that public administration is not particularly successful in developing profitable prison industry. Provided that some long-outmoded restrictive legislation is removed, the private sector is much better placed to make productive prison labor profitable and politically acceptable. A private industrial prison might work in cooperation with a state system by receiving transfer applications from prisoners. Only those prisoners who had shown a good disciplinary and work attitude while in the state prison would be eligible for transfer, and misbehavior could result in various penalties, including removal from the industrial prison. A scheme of this type might offer a more effective, substantial, and politically dramatic chance to advance Chief Justice Burger's campaign for "factories within fences" than many of the very limited joint state-private ventures now under way.

It is a debatable question whether private enterprise should be allowed to tender for "supermax" prisoners. On the one hand, these prisoners could be represented as a specialist population, and a case made for the private provision of the service on a regional basis, as described above. In practical political terms, however, it must be recognized that private prisons have yet to win public confidence. It would probably be risky and counterproductive to go too far beyond public opinion, and one cannot easily contemplate the type of population now housed at the federal prison at Marion, Illinois (a number of whom are held on contracts from state systems), being handed over to a private concern for confinement. That time may come, but it does not seem to be a practical or wise political venture.

CONCLUSION

Encouraged to do what the private sector does best—to innovate and provide resources quickly and flexibly—there seems every reason to believe that private correctional concerns would make an appreciable and welcome contribution to an easing of crowding problems. There will undoubtedly be errors, and there may even be some public relations catastrophes. Provided that these do not exceed in gravity what we would expect from the public sector prisons, excessive criticism and panic should be avoided by politicians and other community leaders. There is a need for effective contract drafting and bid judging and negotiating, but these are everyday and commonplace state and public administration activities. There must also be highly effective contract monitoring bodies, and there may be a need here to supplement state expertise with private auditing and inspecting services, and for a lay presence to assure the public that in the search for profits the rules and decencies continue to be observed behind closed doors and high walls.

All of this is tentative and highly contingent. A major scandal, developments in the national economy, a change in tax structure, a shift in political sentiment, all could drive these new ventures and initiatives off course. But should they continue, develop, and expand, might it be to hope too much that the benefits will be both immediate and long term, and that the publicly administered prisons and jails, while remaining the mainstay of our system, will be energized and improved by the spirit of innovation, efficiency, and confidence generated by the new institutions? The very possibility of such assistance and stimulation is a solace much needed by those who contemplate our contemporary penal doldrums.

NOTES

1. Thus at the winter 1986 meeting of the National Governors' Association, several governors mentioned privatization as a possible solution to

their crowding problems. See *New York Times*, March 2, 1986, sec. 1, p. 21.

2. See, for example, Timothy J. Flanagan and Maureen McLeod, eds., *Sourcebook of Criminal Justice Statistics—1982*, U.S. Department of Justice, Bureau of Justice Statistics (Washington, DC: U.S. Government Printing Office, 1983), pp. 207–89, passim.

3. Thorsten Sellin, *Slavery and the Penal System* (New York: Elsevier, 1976), pp. 152–54, 157. Under the lease system contractors took charge of prisoners, either free of charge or for a small fee, and made their profit from the prisoners' labor. Since the contractors' income depended on the productivity of the prisoners, the system (which in the eighteenth century was also used by some counties and towns to dispose of their paupers) intrinsically lent itself to abuse.

4. Ibid., p. 176; see chap. 12, passim.

5. Ibid., chaps. 11 and 12 (pp. 145–76).

6. "Panopticon: Postscript," Part II, in Jeremy Bentham, *Works*, ed. J. Bowring (Edinburgh, 1843), 4:125.

7. Jeremy Bentham, *The Rationale of Punishment* (London: Robert Heward, 1830), p. 351.

8. Jeremy Bentham had met John Howard in 1778 and had the greatest admiration for the man and his work: "He is . . . one of the most extraordinary men this age can shew." *Correspondence of Jeremy Bentham*, ed. T. L. S. Sprigge (New York: Oxford University Press, 1968), 2:106.

9. American Bar Association, "Report on the Privatization of Prisons," 1986 Midyear Meeting, pp. 5–9.

10. Ibid., p. 12.

11. See Joan Mullen, "Corrections and the Private Sector," *NIJ Reports*, May 1985, pp. 2–7; *ACLU State Lobbyist* 4, no. 1 (March 1985): 3–6; American Bar Association, "Report on the Privatization of Prisons"; Joan Mullen, Kent John Chabotar, and Deborah M. Carrow, *The Privatization of Corrections* (Washington, DC: National Institute of Justice, 1985); Sean McConville and Eryl Hall Williams, *Crime and Punishment: A Radical Rethink* (London: Tawney Society, 1986).

12. Mullen, "Corrections and the Private Sector," p. 4, table 1.

13. *New York Times*, May 21, 1985, sec. 1, p. 14.

14. Telephone confirmation, Bureau of Justice Statistics, June 16, 1986.

15. This is discussed in detail in Sean McConville, *A History of English Prison Administration* (London and Boston: Routledge and Kegan Paul, 1981), vol. 1, chap. 3.

16. It is interesting to note that vestiges of the old, differentiated provision of accommodation remain in the English prison system, where a pretrial prisoner may purchase prepared food from an outside restaurant

or hotel. He may also pay for a special cell, which he may furnish at his own expense, and may hire a fellow prisoner to clean it. See Home Office, *Prison Rules*, 21 (1); 25 (a) and (b).

17. This prejudicial quality may be one of the elements at work in the shaping of differential conviction rates for those who have been granted bail and those who have been detained prior to trial.

18. Bureau of Justice Statistics, *The 1983 Jail Census* (Washington, DC: U.S. Department of Justice, 1984), p. 5.

19. Camille G. Camp and George M. Camp, *Private Sector Involvement in Prison Services and Operations* (Washington, DC: National Institute of Corrections, 1984), p. 14.

20. National Sheriffs' Association, resolution adopted at the 1984 Annual Symposium.

Bibliographical Essay

BACKGROUND READING

In considering almost any topic in public policy and administration, the King's advice to Alice is not entirely inappropriate: "Begin at the beginning... and go on till you come to the end: then stop." While the exact location of "the beginning" is usually a matter of considerable dispute, and the tracing of origins may test the patience and resources of all but the most scholarly, it is proper to make reference here to some of the voluminous background literature to imprisonment.

There is, sadly, no historical conspectus of the American penal system. Three works provide a useful basis for at least a partial understanding of developments. Blake McKelvey's pioneering general history *American Prisons: A History of Good Intentions (NJ: Paterson Smith, 1977) serves as a good introduction. David J. Rothman's two elegantly-written books, The Discovery of the Asylum: Social Order and Disorder in the New Republic* (Boston: Little, Brown, 1971) and *Conscience and Convenience* (Boston: Little, Brown, 1980) provide insights into important ideological and social dynamics of the development of prisons and kindred institutions. There are references to crowding in these works, but the foundation volume, which should be read by all who doubt the maxim *plus ça change, plus c'est le même chose*, is John Howard's *The State of the Prisons* (Warrington: 1777, with several successive editions and numerous reprints).

The philosophy of imprisonment is, of course, embedded in the more general philosophy of punishment. Stanley S. Grupp, *Theories of Punishment* (Bloomington: Indiana University Press, 1971) probably remains the most convenient and comprehensive collection of essays for those who seek an introduction to this field. Grupp's volume was, however, compiled before the publication of certain works that have had a significant influence on recent thinking about imprisonment. These later pieces include Alfred Blumstein and Jacqueline Cohen, "A Theory of the Stability of Punishment," *The Journal of Criminal Law and Criminology* (64 [1973]: 198–207; David Fogel, ". . . *We Are the Living Proof. . . " The Justice Model for Corrections* (Cincinnati: W. H. Anderson, 1975); and the compilation by Douglas Lipton, Robert Martinson, and Judith Wilks, *The Effectiveness of Correctional Treatment: A Survey of Treatment Evaluation Studies* (New York: Praeger, 1976). A good summary of this last rather voluminous book is available in Robert Martinson, "What Works - Questions and Answers About Prison Reform," *The Public Interest* (35 [1974]: 22–54).

The prison is in large part what the legislators and administrators make it, but is also what the prisoners themselves make of their experience of captivity. It is quite impossible to understand the central issues in prison policy, and to grasp many of the consequences of crowding, without some knowledge of the structures of the social life of the prison. Two classic sociological studies are Donald Clemmer, *The Prison Community* (New York: Holt, Rinehart and Winston, 1940) and Gresham M. Sykes, *The Society of Captives* (New York: Atheneum, 1958). Many have followed these authors in seeking a better understanding of the pains of imprisonment and prisoners' collective and individual adaptations. Of the several titles available, Hans Tochs, *Men in Crisis: Human Breakdowns in Prison* (Chicago: Aldine, 1966) is particularly relevant to the issue of overcrowding. The distinctive life of women's prisons is addressed in David Ward and Gene Kassebaum, *Women's Prison: Sex and Social Structure* (Chicago: Aldine, 1965), and in Esther Heffernan, *Making it in Prison: The Square, the Cool and the Life* (New York: Wiley, 1972).

PRISON CROWDING ISSUES

We have sought to make this volume as comprehensive as possible, while at the same time retaining reasonable conciseness. But whatever level of success we have enjoyed, many issues have been dealt with in a manner which may leave readers with unanswered questions and problems with which they may require further guidance. Each of the book's chapters has its own set of references which, taken together, should provide a thorough overview of the literature. What follows is simply a highlighting of some of the principal texts and issues.

Three collections of essays which provide general overviews are "Our Crowded Prisons," a volume of *The Annals of the American Academy of Political and Social Science* (478 [March, 1985]); "Prison Crowding," a special edition of the *University of Illinois Law Review*, (1984, no. 2 [1984]); and "Prison Overcrowding," a special edition of the *New York University Review of Law and Social Change* (12, no. 1 [1983–1984]).

A detailed description of the magnitude of the crowding problem and its enormous increase over the past 15 years is given in S. D., Gottfredson, "The dynamics of prison populations" (paper prepared for the National Academy of Sciences, October, 1986, and available from the National Criminal Justice Reference Service, Silver Spring, Maryland). Two basic surveys and reviews that are now showing signs of age, but remain good sources for statistical information concerning prison conditions and crowding are A. Rutherford, P. Evans, J. Flanagan, D. Fogel, I. Greenberg, and R. Ku, *Prison Populations and Policy Choices* vols. I and II (Cambridge, Mass.: Abt Associates, 1977) and J. Mullen, K. Carlson, and B. Smith, *American Prisons and Jails, Volume I: Summary Findings and Policy Implications of a National Survey* (Washington, D.C.: U.S. Government Printing Office, 1980). More recent information is available from a variety of extremely clear and well-presented Justice Department publications such as those of the Bureau of Justice Statistics. (See, for example, *Prisoners in 1985* and *State and Federal Prisoners, 1925–85* (Washington, D.C.: United States Department of Justice, June 1986 and October 1986, respectively).

Information concerning litigation on prison conditions is given in G. P. Alpert, ed., *Legal Rights of Prisoners* (Beverly Hills, Calif.: Sage, 1980) and the American Correctional Association, *Correctional Law: A Bibliography of Selected Books and Articles* (College Park, Md.: American Correctional Association, 1977). Much of the foregoing is presented in a commendably clear and concise fashion in Daniel E. Manville's handbook, *Prisoners' Self-Help Litigation*

Manual (New York: Oceana Publications, 1983). For a description of current litigation and the status of cases in each state, the American Civil Liberties Union Foundation, *Status Report: The Courts and Prisons* (Washington, D. C.: American Civil Liberties Union Foundation, February, 1986) should prove useful.

Approaches to the costing of corrections and some of the associated policy issues are dealt with in D. McDonald's *The Price of Punishment: Public Spending for Corrections in New York* (Boulder, Colo.: Westview, 1980) and in T. R. Clear, P. M. Harris, and A. L. Record, "Managing the Cost of Corrections," *Prison Journal* (62, no. 1 [1982]:1–63).

S. D. Gottfredson and R. B. Taylor describe how public opinion and the policy process affect corrections and correctional reform in *The Correctional Crisis* (Washington, D. C.: National Institute of Justice, June, 1983). This topic is also dealt with by R. A. Berk and P. H. Rossi, *Prison Reform and State Elites* (Cambridge, Mass.: Ballinger, 1977) and P. J. Riley, and McN. Rose, "Public Opinion vs. Elite Opinion on Correctional Reform," *Journal of Criminal Justice* (8 [1980]: 345–56). For a discussion of the basic policy debate, refer to M. Sherman and G. Hawkins, *Imprisonment in America: Choosing the Future* (Chicago: University of Chicago Press, 1981), and to J. B. Jacobs, *The Politics of Prison Construction* (New York: New York University School of Law, 1983).

Sentencing plays a major role in the problem of prison crowding. Issues relating to sentencing reform are discussed in A. Blumstein, J. Cohen, S. Martin, and M. Tonry, *Research on Sentencing: The Search for Reform* (Washington, D. C.: National Academy Press, 1983). Recently, much attention has been given the concept of "selective incapacitation"—the notion of attempting to identify "career criminals," and selectively providing forms of preventive imprisonment for this small group of highly active offenders. This controversial concept is treated in some detail in A. Blumstein, J. Cohen, and J. Roth, *Criminal Careers and "Career Criminals"* (Washington, D. C.: National Academy Press, 1986), in A. von Hirsch and D. M. Gottfredson, "Selective Incapacitation: Some Queries about Research Design and Equity," *New York University Review of Law and Social Change* (12, no. 1 [1983–1984]), and in J. Cohen, "Incapacitation as a Strategy for Crime Control: Possibilities and Pitfalls," in M. Tonry and N. Morris, eds., (*Crime and Justice: An*

Annual Review of Research, Vol. 5 (Chicago: University of Chicago Press, 1983). A detailed assessment of several sentencing strategies can be found in Franklin Zimring, "A Consumer's Guide to Sentencing Reform," in F. Zimring and R. Frase, eds., *The Criminal Justice System* (Boston: Little, Brown, 1980).

Sentencers and legislators are, of course, constrained by the range of penalties available. Martin Wright, *Making Good* (London: Hutchinson, 1982) is a useful survey and discussion of a variety of non-custodial penalties, and the problems and opportunities associated with them. Kay Harris writes engagingly and with much experience on this topic in "Reducing Prison Crowding and Non Prison Penalties," *The Annals*, (478 [March 1985]: 150–60).

It has proven very difficult accurately to predict prison populations, yet the importance of reliable projections as a basis for practical and political action is paramount. Discussions can be found in Rutherford et al., *Prison Populations* (1977); A. Blumstein, J. Cohen, and H. Miller, "Demographically disaggregated projections of prison populations," *Journal of Criminal Justice* (8 [1980]: 1–26); and the report of the Pennsylvania Commission on Crime and Delinquency, *A Strategy to Alleviate Overcrowding in Pennsylvania's Prison and Jails* (Philadelphia: Pennsylvania Commission, 1985).

In recent years increasingly sophisticated attempts have been made to conceptualize and to measure the physiological and psychological effects of prison crowding on staff and on inmates. This subject is dealt with in P. Paulus, V. Cox, G. McCain, and J. Chandler, "Some Effects of Crowding in a Prison Environment," *Journal of Applied Social Psychology*, (5 [1975]: 86–91), E. Megargee, "Population Density and Disruptive Behavior in a Prison Setting," in A. Cohen, G. Coal, and R. Bailey, eds., *Prison Violence* (Lexington, Mass.: Lexington Books, 1976), and D.P. Farrington and C. P. Nuttall, "Prison Size, Overcrowding, Prison Violence, and Recidivism," *Journal of Criminal Justice* (8 [1980]: 221–31). A very useful analytical summary of the literature is provided by Gerald R. Gaes, "The Effects of Overcrowding in Prison" in Michael Tonry and Norval Morris eds., *Crime and Justice* vol. 6 (Chicago: University of Chicago Press, 95–146).

Finally, international comparisons can provide lessons, positive as well as negative, and may sometimes be the source of a grim form of solace. A book which looks at burgeoning prison populations in a provocative manner and with a firm strategy in mind is Andrew Rutherford, *Prisons and the Process of Justice: The Reductionist Challenge* (London: William Heinemann, 1984). A more descriptive and less polemical survey of the prison systems of several nations is offered in R. J. Wicks and H. H. C. Cooper, eds., *International Corrections* (Lexington, Mass.: Lexington Books, 1979).

Index

About the Editors and Contributors

ALFRED BLUMSTEIN is J. Erik Jonsson Professor of Urban Systems and Operations Research and Director of the Urban Systems Institute in the School of Urban and Public Affairs at Carnegie-Mellon University. He has served as Director of the Task Force on Science and Technology for President Johnson's Crime Commission, as Chairman of the National Academy of Sciences' Committee on Research on Law Enforcement and the Administration of Justice and various of its panels, and as Chairman of the Pennsylvania Commission on Crime and Delinquency. His Ph.D. is from Cornell University.

TODD R. CLEAR is Associate Professor at the School of Criminal Justice, Rutgers University. He has written numerous articles and has provided training to criminal justice practitioners across the country on the subjects of probation case management and prison crowding. He is co-author of *Supervising the Offender in the Community*, and is currently engaged in the study of the impact of changes in resources on corrections decision-making. His Ph.D. (criminal justice) is from the State University of New York at Albany.

DON M. GOTTFREDSON is Professor of Criminal Justice at Rutgers University. Previously Chairman of the New Jersey Correctional Master Plan Policy Council, he currently is a member of the New Jersey Department of Corrections Advisory Council, Chairman of the New Jersey Criminal Disposition Commission, and President of the American Society of Criminology. Dr. Gottfredson received his Ph.D. (in psychology) from Claremont University.

STEPHEN D. GOTTFREDSON is Associate Professor of Criminal Justice at Temple University. Previously Associate Director of The Johns Hopkins University's Center for Metropolitan Planning and Research, he also has served as Executive Director of the Maryland Criminal Justice Coordinating Council. Dr. Gottfredson's degrees are from the University of Oregon and The Johns Hopkins University (Ph.D., psychology).

ALAN T. HARLAND is Chairman and Associate Professor in the Department of Criminal Justice, Temple University. He was formerly Director of the Criminal Justice Research Center, Albany, New York, where he directed several research projects in the corrections area. He has contributed numerous publications to the corrections literature and holds law degrees from the University of Pennsylvania and Oxford University. His Ph.D. (criminal justice) is from SUNY Albany.

M. KAY HARRIS is Associate Professor of Criminal Justice at Temple University. She formerly served as Director of the Washington D.C. office of the National Council on Crime and Delinquency and has held positions with the American Bar Association, the Unitarian Universalist Service Committee, and the U. S. Department of Justice. Her degree is from the University of Chicago.

PATRICIA M. HARRIS is Assistant Professor of Criminal Justice at Temple University. She currently is exploring justifications for reform of the juvenile justice system, and is participating with Dr. Clear in a longitudinal study of the impact of changes in resources on corrections decision-making. Her Ph.D. (criminal justice) is from Rutgers University.

PHILIP W. HARRIS is Associate Professor of Criminal Justice at Temple University. Before joining Temple, Dr. Harris obtained his Ph.D. in criminal justice from the State University of New York at Albany, and worked in juvenile corrections in Canada. His research and publications have focused on capital punishment and on classification systems in juvenile justice. He currently is President of the International Differential Treatment Association.

BARTON L. INGRAHAM is Associate Professor of Criminal Justice at the University of Maryland (College Park Campus). He is a graduate of Harvard University and Harvard Law School (1957) and received his doctorate in Criminology from the University of California (Berkeley, 1972), after leaving the practice of law.

SEAN McCONVILLE is Associate Professor of Criminal Justice at the University of Illinois at Chicago. He received his Ph.D. from the University of Cambridge, and has taught at several universities in England and the United States. Dr. McConville has written on the history and contemporary administration of punishment, and has served as a consultant to governments on both sides of the Atlantic.

JOAN MULLEN is a Vice-President and Manager of the Law and Justice Area of Abt Associates, Inc., a public policy research organization. In 1979-80 she directed the preparation of a five-volume congressionally mandated study, *American Prisons and Jails*, sponsored by the National Institute of Justice. This was followed in 1983-84 by a survey on state responses to prison crowding that forms the basis for this chapter.

RALPH B. TAYLOR is Associate Professor of Criminal Justice at Temple University. Previously, he directed the Criminal Justice Program in the Center for Metropolitan Planning and Research, The Johns Hopkins University. He has written extensively in the areas of environmental criminology, social psychology, and community crime prevention. His Ph.D. (psychology) is from The Johns Hopkins University.

CHARLES F. WELLFORD has been Director of the University of Maryland's Institute of Criminal Justice and Criminology since 1981. He serves on numerous state and federal advisory boards and commissions and is Executive Secretary of the American Society of Criminology. Previously, he served in the Office of the United States

Attorney General, where he directed the Federal Justice Research Program. Dr. Wellford received his Ph.D. in 1969 from the University of Pennsylvania.

ERYL HALL WILLIAMS is Professor of Criminology, with special reference to penology, at the London School of Economics and Political Science. He is a former member of the English Parole Board. Professor Hall Williams has taught criminal law and criminology for many years. He has published two books on prisons, and a popular textbook. He has been active in the work of the European Committee on Crime Problems, Council of Europe.